"In big cities, in small towns, in villages and on the plains, you see – waiting impatiently at the side of the road – old ladies and little girls, school teachers and priests..."

The universal appeal of the Tour de France, as described by
French writer Pierre Bost in the newspaper *Marianne*, July 1935

ELLIS BACON

MAPPING
LE
TOUR

FOREWORD BY
MARK CAVENDISH

Mapping le Tour

Collins
An imprint of HarperCollins Publishers
Westerhill Road
Bishopbriggs
Glasgow G64 2QT

First published 2013
Paperback edition 2014

Printed in China by South China Printing Co Ltd.

British Library Cataloguing in Publication Data
A catalogue record for this book is available from
the British Library

ISBN 978-0-00-794335-7
Imp 001

Collins Bartholomew, the UK's leading independent
Geographical information supplier, can provide a
digital, custom, and premium mapping service to a
variety of markets.
For further information:
Tel: +44 (0) 208 307 4515
e-mail: collinsbartholomew@harpercollins.co.uk
or visit our website at: www.collinsbartholomew.com

If you would like to comment on any aspect of this book,
please write to
Collins Maps, HarperCollins Publishers, Westerhill Road,
Bishopbriggs, Glasgow G64 2QT
e-mail: collinsmaps@harpercollins.co.uk

Find us at www.harpercollins.co.uk
 HarperCollinsCycling
 @CollinsMaps
and the author @EllisBacon

Contents

Foreword
by Mark Cavendish MBE

The Tour de France is a special race for all professional cyclists. It is the biggest, the best, the toughest and the most competitive on the circuit. This year's race, starting in Yorkshire, is even more special.

I can say from experience that just completing the Tour is an impressive achievement for even the best cyclists in the world. It was not until my third Tour that I had a chance to race down the Champs-Élysées and finish a Tour de France. Since it started, the race was intended to be sport's ultimate physical challenge, a sentiment that comes across clearly in this book. Since that first completion, I've finished the race a further four times, and every year has offered a uniquely challenging experience.

One of the reasons we get drawn back to racing around France every year is that a different route, with new tests and problems to overcome, is picked for each edition. The route is just as much of a challenge in the Tour as the other riders, but it also gives us a chance to travel to new places each year, experiencing different areas of France with our team-mates.

The highlight of every race for me is definitely that sprint finish along the Champs-Élysées. When that also ends with winning the final stage in front of the Paris crowds it becomes the dream of any competitive cyclist. I feel privileged to have done it four times and I'm looking forward to doing it a few more!

After a hundred races across the fields and mountains of France and its neighbouring countries, it's amazing to think of the history of the Tour, the legends it has made, and the tragedies that have happened. From the gentlemen disqualified in 1904 for taking the train to the latest issues that the sport has experienced, the route, rather than any individual rider, is always the star of the event. Perhaps this is why the Tour has survived and flourished despite all of its controversies.

This book is a detailed textual and visual biography of the Tour itself, and one which uniquely places the document we refer to the most, the map, at its core.

Each stage of the Tour has characteristics that cyclists all over the world can recognise and be inspired by. This can most easily be imagined through maps. I study the route map in detail, both before the first stage and throughout the Tour. It's the key to planning my race strategy, and the team's. Sometimes you have to pick your battles and know which stages to target to try to win, and in which ones you're just going to have to fight it out for survival in the peloton while the climbers slog it out at the front. We get all this by studying the route map along with the stage profiles.

When I was young I followed the Tour de France, watching it avidly on television. It inspired me on my bike rides around the Isle of Man and led to dreams about competing in the race. It is great to see a book that captures the history of this incredible event and lets us look back at the Tour with fond memories, whether following or taking part in the race as it travels around France.

Introduction
by Ellis Bacon

The Tour de France is all about mapping and geography – it is its very lifeblood. It seems fitting, then, that the Tour came about as a result of some geographical wranglings, of sorts: the so-called Dreyfus Affair.

In 1894, Alfred Dreyfus, a Jewish officer in the French Army, was accused of spying for Germany, although it later came to light that he had been framed by an anti-Semitic army colleague.

France was divided by the case, and the editor of sports newspaper *Le Vélo*, Pierre Giffard, was very much on Dreyfus's side. That grated with the paper's advertisers, such as bike and tyre manufacturers Adolphe Clément, Edouard Michelin and Count Jules-Albert de Dion, who were very much anti-Dreyfusards, and so began looking for somewhere else to advertise their wares. Feelings were such that Giffard certainly didn't want them in his paper anymore, either.

Clément turned to his director of publicity, Henri Desgrange – a former racing cyclist who had already published a book about bike training called *La Tête et les Jambes* ('The Head and the Legs') – and on 16 October 1900, new newspaper *L'Auto* was first published, with Desgrange at the helm.

Despite the proliferation of anti-Dreyfusard advertisers, the new title struggled when it came to sales, and in November 1902 – over lunch, *bien sûr* – one of *L'Auto's* writers, Géo Lefèvre, came to his ailing paper's rescue by proposing a 'Tour de France' bicycle race. The rest is history.

Except it's not that simple, as the 1904 edition of the race – as you can read in these pages – was almost its last, thanks to cheating.

Then in 1998 the race was rocked to its core once more thanks to the Festina doping affair. So serious was it, in fact, that then-race director Jean-Marie Leblanc feared that the '98 edition genuinely would be the race's last. It has been shaken yet further by more recent events, too, but still it survives – simply 'there', year after year, it seems, as much a part of France as baguettes or the Eiffel Tower.

Compiling this book has been a true labour of love and, fittingly, a journey, as I delved as deeply into my own experiences and memories as I did into my collection of cycling books and magazines, and even my university dissertation.

It all came back to me: the reason why I, and millions like me, are so enamoured with the Tour de France and its history, and in particular the places it's visited, the riders it's created and the lives it's touched. Hopefully 'Mapping le Tour' will convey all of that.

Did my love of all things French come before or after my awareness of the Tour? I don't remember any more, but what I do know is that they have always been inextricably linked: it may be a cliché, but the Tour is truly a French institution.

This, though, is a book that focuses more on the geographical side of the race than simply the epic tales that make up the Tour's history, although of course they, too, are inextricably linked.

In 2014, the race celebrates its 101st edition, having started in 1903 but having been interrupted by the two world wars. The first Tour I saw was the finish of the 1986 edition when it was shown on UK television by Channel 4. By the following year, I was hooked, and my next French project at school was about the Tour, and in particular about British rider Tom Simpson and his collapse on Mont Ventoux in 1967. I devoured the race's history, its geography and its language – the latter then very much French; now increasingly, and a little disappointingly, English.

I studied French at university; my third year abroad was a toss-up between spending it in Avignon (close to Mont Ventoux) or in Chambéry – near to the legendary climb of Alpe d'Huez. Provence won out in the end – helped, a little, by Marcel Pagnol and Peter Mayle's tales, *sans doute* – and I soon found out that the university hall of residence in which I was to live had been the old hospital in which Simpson had died.

My dissertation that year, written in French, could only be about the Tour, and I subtitled it *La Grande Boucle* – 'The Big Loop' – as it's affectionately known in France.

L'Auto

AUTOMOBILE — CYCLISME

ATHLÉTISME, YACHTING, AÉROSTATION, ESCRIME, POIDS et HALTÈRES, HIPPISME, GYMNASTIQUE, ALPINISME

Directeur-Rédacteur en Chef :
HENRI DESGRANGE

RÉDACTION, ADMINISTRATION
PUBLICITÉ
10, Rue du Faubourg-Montmartre, 10
PARIS (9e Arr.)

LE TOUR DE FRANCE — LE DÉPART

Organisé par L'AUTO du 1er au 19 Juillet 1903

LA SEMENCE

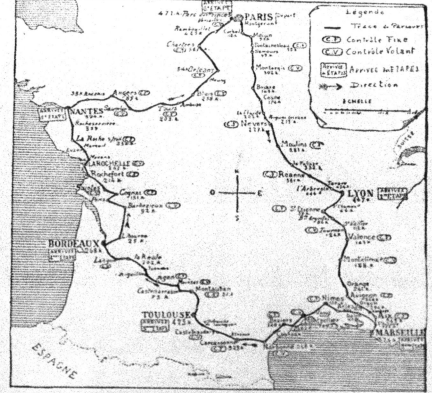

L'ITINÉRAIRE DU TOUR DE FRANCE

QUI ?

Maurice GARIN

That same year – 1998, which, thanks to the aforementioned Festina doping affair, was also memorable for all the wrong reasons – I managed to watch the race live for the first time on French soil, at Carpentras for the finish of stage 13, and again the next day for the start of the fourteenth stage in nearby Valréas. (I'd already skipped school in 1994 to watch the race come through Brighton when it came to the UK – with my parents' blessing, of course.)

In 2001, when I was living in Denmark, I met up with my dad to watch the start of the Tour in Dunkirk. That night, after the prologue – won by Christophe Moreau – we slept in the car at some motorway services to save money, and then continued on to the start of stage 1 in St-Omer. Incidentally, my dad now always buys those small bottles of St-Omer lager, proving that the commercial side of the Tour definitely 'works'.

After hours slumped on a metal crowd barrier at the finish of the stage in Boulogne-sur-Mer, waiting for the race to arrive, our trip was rounded off nicely by watching Erik Zabel show Romans Vainsteins a clean pair of heels to take the bunch sprint.

I'd enjoyed following the Tour as a fan and, just two years later in 2003, I would follow it for the first time as a journalist.

Since then, I've returned year after year, which strangely means that I haven't really noticed the race's rather swift evolution from French holiday to English-speaking-dominated sports event. That dominance looks set to continue, but the race remains fiercely French in its goal of showcasing the country's stunning countryside and terrain.

Each October, the unveiling of the following year's route in Paris is eagerly awaited by the world's press, and by the Tour's millions of fans at home. Once that familiar hexagonal shape of France with the race route laid out across it is beamed around the world, people begin to plan their holidays around it. The riders, meanwhile, get straight to work, scouting out the roads – and the climbs in particular – named on the following year's itinerary. It is that hard work and attention to detail, across the winter and in the early part of the season, that marks out the true contenders from the also-rans come the summer.

The Tour has also gone beyond the confines of France, and over the years has enjoyed sojourns to Belgium, Italy, Spain and Switzerland, as well as seeking out new roads further afield, in the Netherlands, Ireland and Britain. The Pyrenees made their first appearance in 1910, while the Alps followed in 1911. It also makes regular visits to the Massif Central, and the Vosges mountains in eastern France, where the riders have tackled the Puy de Dôme and the Ballon d'Alsace, respectively.

Host cities such as Paris, Lyon, Marseille and Bordeaux have appeared regularly on the route since the Tour's first edition in 1903, and as cities in countries other than France were added, so, too, grew the breadth of contenders. As well as ever-increasing numbers of riders from neighbouring countries like Belgium, Luxembourg, Switzerland, Italy and Spain, 'international milestones' include the first participation by an African rider, Tunisian Ali Neffati, at the 1913 Tour, and the first riders from Australia – Snowy Munro and Don Kirkham – a year later in 1914. In 1937 came the first British riders – Bill Burl and Charles Holland – although neither finished; it wasn't until 1955 that Brian Robinson and Tony Hoar became the first Brits to complete the Tour. Greg LeMond became the first American stage winner in 1985 and, after the Colombia-Varta team's appearance at the Tour in 1983, Victor Hugo Peña becoming the first Colombian to wear the yellow jersey, albeit for only three days, in 2003.

Today, the Tour organisation is faced with the task of ensuring that the enduring image of riders toiling up fan-filled mountain sides and streaming past sunflower-filled fields does indeed endure... To paraphrase Tour boss Christian Prudhomme's message, which he is at pains to get across: the Tour exists to allow people to dream.

The scenery and routes used allow people in far-flung corners of the world to see France in a justly flattering light: laid bare in all its glory for the riders to fight against and the spectators – both roadside and televisual – to appreciate. It is an event that has made national and international heroes of previously local heroes, and has brought life to corners of France, and the globe, that needed it...

Long may it continue.

How to use this book

Map symbols

⚑	Race start
⚑	Race finish
⚑⚑	Race start/finish
◑	Stage start
◑	Stage finish
◑	Stage start/finish
BORDEAUX	Stage town
⟶	General race direction
┅┅┅	Non-race route
★	Memorable place location

6 15	Flat stage number
6 15	Hilly stage number
6 15	Mountain stage number
6 15	Individual time trial (ITT) stage number
6 15	Team time trial (TTT) stage number
6 15	Mountain ITT stage number
6 15	Mountain TTT stage number

228.5 km	Flat stage distance
228.5 km	Hilly stage distance
228.5 km	Mountain stage distance
228.5 km	Individual time trial (ITT) stage distance
228.5 km	Team time trial (TTT) stage distance

Statistics symbols

🏁	Start/finish town
🚲	Riders
👕	Jerseys
〰	Distance
⏱	Winning time and speed
📅	Stage numbers (2013 route)
⛰	Mountains
🎲	Podium
𝑖	Tour Detour (2013 route)

The Route

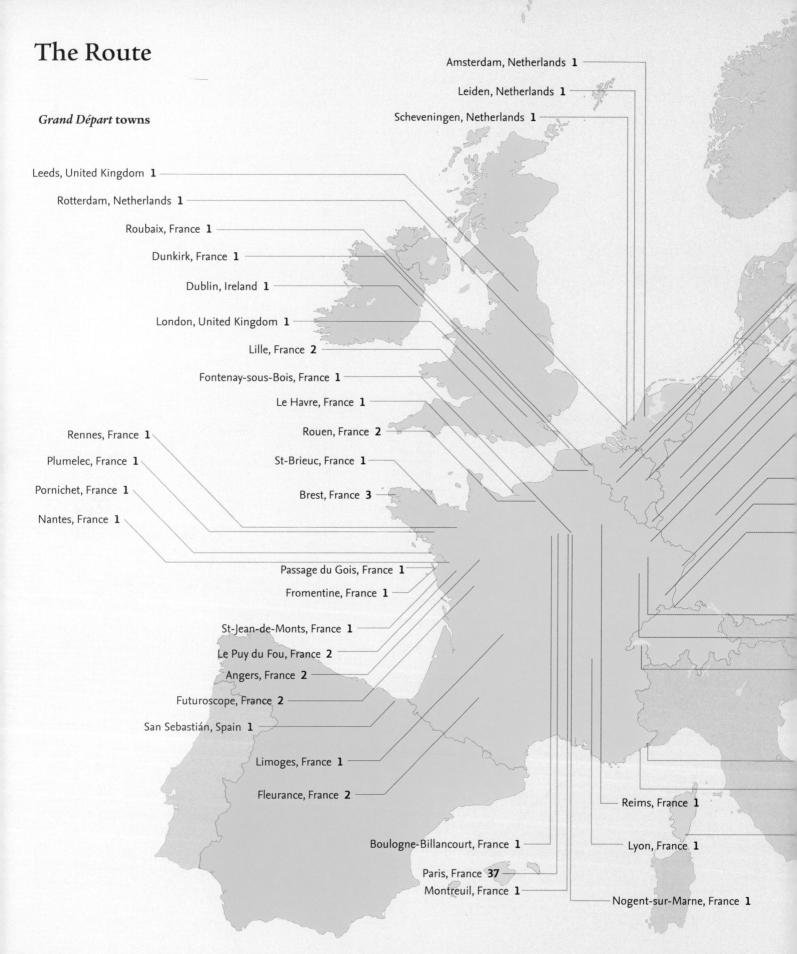

Grand Départ towns

Amsterdam, Netherlands **1**

Leiden, Netherlands **1**

Scheveningen, Netherlands **1**

Leeds, United Kingdom **1**

Rotterdam, Netherlands **1**

Roubaix, France **1**

Dunkirk, France **1**

Dublin, Ireland **1**

London, United Kingdom **1**

Lille, France **2**

Fontenay-sous-Bois, France **1**

Le Havre, France **1**

Rennes, France **1**

Plumelec, France **1**

Pornichet, France **1**

Nantes, France **1**

Rouen, France **2**

St-Brieuc, France **1**

Brest, France **3**

Passage du Gois, France **1**

Fromentine, France **1**

St-Jean-de-Monts, France **1**

Le Puy du Fou, France **2**

Angers, France **2**

Futuroscope, France **2**

San Sebastián, Spain **1**

Limoges, France **1**

Fleurance, France **2**

Reims, France **1**

Boulogne-Billancourt, France **1**

Lyon, France **1**

Paris, France **37**

Montreuil, France **1**

Nogent-sur-Marne, France **1**

12

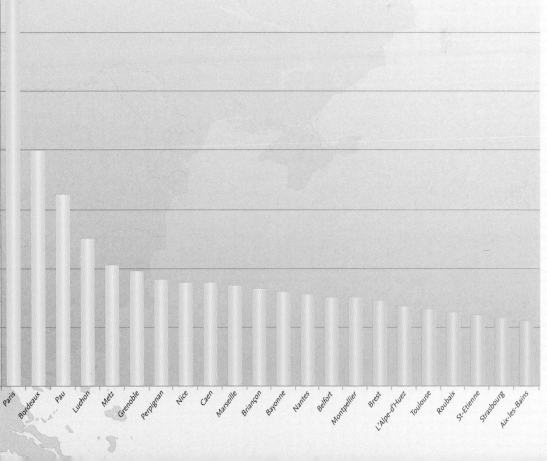

Grand Départ *host country*

France	**81**
Netherlands	**5**
Belgium	**4**
Germany	**3**
Luxembourg	**2**
United Kingdom	**2**
Ireland	**1**
Monaco	**1**
Spain	**1**
Switzerland	**1**

's-Hertogenbosch, Netherlands **1**

Brussels, Belgium **1**

Charleroi, Belgium **1**

Liège, Belgium **2**

Cologne, Germany **1**

Luxembourg **2**

Metz, France **1**

Frankfurt, Germany **1**

Berlin, Germany **1**

Strasbourg, France **2**

Mulhouse, France **2**

Basel, Switzerland **1**

Nancy, France **2**

Vittel, France **1**

Évian, France **1**

Monaco **1**

Nice, France **1**

Porto-Vecchio, France **1**

Host town (start or finish) 1903-2012

Paris, Bordeaux, Pau, Luchon, Metz, Grenoble, Perpignan, Nice, Caen, Marseille, Briançon, Bayonne, Nantes, Belfort, Montpellier, Brest, L'Alpe-d'Huez, Toulouse, Roubaix, St-Etienne, Strasbourg, Aix-les-Bains

The Climbs

Many battles have been won and lost over the Tour's mountain stages. Whether it is in the Alps, Pyrenees or the Massif Central, riders need grit, determintaion and extraordinary fitness to overcome the punishing ascents of these now famous climbs.

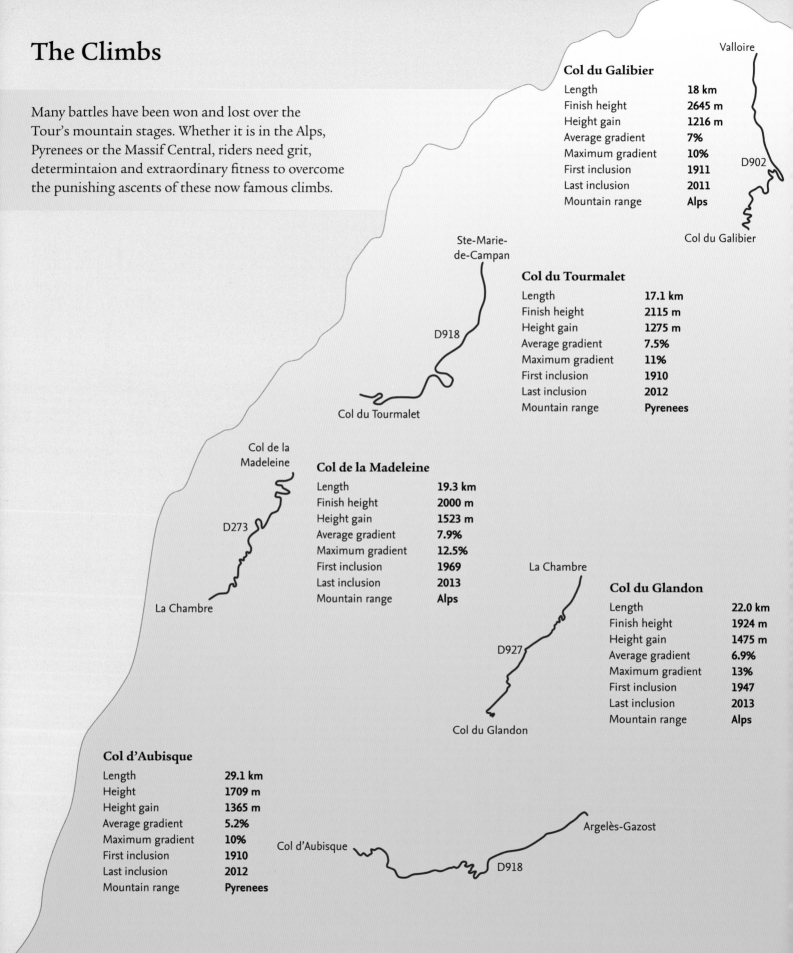

Valloire

Col du Galibier

Length	**18 km**
Finish height	**2645 m**
Height gain	**1216 m**
Average gradient	**7%**
Maximum gradient	**10%**
First inclusion	**1911**
Last inclusion	**2011**
Mountain range	**Alps**

D902

Col du Galibier

Ste-Marie-de-Campan

Col du Tourmalet

Length	**17.1 km**
Finish height	**2115 m**
Height gain	**1275 m**
Average gradient	**7.5%**
Maximum gradient	**11%**
First inclusion	**1910**
Last inclusion	**2012**
Mountain range	**Pyrenees**

D918

Col du Tourmalet

Col de la Madeleine

Col de la Madeleine

Length	**19.3 km**
Finish height	**2000 m**
Height gain	**1523 m**
Average gradient	**7.9%**
Maximum gradient	**12.5%**
First inclusion	**1969**
Last inclusion	**2013**
Mountain range	**Alps**

D273

La Chambre

La Chambre

Col du Glandon

Length	**22.0 km**
Finish height	**1924 m**
Height gain	**1475 m**
Average gradient	**6.9%**
Maximum gradient	**13%**
First inclusion	**1947**
Last inclusion	**2013**
Mountain range	**Alps**

D927

Col du Glandon

Col d'Aubisque

Length	**29.1 km**
Height	**1709 m**
Height gain	**1365 m**
Average gradient	**5.2%**
Maximum gradient	**10%**
First inclusion	**1910**
Last inclusion	**2012**
Mountain range	**Pyrenees**

Argelès-Gazost

Col d'Aubisque

D918

*"I had one of the hardest moments ever on the Col du Glandon in 1977.
I was at the end of my career, and what I had was gone by then."*

Eddy Merckx

Top 10 highest climbs

Climb	Range	Highest point
Cime de la Bonette	*Alps*	2802 m
Col de l'Iseran	*Alps*	2770 m
Col Agnel	*Alps*	2744 m
Col du Galibier	*Alps*	2645 m
Col du Grand St-Bernard	*Alps*	2473 m
Col du Granon	*Alps*	2413 m
Col d'Izoard	*Alps*	2360 m
Col de la Lombarde	*Alps*	2351 m
Col de la Cayolle	*Alps*	2326 m
Val-Thorens	*Alps*	2275 m

Col d'Izoard

Length	31.7 km
Finish height	2360 m
Height gain	1438 m
Average gradient	4.5%
Maximum gradient	7%
First inclusion	1922
Last inclusion	2011
Mountain range	**Alps**

Col de la Croix de Fer

Length	31.6 km
Finish height	2067 m
Height gain	1502 m
Average gradient	5%
Maximum gradient	12%
First inclusion	1947
Last inclusion	2012
Mountain range	**Alps**

Mont Ventoux

Length	21.0 km
Finish height	1909 m
Height gain	1610 m
Average gradient	7.6%
Maximum gradient	10.7%
First inclusion	1951
Last inclusion	2013
Mountain range	**Alps**

Alpe d'Huez

Length	14.5 km
Finish height	1850 m
Height gain	1150 m
Average gradient	8%
Maximum gradient	13%
First inclusion	1952
Last inclusion	2013
Mountain range	**Alps**

Puy de Dôme

Length	4.4 km
Finish height	1415 m
Height gain	488 m
Average gradient	11%
Maximum gradient	13%
First inclusion	1952
Last inclusion	1988
Mountain range	**Massif Central**

Col d'Izoard

D902

Guillestre

Col de la Croix de Fer

D526

N91

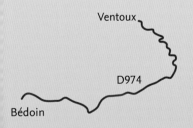

Ventoux

D974

Bédoin

L'Alpe-d'Huez

D211

Le Bourg-d'Oisans

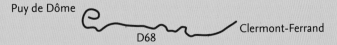

Puy de Dôme

D68

Clermont-Ferrand

The Winners

Tour wins by country

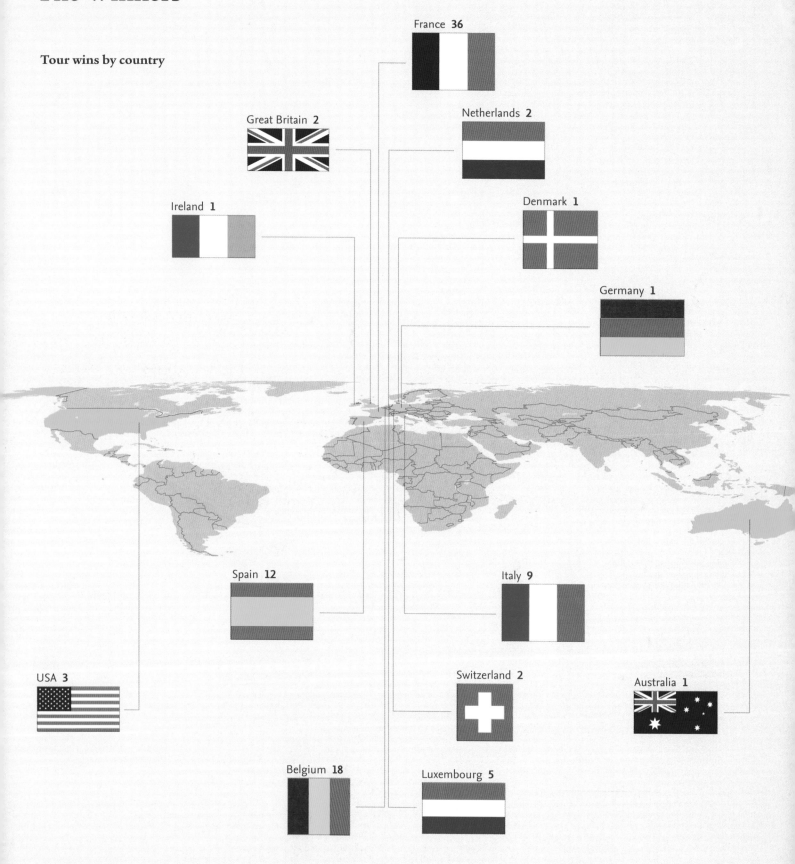

France **36**

Netherlands **2**

Great Britain **2**

Denmark **1**

Ireland **1**

Germany **1**

Spain **12**

Italy **9**

USA **3**

Switzerland **2**

Australia **1**

Belgium **18**

Luxembourg **5**

Most days in yellow jersey

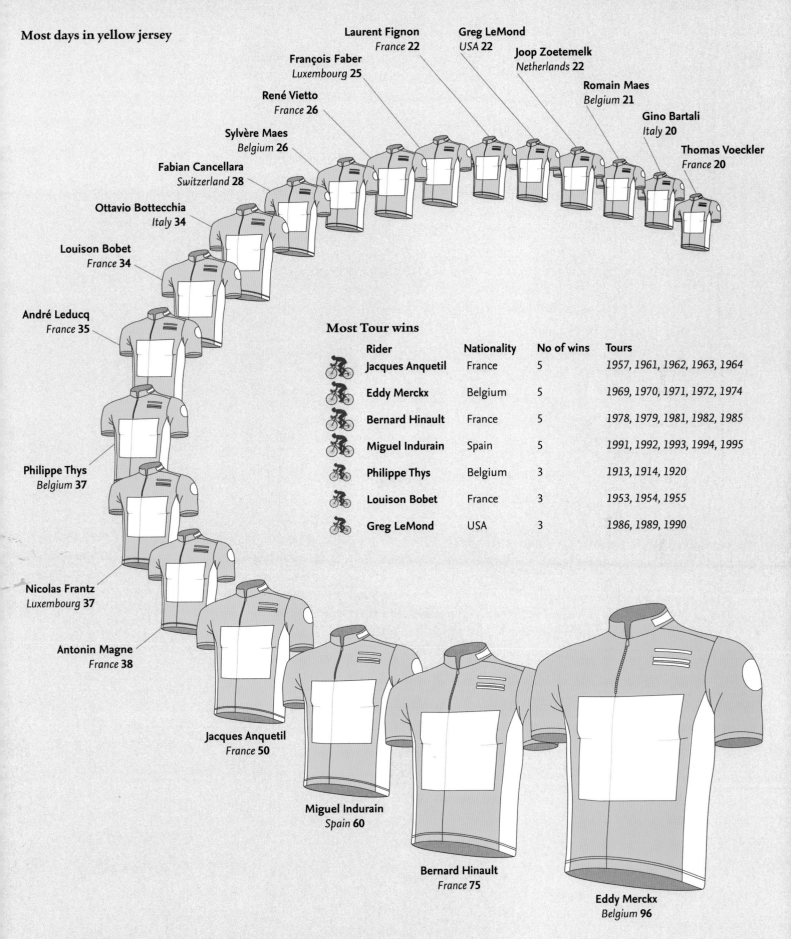

Laurent Fignon
France **22**

Greg LeMond
USA **22**

François Faber
Luxembourg **25**

Joop Zoetemelk
Netherlands **22**

René Vietto
France **26**

Romain Maes
Belgium **21**

Sylvère Maes
Belgium **26**

Gino Bartali
Italy **20**

Fabian Cancellara
Switzerland **28**

Thomas Voeckler
France **20**

Ottavio Bottecchia
Italy **34**

Louison Bobet
France **34**

André Leducq
France **35**

Philippe Thys
Belgium **37**

Nicolas Frantz
Luxembourg **37**

Antonin Magne
France **38**

Jacques Anquetil
France **50**

Miguel Indurain
Spain **60**

Bernard Hinault
France **75**

Eddy Merckx
Belgium **96**

Most Tour wins

	Rider	Nationality	No of wins	Tours
	Jacques Anquetil	France	5	*1957, 1961, 1962, 1963, 1964*
	Eddy Merckx	Belgium	5	*1969, 1970, 1971, 1972, 1974*
	Bernard Hinault	France	5	*1978, 1979, 1981, 1982, 1985*
	Miguel Indurain	Spain	5	*1991, 1992, 1993, 1994, 1995*
	Philippe Thys	Belgium	3	*1913, 1914, 1920*
	Louison Bobet	France	3	*1953, 1954, 1955*
	Greg LeMond	USA	3	*1986, 1989, 1990*

Riders make their way from Lyon to Marseille during stage 2 of the first Tour de France. Only twenty-one competitors would complete the race, covering 2428 km (1509 miles) in six days.

"The ideal Tour would be one that only one rider was capable of finishing."

Henri Desgrange, founder of the Tour de France

Maurice Garin (in white) becomes the Tour's first champion

Start: Paris, France, on 1 July
Finish: Paris, France, on 19 July

Total distance:
2428 km (1509 miles)
Longest stage:
471 km (293 miles)

Highest point:
Col de la République:
1161 m (3809 ft)
Mountain stages: 1

Starters: 60
Finishers: 21

Winning time:
94 h 33' 14"
Average speed:
25.679 kph (15.956 mph)

1. Maurice Garin (Fra)
2. Lucien Pothier (Fra)
   at 2 h 59' 02"
3. Fernand Augereau (Fra)
   at 4 h 29' 24"

Just six stages made up the route of the first Tour de France in 1903. Rather than the race being easy by today's standards, however, the shortest stage – between Toulouse and Bordeaux – was still 268 km (167 miles), while most of the rest were well over 400 km (250 miles).

Where the stages were easier compared to today's, however, was in their relative lack of climbing, with a route that avoided both the Alps and the Pyrenees, instead focusing on featuring France's major towns and cities.

While the Ballon d'Alsace, in the Vosges, is widely credited with being the first major climb to have been included on the Tour route, in 1905, the inaugural race did in fact include a number of climbs, although they were not noted as particular challenges to the riders.

Stage 1, between Montgeron, on the southeast edge of Paris, and Lyon featured both the Col des Echarmeaux and the Col du Pin-Bouchain – 712 m (2336 ft) and 759 m (2490 ft) high, respectively – while on the second stage

riders had to tackle the Col de la République, near St-Étienne, with France's Hippolyte Aucouturier the first rider to reach the top of the 1161-m (3809-ft)-high pass.

Named as one of the pre-race favourites, Aucouturier, riding as an 'independent', had failed to finish the Tour's opening stage due to stomach cramps, but was allowed to start stage 2 under rules that said that he could no longer remain in the hunt for the overall prize. He went on to win the second stage in Marseille, and repeated the feat on stage 3.

The first Tour ended in front of an enthusiastic crowd at the Parc des Princes velodrome, where another pre-race favourite, Frenchman Maurice Garin, riding in the colours of bicycle manufacturer La Française, took his third stage win of the race, and with it the honour of being the first Tour de France winner, having held the lead since his victory on the opening stage in Lyon.

The Tour was born, but its second edition was to be a lot less celebrated.

Publié par ATTINGER FRÈRES, éditeurs - PARIS

1904
2nd Edition

"The Tour de France is over, although its second edition will have been, I fear, its last – a victim of its own success."

Henri Desgrange, founder of the Tour de France, following the 1904 race

Spectators use tacks and pebbles to sabotage the stage between Nantes and Paris

Start: Paris, France, on 2 July
Finish: Paris, France, on 24 July

Total distance:
2428 km (1509 miles)
Longest stage:
471 km (293 miles)

Highest point:
Col de la République:
1161 m (3809 ft)
Mountain stages: 1

Starters: 88
Finishers: 15

Winning time:
96 h 05' 55"
Average speed:
25.265 kph (15.699 mph)

1. Henri Cornet (Fra)
2. Jean-Baptiste Dortignacq (Fra)
   at 2 h 16' 14"
3. Aloïs Catteau (Bel)
   at 9 h 01' 25"

It's become somewhat of a cliché, but the second edition of the Tour de France, in 1904, was almost its last.

Geographically, the 1904 Tour followed the same route as the first edition the previous year, again starting in Paris and taking in the major cities of Lyon, Marseille, Toulouse, Bordeaux and Nantes, before finishing once more in the Parc des Princes, Paris.

However, the race was marred by interventions from a by-now feverish public, while following the race it was discovered that the first four in the overall classification, including defending champion Maurice Garin, had cheated, and were disqualified from the race, handing victory to 19-year-old Henri Cornet, who remains the race's youngest-ever winner.

On the race's second, hilliest stage, between Lyon and Marseille, local Lyon lad Antoine Fauré led the race over the Col de la Rébublique while behind him the race favourites, including Garin and his brother, César, were set upon by masked men, believed to be Fauré's supporters.

That year was also the first recorded instance of tacks being thrown onto the road by partisan crowds – something that would happen intermittently throughout the Tour's history, including as recently as the 2012 Tour when the race passed over the Mur de Péguère on stage 14.

It took some time for the organisers of the 1904 Tour to wade through all the accusations and rumours at the end of the race, but in November they came to the decision to ban the two Garin brothers – who had finished first and third – with the older Maurice having apparently illegally been given food by one of the race organisers themselves, as well as allegedly having covered part of the route by train.

Runner-up Lucien Pothier was handed a lifetime ban by French governing body the Union Vélocipédique Française (although he was later permitted to start the Tour again, in 1907), while fourth-placed Hippolyte Aucouturier, again one of the race favourites, having failed to finish the first stage of the 1903 race due to illness, was one of those believed to have cheated by gripping a cork in his mouth that was attached to a string tied to the back of a car.

Publié par ATTINGER FRÈRES, éditeurs · PARIS

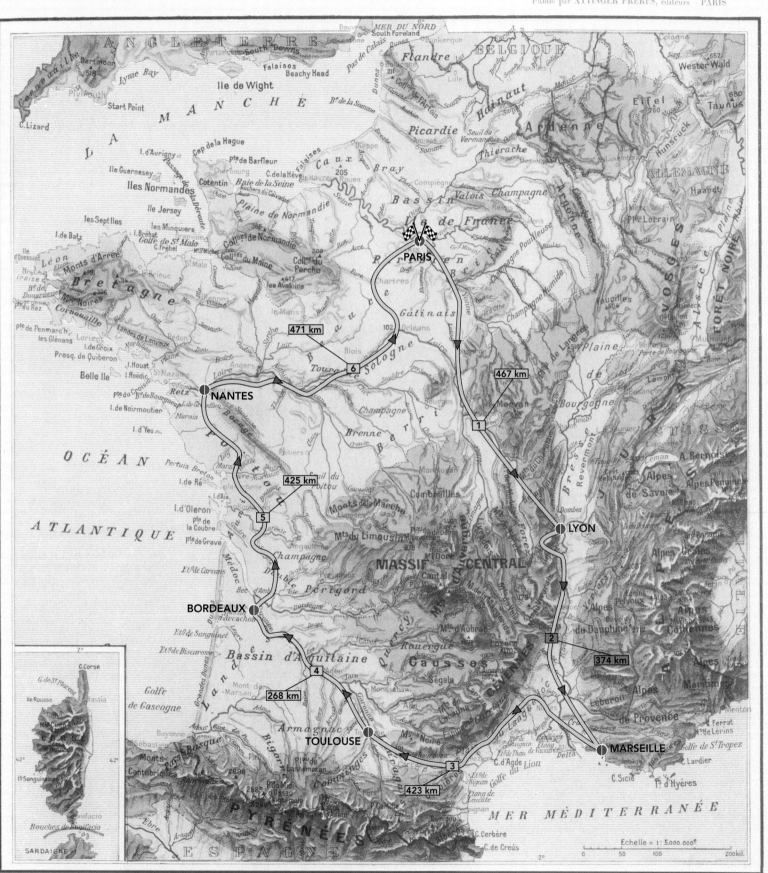

Despite the race having tackled the Col de la République in its previous two editions, the third Tour de France entered new territory in 1905 by introducing its first serious, leg-crunching, lung-busting climb in the shape of the Ballon d'Alsace. It was also made up of shorter stages, albeit with an increase in their number – up to eleven from six.

After his despair at the previous year's mass cheating, race director Henri Desgrange almost cancelled the 1905 Tour as early as its first stage, during which tacks were again thrown onto the road. All the riders punctured apart from 1904 runner-up Jean-Baptiste Dortignacq, though eventual overall race winner, Louis Trousselier, was nevertheless able to recover and win stage 1 from Paris to Nancy.

For stage 2, between Nancy and Besançon, it was out with the Col de la République and in with the Ballon d'Alsace, in the Vosges mountains. Wrongly, the Ballon d'Alsace is considered the Tour's first major climb, but it was recognised as such by the race organisers more for its steepness than its height: at 1178 m (3865 ft), it is just 17 m (56 ft) higher than the Col de la République. Indeed, the Col Bayard, climbed later, on stage 4 of the 1905 Tour, stands at 1246 m (4088 ft).

With an average grade of 6.9 per cent, climbed from the north from the town of St-Maurice-sur-Moselle, Desgrange predicted that none of his race's participants would be able to ride over the Ballon d'Alsace. René Pottier, however, had other ideas, stomping on the pedals to become the first rider to the top of the climb, although he was overtaken later in the stage by Hippolyte Aucouturier.

Overall race winner Trousselier – victorious thanks to five stage wins and Desgrange's newly introduced points, rather than time, system of determining the winner – was a deserving Tour champion, but gambled his winnings away in a single, celebratory evening after the finish in Paris.

Frenchman Louis Trousselier was the first rider to win the Tour de France on points

Start: Paris, France, on 9 July
Finish: Paris, France, on 30 July

Total distance:
3021 km (1877 miles)
Longest stage:
348 km (216 miles)

Highest point:
Col Bayard: 1246 m (4088 ft)
Mountain stages: 2

Starters: 60
Finishers: 24

Winning time: 35 points
Average speed:
27.481 kph (17.075 mph)

1. Louis Trousselier (Fra)
   35 points
2. Hippolyte Aucouturier (Fra)
   61 points
3. Jean-Baptiste Dortignacq (Fra)
   64 points

Publié par ATTINGER FRÈRES, éditeurs · PARIS

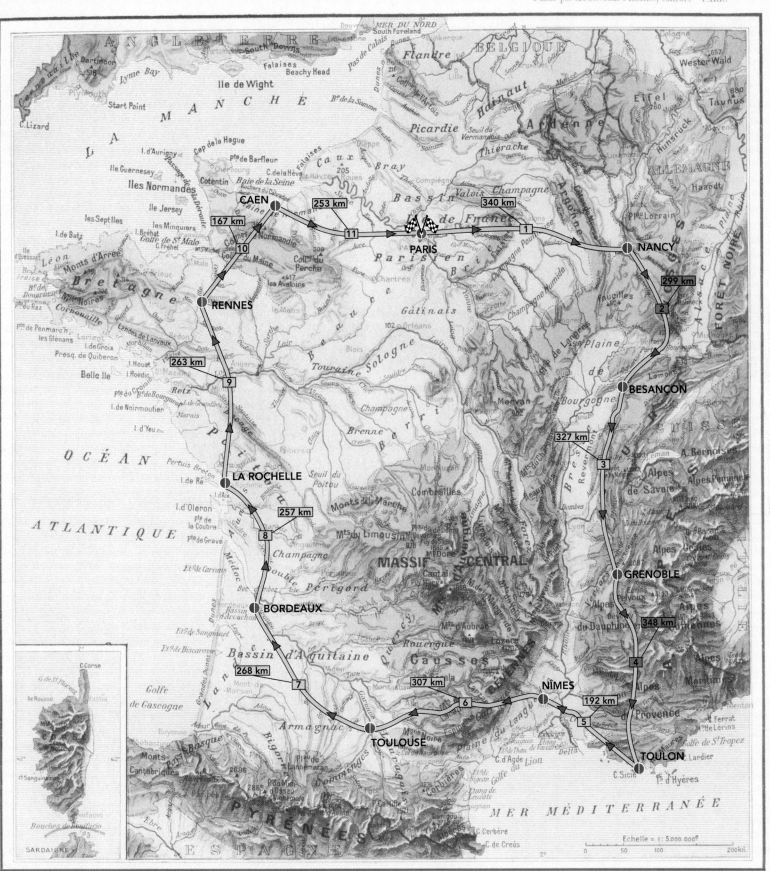

The 1906 edition of the Tour was a true tour of France, increased to thirteen stages from eleven, and reaching further afield than ever before: up to Lille in the north, Nice in the southeast, Bayonne in the furthest southwest corner, close to the Spanish border, and Brest, in Brittany, to the northwest.

It was also the first time that a stage started in a different town to the finish the previous day, when Douai hosted the start of stage 2, some 40 km (25 miles) from the Lille finish of stage 1.

It was a real Tour of 'firsts': for the first time, too, the race ventured outside French territory, when the stage from Douai dipped into German-held Alsace-Lorraine, and the city of Metz (today inside the French border), on its way to Nancy.

When it came to the competition, René Pottier, the man who had stunned the cycling world the previous year by managing to ride up the supposedly unridable Ballon d'Alsace, did it again, making it first to the top of the same climb when it featured on stage 3, and this time holding his advantage all the way to the finish in Dijon.

Having already won stage 2, and by taking another four stage wins en route to Paris, including the tough fifth stage over the Côte de Laffrey and the Col Bayard, Pottier beat the always-consistent Georges Passerieu – a Frenchman who finished in the top ten in every stage, including winning two stages – on points, 31 to 39. It was the rider with the fewest points who won, stage winners being awarded one point, two points being awarded for second place, etc., and was a system race organiser Henri Desgrange was to retain until the 1913 Tour, which reverted to being contested on time.

Pottier, it seemed, had an illustrious career ahead of him, having proved himself at the Tour as the sport's best climber.

Start: Paris, France, on 4 July
Finish: Paris, France, on 29 July

Total distance:
4546 km (2825 miles)
Longest stage:
480 km (298 miles)

Highest point:
Col Bayard: 1246 m (4088 ft)
Mountain stages: 2

Starters: 76
Finishers: 14

Winning time: 31 points
Average speed:
24.463 kph (15.201 mph)

1. René Pottier (Fra) 31 points
2. Georges Passerieu (Fra) 39 points
3. Louis Trousselier (Fra) 59 points

René Pottier was unbeatable in the mountains

Publié par ATTINGER FRÈRES, éditeurs · PARIS

Echelle = 1:5.000.000e

Overall winner Lucien Petit-Breton leads the stage between Toulouse and Bayonne

Start: Paris, France, on 8 July
Finish: Paris, France, on 4 August

Total distance:
4488 km (2789 miles)
Longest stage:
415 km (258 miles)

Highest point:
Col de Porte: 1326 m (4350 ft)
Mountain stages: 4

Starters: 93
Finishers: 33

Winning time: 47 points
Average speed:
28.470 kph (17.690 mph)

1. Lucien Petit-Breton (Fra)
   47 points
2. Gustave Garrigou (Fra)
   66 points
3. Émile Georget (Fra) 74 points

The 1907 Tour started on a sombre note as the 1906 champion, gifted 27-year-old climber René Pottier, had committed suicide in January.

The fifth edition's opening stage followed the route of the famous cobbled Classic, Paris-Roubaix, which had run since 1896, and although 1906 Tour runner-up – and now race favourite – Georges Passerieu had won the 1907 edition of the one-day race, it was 1905 Tour champ Louis Trousselier who took the victory in Roubaix in July.

The race followed a very similar route around the edge of France to that of 1906, again taking in the city of Metz, then still in Germany, and adding a second foreign sojourn by briefly drifting onto Swiss soil on stage 4 from Belfort to Lyon. The total number of stages ramped up to fourteen, and the race included its highest mountain pass yet by adding the 1326-m (4350-ft) Col de Porte, in the Chartreuse mountains of southeast France, to the route of stage 5 from Lyon to Grenoble.

There was a South American flavour added to the mix, too, in that Lucien Petit-Breton – a Frenchman born in Brittany who had moved to Buenos Aires, Argentina, as a child with his family, only returning to France in 1902 to enlist in the French army – was a very real contender for overall victory, having finished fifth overall at the 1905 Tour and fourth in 1906. Winning the very first edition of the Italian one-day Classic, Milan-San Remo, earlier in the 1907 season hadn't done his prospects much harm, either.

Petit-Breton – real name Lucien Mazan – had adopted the pseudonym while bike racing in Argentina, a moniker presumably given to him by Buenos Aires locals, to hide the fact that he raced from is disapproving father.

After taking control of the race on stage 10 to Bordeaux, the little Breton held on to the lead the rest of the way to the finish in Paris.

Publié par ATTINGER FRÈRES, éditeurs - PARIS

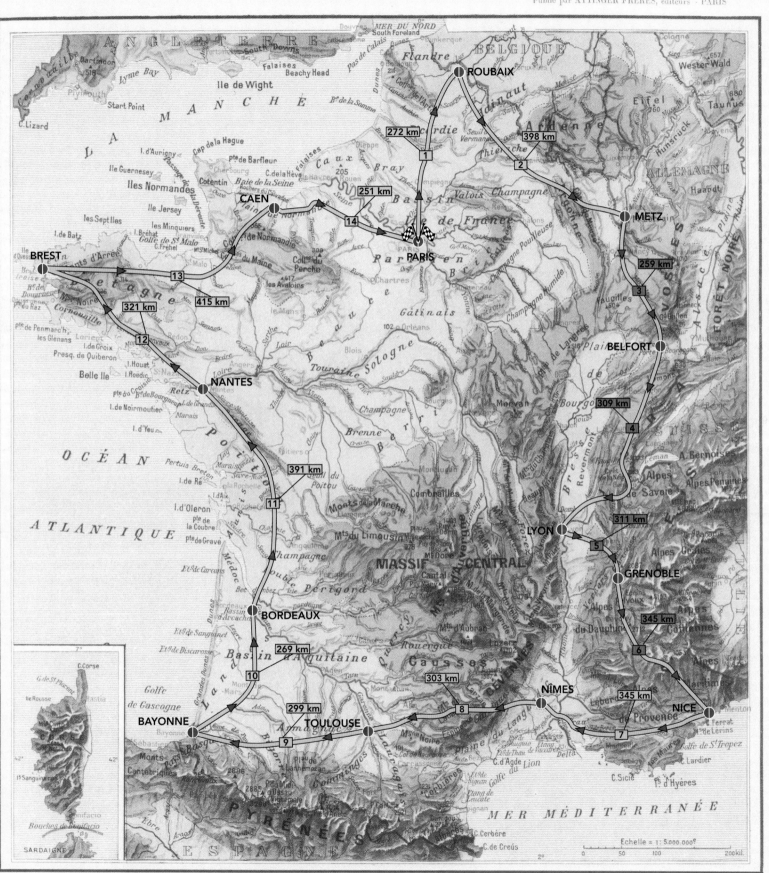

The Tour takes on the Ballon d'Alsace, in the Vosges mountains of eastern France, in 1908. The Ballon, the first ever genuine mountain climb in the Tour, first featured in the 1905 race, five years before the first appearance of the Pyrenees, and six years before the Alps.

1908
6th Edition

"It's time to hand over the mantle. Next year's Tour is for Faber."

1908 Tour champion Lucien Petit-Breton following his second consecutive overall victory, suggesting that Luxembourg's François Faber, his Peugeot team-mate, is the rightful heir to the Tour crown

Start: Paris, France, on 13 July
Finish: Paris, France, on 9 August

Total distance:
4488 km (2789 miles)
Longest stage:
415 km (258 miles)

Highest point:
Col de Porte: 1326 m (4350 ft)
Mountain stages: 4

Starters: 114
Finishers: 36

Winning time: 36 points
Average speed:
28.740 kph (17.858 mph)

1. Lucien Petit-Breton (Fra)
   36 points
2. François Faber (Lux) 68 points
3. Georges Passerieu (Fra)
   75 points

Lucien Petit-Breton arrived at the 1908 edition of the Tour in rude form, having already won that year's Paris-Brussels – a one-day race still in existence, now held in September, but then held in April.

The 1908 Tour followed the exact route of the previous edition, both starting on Paris's Ile de la Jatte and finishing at the Parc des Princes. The only real change was the number of starters – up to 114 from 93 the year before – and Petit-Breton's absolute dominance of the race this time, becoming the first rider to win two Tours (winner of the inaugural Tour, Maurice Garin, having been disqualified after cheating to win the 1904 edition).

Although London-born Georges Passerieu – second at the 1906 Tour to the late René Pottier – put up a good fight, winning stages 1, 5 and 13, and standing out as the only rider capable of getting over the Col de Porte and 'Pottier's mountain', the Ballon d'Alsace, without walking, his Peugeot-Wolber 'team-mates' (riders often simply shared the same sponsors rather than necessarily working as a team), Petit-Breton and François Faber, dominated the race with five and four stage victories apiece, respectively.

René Pottier's younger brother, André, helped to keep the family name alive by leading the race over the Col Bayard and Côte de Laffrey, but simply wasn't in the same league as his more famous sibling, and could only finish seventeenth overall in Paris.

François Faber struggles over the summit of the Ballon d'Alsace

François Faber won six stages on his way to overall victory in 1909

Start: Paris, France, on 5 July
Finish: Paris, France, on 1 August

Total distance:
4488 km (2789 miles)
Longest stage:
415 km (258 miles)

Highest point:
Col de Porte: 1326 m (4350 ft)
Mountain stages: 4

Starters: 150
Finishers: 55

Winning time: 37 points
Average speed:
28.658 kph (17.807 mph)

1. François Faber (Lux) 37 points
2. Gustave Garrigou (Fra)
   57 points
3. Jean Alavoine (Fra) 66 points

True to his word, 1907 and 1908 winner Lucien Petit-Breton retired from racing and followed the 1909 Tour as a journalist, leaving the door open for his former team-mate, François Faber, to take the race.

At 6 ft 2 in and weighing 91 kg, 'The Giant of Colombes' must have taken advantage of his bulk to help keep him warm in a race run in freezing conditions, and thought to still be the coldest weather ever encountered by the Tour.

Faber, to all extents and purposes a Frenchman but officially a Luxembourger, blazed to six stage wins – five of them consecutive – on his way to becoming 1909 Tour champion, and the race's first non-French winner.

Mondialisation – globalisation – is an oft-bandied-around term in modern Tour de France circles to describe the ever-growing number of countries that the race has visited and the ever-increasing number of nationalities that have taken part as riders. But the 1909 Tour saw not only its first foreign winner in Faber, but after Belgium's Cyrille van Hauwaert won the opening stage, non-French riders and French riders shared the fourteen stages with seven wins apiece.

The 1909 race had again followed a very similar route to that used in both 1907 and 1908, but the Tour was about to become much more mountainous...

Publié par ATTINGER FRÈRES, éditeurs - PARIS

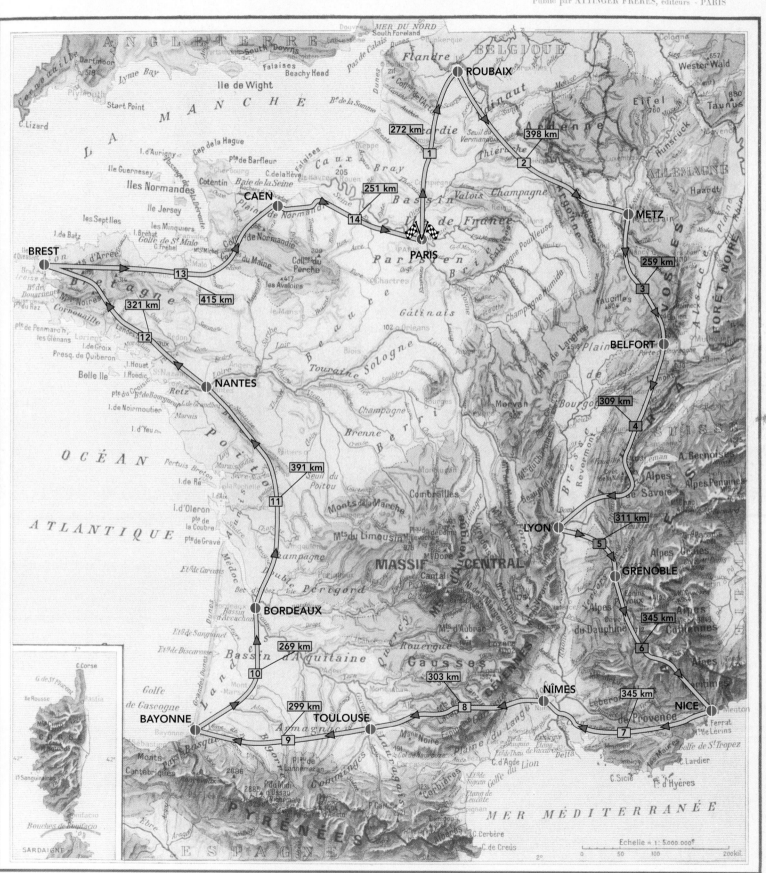

ROUBAIX

272 km
1

398 km
2

METZ

251 km
14

CAEN

259 km
3

BREST

13

BELFORT

415 km

321 km
12

309 km
4

NANTES

311 km
5

LYON

391 km
11

GRENOBLE

345 km
6

BORDEAUX

269 km
10

303 km
8

NÎMES

345 km
7

299 km
TOULOUSE

NICE

BAYONNE

9

PARIS

France's Octave Lapize trudges up the Col du Tourmalet in 1910. It was the first time that the 2115-m (6939-ft) pass had been used at the Tour, and was in fact the first time that the Pyrenees had been used at all. Despite having to walk, he was the first rider across the summit, and on the next climb — the Col d'Aubisque — he accused the race organisers of being murderers for taking the race over such difficult terrain. Lapize nevertheless went on to win the 1910 Tour overall.

"Crossed the Tourmalet. Very good road. Perfectly passable. Steines."

Alphonse Steines' telegram to boss Henri Desgrange having
failed to cross the Col du Tourmalet in January 1910

Although the overall race distance changed little, with only one extra stage added to make fifteen at the 1910 edition of the Tour, the big change was the addition of Pyrenean climbs to the race.

The Portet d'Aspet, Col du Peyresourde, Col d'Aspin, Col du Tourmalet and Col d'Aubisque all featured for the first time.

It was one of Henri Desgrange's employees, Alphonse Steines, whose job it had been to map the race since its 1903 beginnings, and it was therefore Steines that Desgrange sent to scout out the Pyrenees in January 1910 in the hope of including some tougher climbs that summer.

Steines almost killed himself trying to cross an impassable, blocked-by-snow Tourmalet but, for reasons only known to himself – perhaps not wishing to upset Desgrange – he sent his boss a telegram to say that the 2115-m (6939-ft) climb was "perfectly passable".

Come July, the snow had indeed gone, but 18 km of riding and walking up gradients of up to 10 per cent on unmade roads would test even the Tour's best riders in 1910.

Reaching the top of the Tourmalet without stopping – an easily quantifiable feat of strength in those early days of the Tour's climbs – earned Gustave Garrigou a 100-franc prize for his no-doubt considerable trouble.

He wasn't even first over the Tourmalet, though; that honour fell to overall race winner Octave Lapize, who then crested the summit of the stage's next climb, the 1709-m (5606-ft)-high Col d'Aubisque hollow-eyed and spitting, "You're all murderers!" in the race organisation's general direction.

1910 also saw the first appearance of the *voiture balai* – the broomwagon – so called because it's the final vehicle in the race convoy, 'sweeping up' riders unable to go any further due to exhaustion or injury. With the Pyrenees making their first appearance in the race, there were plenty of riders who needed it.

The inclusion of Pyrenean climbs takes its toll on a shattered Octave Lapize as he reaches the summit of the Col du Tourmalet during stage 10

Start: Paris, France, on 3 July
Finish: Paris, France, on 31 July

Total distance:
4737 km (2944 miles)
Longest stage:
424 km (264 miles)

Highest point: Col du Tourmalet:
2115 m (6939 ft)
Mountain stages: 6

Starters: 110
Finishers: 41

Winning time: 63 points
Average speed:
28.680 kph (17.822 mph)

1. Octave Lapize (Fra) 63 points
2. François Faber (Lux) 67 points
3. Gustave Garrigou (Fra)
   86 points

Publié par ATTINGER FRÈRES, éditeurs - PARIS

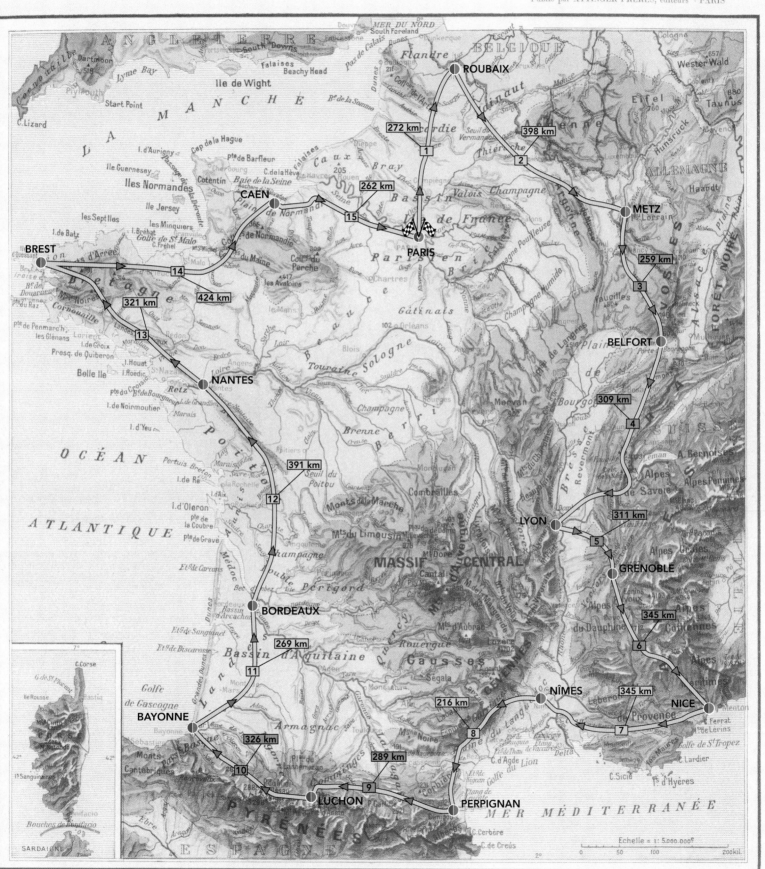

"Oh Sappey, oh Laffrey, oh Col Bayard, oh Tourmalet...
You are nothing compared to the Aubisque."

Henri Desgrange congratulates himself for having organised such a spectacular 1911 Tour

Gustave Garrigou battles the Col d'Aubisque on his way to overall victory

Start: Paris, France, on 2 July
Finish: Paris, France, on 30 July

Total distance:
5344 km (3321 miles)
Longest stage:
470 km (292 miles)

Highest point:
Col du Galibier: 2556 m (8386 ft)
Mountain stages: 7

Starters: 84
Finishers: 28

Winning time: 43 points
Average speed:
27.322 kph (16.977 mph)

1. Gustave Garrigou (Fra)
   43 points
2. Paul Duboc (Fra) 61 points
3. Émile Georget (Fra) 84 points

With Pyrenean climbs appearing for the first time in the 1910 Tour, it was only natural that the 1911 Tour should visit France's other great mountain range, the Alps.

As it had been every year since 1905, the climb of the Ballon d'Alsace was on the menu again, but stage 5 saw the riders face nothing short of an epic day as they tackled the Col des Aravis, the Col du Télégraphe, the Col du Lautaret and the monstrous Col du Galibier – all now today very familiar and oft-used climbs in the Tour.

Despite the anger of the previous year at having been sent over such an inhumane route as that through the Pyrenees, and despite the Alps being higher and arguably harder, the riders surprised even themselves by being dazzled by the beauty of these new Alpine climbs.

Émile Georget – who was to eventually finish third overall – was the first over the top of a still-snow-covered Galibier, having heaved his way up its muddy, unmade roads. He held his lead all the way to the finish of that fifth stage between Chamonix and Grenoble, too, taking the stage win over Paul Duboc by a whopping 15 minutes.

There was a step backwards, however: Germany no longer allowed the race to cross its borders and, with no Swiss visit this time, the race remained entirely within the borders of France.

Publié par ATTINGER FRÈRES, éditeurs - PARIS

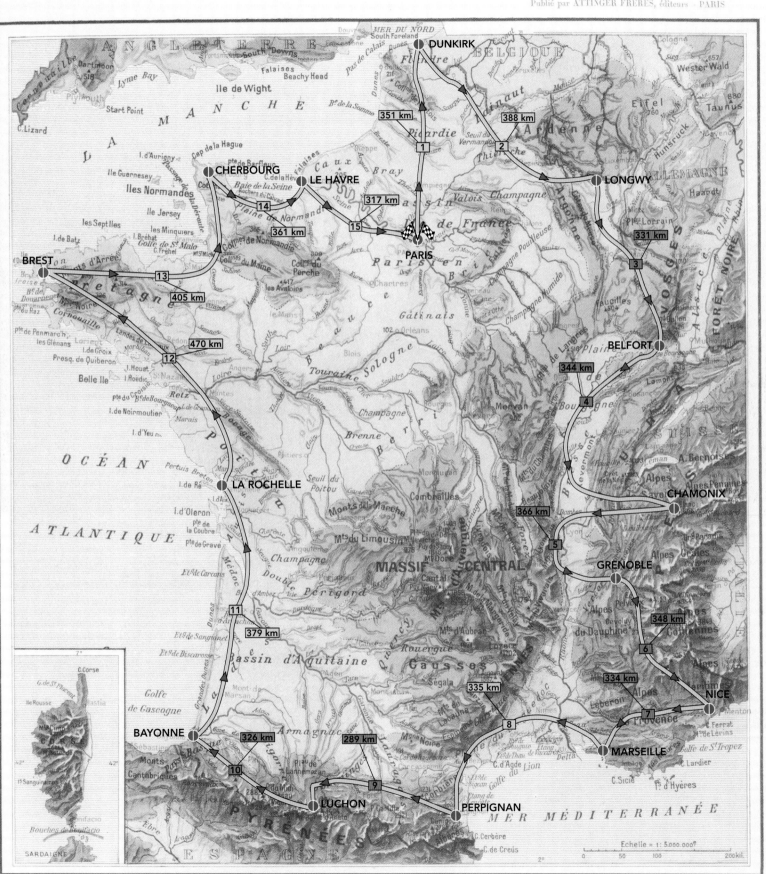

Eugène Christophe on his incredible 315-km breakaway

Start: Paris, France, on 30 June
Finish: Paris, France, on 28 July

Total distance:
5319 km (3305 miles)
Longest stage:
470 km (292 miles)

Highest point:
Col du Galibier: 2556 m (8386 ft)
Mountain stages: 7

Starters: 131
Finishers: 41

Winning time: 49 points
Average speed:
27.894 kph (17.333 mph)

1. Odile Defraye (Bel) 49 points
2. Eugène Christophe (Fra)
   108 points
3. Gustave Garrigou (Fra)
   140 points

The 1912 Tour followed the same route as the 1911 edition, save for a slightly shortened sixth stage. This time, the French fans' hero was to be Eugène Christophe, who effectively replaced Émile Georget in their hearts after the third-placed finisher in 1911 abandoned on the third stage of the 1912 race.

Christophe's was a name that was about to become synonymous with the Tour de France for a number of reasons in the years following the 10th edition of the race, but became legendary enough in 1912 when the French rider staged the race's longest-ever successful breakaway.

Just as Georget had done the year before, it was Christophe who led the race over the Aravis, Télégraphe, Lautaret and Galibier as part of a 315-km (196-mile) break, winning in Grenoble with only two-and-a-half minutes to spare over countryman Octave Lapize.

With that 315 km (196 miles) being around 100 km (62 miles) longer than any complete stage in the modern era, it's not going to be beaten any time soon – read, ever.

By virtue of winning three stages – stage 4 by a considerable margin of more than 13 minutes – it's likely that Christophe would have won the race overall in 1912 had it been contested on time. Instead, for the final time that it was decided on points, it was Odile Defraye who became the first ever Belgian winner of the Tour, easily beating Christophe for consistency by finishing in the top ten on every one of the race's fifteen stages, bar one.

From 1912 on, Belgian riders would come to play a huge part in the race's success and history.

Publié par ATTINGER FRÈRES, éditeurs · PARIS

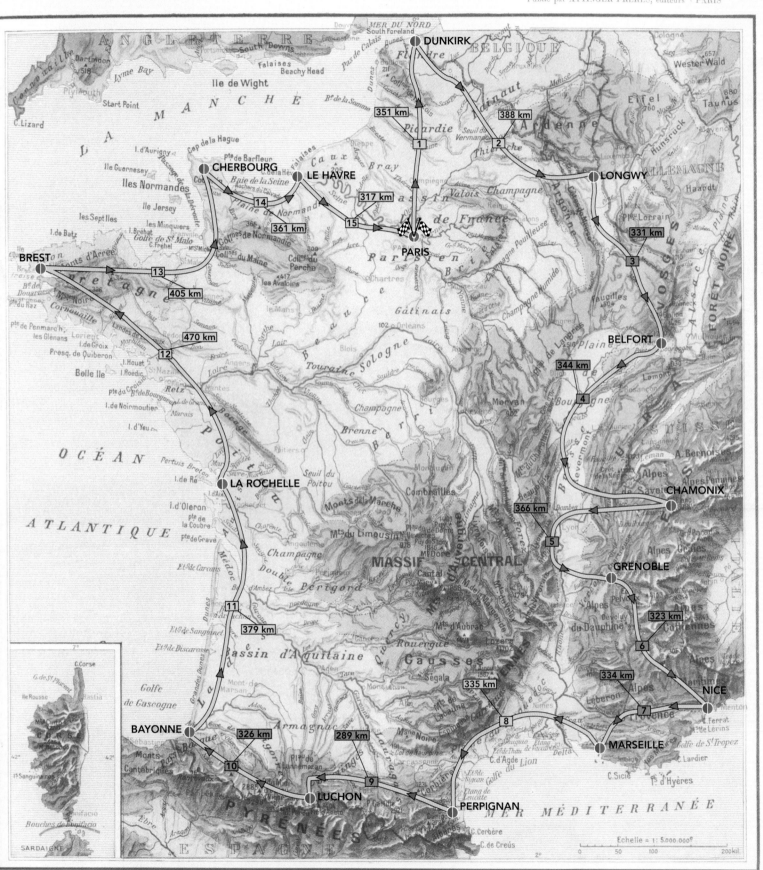

1913
11th Edition

Start: Paris, France, on 29 June
Finish: Paris, France, on 27 July

Total distance:
5388 km (3348 miles)
Longest stage:
470 km (292 miles)

Highest point:
Col du Galibier: 2556 m (8386 ft)
Mountain stages: 7

Starters: 140
Finishers: 25

Winning time: 197 h 54' 00"
Average speed:
26.715 kph (16.600 mph)

1. Philippe Thys (Bel)
2. Gustave Garrigou (Fra)
   at 8' 37"
3. Marcel Buysse (Bel)
   at 3 h 30' 55"

As well as reverting back to cumulative time rather than points deciding the race's overall winner, the Tour headed off from Paris for an anti-clockwise circuit of France for the first time in 1913. That said, it followed an extremely similar route to the previous two editions of the race, visiting almost all of the same towns, from the other direction.

Some went as far as to say that organiser Desgrange's decision to revert to time as the measure of his race's winner was in an effort to help a Frenchman win – namely Eugène Christophe, runner-up in 1912.

However, what happened to Christophe on stage 6, on the road between Bayonne and Luchon, soon put the kibosh on that theory. While descending the Col du Tourmalet, Christophe's forks snapped, requiring him to run the rest of the way down the mountain to the town at the bottom – Ste-Marie-de-Campan – where he found a blacksmith willing to allow him to use his tools to effect a repair. However, the fact that the blacksmith's assistant operated the bellows to help Christophe contravened race rules that stipulated that a rider couldn't receive any outside assistance.

The Frenchman was handed a time penalty, and Belgian rider Philippe Thys went on to win the race by just eight-and-a-half minutes over Frenchman Gustave Garrigou, meaning that, for the second year in a row, there was a foreign winner, which wouldn't have pleased an organiser trying to promote a French newspaper to a French public.

In fact, Belgian riders would win the race seven times in a row before a French rider would win his home race again.

Anyone who thinks that today's *maladie* of there having been no French winner since 1985 need only look to the past to see that everything goes in cycles.

Eugène Christophe's repairs are in vain as he is subsequently penalised for accepting outside assistance

Publié par ATTINGER FRÈRES, éditeurs - PARIS

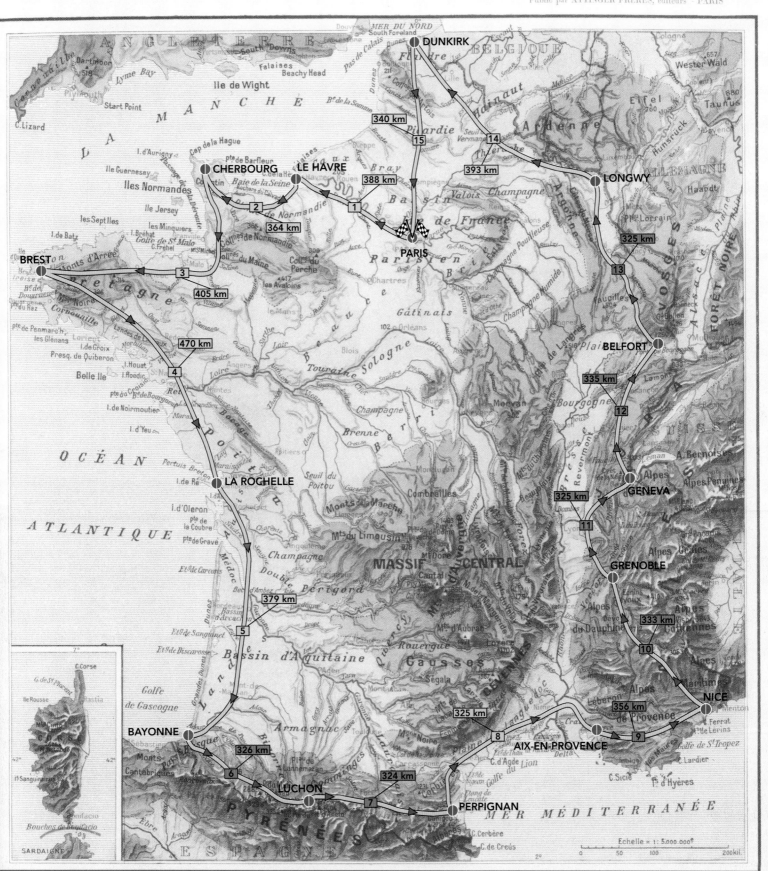

1914
12th Edition

Debutant Henri Pélissier races from Grenoble to Geneva

Start: Paris, France, on 28 June
Finish: Paris, France, on 26 July

Total distance:
5391 km (3350 miles)
Longest stage:
470 km (292 miles)

Highest point:
Col du Galibier: 2556 m (8386 ft)
Mountain stages: 7

Starters: 145
Finishers: 54

Winning time: 200 h 28' 48"
Average speed:
27.028 kph (16.795 mph)

1. Philippe Thys (Bel)
2. Henri Pélissier (Fra) at 1' 50"
3. Jean Alavoine (Fra) at 36' 53"

After 1913's relatively close finish to the race, reigning champion Philippe Thys started the 1914 Tour in earnest, winning the sprint from an eleven-man lead group on stage 1, and then never letting go of the lead again. It looked as though it was going to be a dominating show of riding from the Belgian.

Sure enough, Thys had built up a 35-minute lead over Henri Pélissier, a 25-year-old Frenchman riding his first Tour de France, by the time the race exited the Pyrenees. Pélissier pushed the race leader hard in the Alps, but had only been able to reduce his deficit by a few minutes going into the fourteenth and penultimate stage between Longwy and Dunkirk.

Thys, however, was docked 30 minutes for an illegal wheel change on the stage, and Pélissier trailed Thys by just 1 minute 50 seconds when they reached the finish in the Parc des Princes in Paris the next day, having won three stages along the way.

The 1914 Tour also saw the first participation by an Australian rider, with two of them – Don Kirkham and Iddo 'Snowy' Munro – lining up together for the off in Paris at the end of June.

Both made it all the way around and back to Paris, in seventeenth and twentieth place, respectively, but another foreign rider, poor Ali Neffati – a Tunisian riding his second Tour who had garnered a number of fans for choosing to wear a fez while he rode – was less fortunate, hit by one of the organisation's cars on stage 6, and forced to abandon for the second year in a row.

Two days after the race finished in Paris, Austria-Hungary declared war on Serbia, following the assassination of Archduke Franz Ferdinand a month earlier, on the day the Tour had started. The First World War would put paid to the Tour de France for the next five years.

Publié par ATTINGER FRÈRES, éditeurs - PARIS

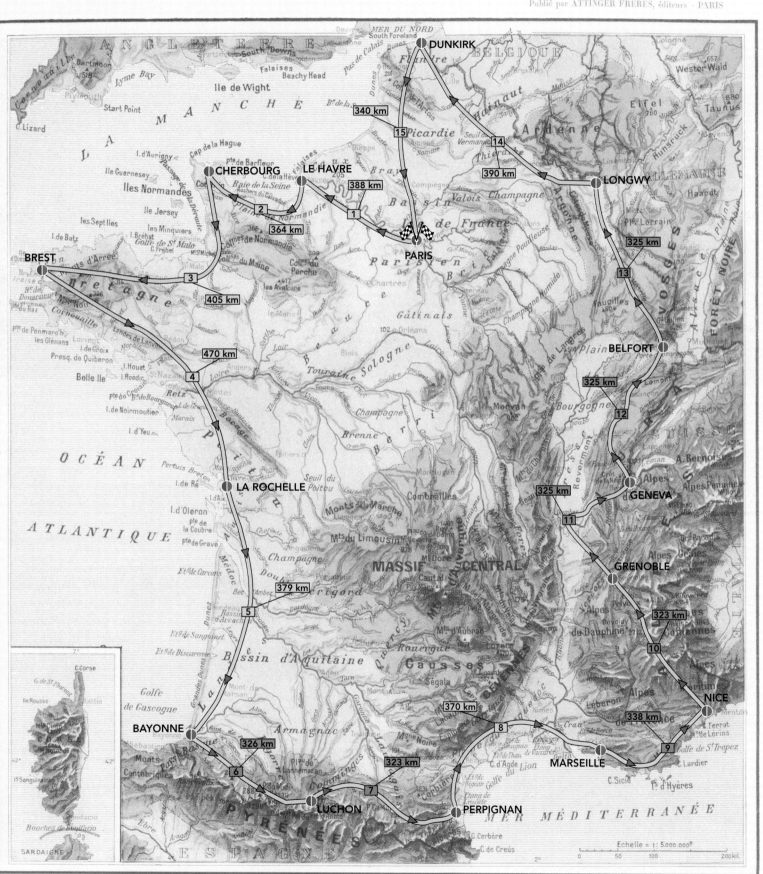

"No rider deserves it more than he does."

Henri Desgrange on Eugène Christophe's credentials
for being the first rider ever to wear the Tour's yellow jersey

Firmin Lambot is congratulated after claiming the yellow jersey in Dunkirk

Start: Paris, France, on 29 June
Finish: Paris, France, on 27 July

Total distance:
5560 km (3455 miles)
Longest stage:
482 km (300 miles)

Highest point:
Col du Galibier: 2556 m (8386 ft)
Mountain stages: 6

Starters: 67
Finishers: 10

Winning time: 231 h 07' 15"
Average speed:
24.056 kph (14.948 mph)

1. Firmin Lambot (Bel)
2. Jean Alavoine (Fra)
    at 1 h 42' 54"
3. Eugène Christophe (Fra)
    at 2 h 26' 31"

The Tour resurfaced with a cold, wet and just downright miserable schlep of a 1919 edition through a war-ravaged France. Three past winners – Lucien Petit-Breton, François Faber and Octave Lapize – had been killed during the First World War, and many of the riders arrived at the race weary and out of shape, which was said to have contributed to what was, and remains, the Tour's slowest ever average speed: 24.056 kph (14.948 mph).

It won't have helped, either, that the organisers saw fit to include the race's longest-ever stage: a 482-km (300-mile) route between Les Sables-d'Olonne and Bayonne. It was a stage the race would then use every year until 1924; it was common in the early years of the Tour to repeat stages year after year, but today, with competition between towns to host stages fierce, the race follows a different route every year.

French darling Eugène Christophe was back in 1919, as was defending champion Philippe Thys, winner in 1913 and 1914.

Thys, however, soon abandoned, ill, on stage 1; he'd be back the following year. Christophe, though, took over the race lead from compatriot Henri Pélissier after stage 4.

After six stages at the head of the race, Christophe was awarded a yellow jersey by race organiser Henri Desgrange at the café L'Ascenseur in Grenoble, at the start of stage 11 on 19 July. The choice of colour to identify the race leader was in order to further publicise Desgrange's newspaper, *L'Auto*, which was printed on yellow paper.

Christophe held the *maillot jaune* for another four stages before bad luck hit. Ironically, just as they had done in 1913 on the Tourmalet, Christophe's forks broke while riding the cobbles between Metz and Dunkirk on stage 14, forcing him to fix them and cede the race lead – and the jersey – to Belgium's Firmin Lambot, who wore it, and defended it, on the next day's final stage to Paris.

DUNKIRK

340 km
15

388 km
1

468 km
14

METZ
315 km
13

STRASBOURG

371 km
12

CHERBOURG

364 km
2

LE HAVRE

PARIS

405 km
3

412 km
4

LES SABLES-
D'OLONNE

GENEVA

325 km
11

482 km
5

GRENOBLE

333 km
10

370 km
8

NICE

338 km
9

BAYONNE

326 km
6

LUCHON

323 km
7

MARSEILLE

PERPIGNAN

49

Invading crowds celebrate with riders as they finish in the Parc des Princes velodrome

Start: Paris, France, on 27 June
Finish: Paris, France, on 25 July

Total distance:
5503 km (3420 miles)
Longest stage:
482 km (300 miles)

Highest point:
Col du Galibier: 2556 m (8386 ft)
Mountain stages: 5

Starters: 113
Finishers: 22

Winning time: 228 h 36' 13"
Average speed:
24.072 kph (14.958 mph)

1. Philippe Thys (Bel)
2. Hector Heusghem (Bel)
   at 57' 21"
3. Firmin Lambot (Bel)
   at 1 h 39' 35"

Following the war, 1913 and 1914 Tour champ Philippe Thys had arrived at the 1919 race out of shape and in ill health, quitting on the first stage. He arrived at the 1920 Tour in June a changed man, and proceeded to dish out a hammering to his rivals, taking the yellow jersey on stage 2 and never relinquishing it, with the added bonus of no fewer than four stage victories along the way.

In Paris, Henri Desgrange's face must have been a picture as three Belgians stood atop his podium in the Parc des Princes.

That made it three Tour victories for Thys – the 'winningest' rider in the race's history so far. The poor performances of the French riders – Honoré Barthélémy was the best placed of them down in eighth – angered Desgrange, who took out his fury on Henri Pélissier, who in turn had quit the race in a huff. Even golden-boy Eugène Christophe couldn't help Desgrange out with any fan-friendly heroics: the unlucky Frenchman's forks may have stayed in one piece on this occasion, but his body didn't, and he was forced to retire on the seventh stage with backache.

It had arguably been an easier Tour than many of the previous editions, with only five mountain stages against the usual six or seven, and the flatter stages seemed to play into the hands of the Belgians. Despite that, and despite Desgrange's desire to see 'his' French riders in the thick of the action, the following two Tours followed much the same format.

DUNKIRK

340 km
15

433 km
14

CHERBOURG

LE HAVRE

364 km
2

388 km
1

METZ

300 km
13

STRASBOURG

405 km
3

PARIS

412 km
4

354 km
12

LES SABLES-
D'OLONNE

GEX

362 km
11

482 km
5

GRENOBLE

333 km
10

BAYONNE

325 km
8

356 km
9

NICE

AIX-EN-PROVENCE

326 km
6

323 km
7

LUCHON

PERPIGNAN

51

The scars of the First World War are still evident as riders make their way through ruins in Montdidier

Start: Paris, France, on 26 June
Finish: Paris, France, on 24 July

Total distance:
5485 km (3408 miles)
Longest stage: 482 km (300 miles)

Highest point:
Col du Galibier: 2556 m (8386 ft)
Mountain stages: 5

Starters: 123
Finishers: 38

Winning time: 221 h 50' 26"
Average speed:
24.720 kph (15.360 mph)

1. Léon Scieur (Bel)
2. Hector Heusghem (Bel)
   at 18' 36"
3. Honoré Barthélémy (Fra)
   at 2 h 01' 00"

A still-sulking Henri Pélissier didn't even turn up to the 1921 Tour, while Tour organiser Henri Desgrange – with whom Pélissier had fallen out – continued to earn a reputation as somewhat of a curmudgeon, with his on-a-whim rules, his constant complaints about riders not trying hard enough and his anger at France's apparent inability to challenge the dominant Belgian riders.

He might have been secretly pleased when 1920 Tour winner Philippe Thys was forced to quit the race after the first stage, suffering from illness, perhaps secretly hoping that it would open the door for France's best hope of overall victory, Honoré Barthélémy.

The Belgians, however, found themselves with strength in numbers, and it was 33-year-old Belgian rider Léon Scieur – who had only learned to ride a bike aged 22 – who came to the fore.

The man who had taught him to ride was none other than 1919 Tour winner Firmin Lambot, who hailed from the same Belgian village – Florennes – as Scieur. In fact, the pair remain the only two riders to come from the same town who have both won the Tour de France.

Barthélémy helped save French blushes by taking third spot overall, albeit more than two hours adrift, but with Scieur's compatriot Hector Heusghem again finishing runner-up, as he had done the year before. The Belgians had more than just arrived; they had positively taken over the Tour de France.

DUNKIRK

340 km
15

433 km
14

388 km
1

CHERBOURG

364 km
2

LE HAVRE

METZ

300 km
13

405 km
3

PARIS

STRASBOURG

412 km
4

371 km
12

LES SABLES-
D'OLONNE

GENEVA

325 km
11

482 km
5

GRENOBLE

333 km
10

BAYONNE

411 km
8

272 km
9

NICE

326 km
6

323 km
7

TOULON

LUCHON

PERPIGNAN

53

1922
16th Edition

Start: Paris, France, on 25 June
Finish: Paris, France, on 23 July

Total distance:
5372 km (3338 miles)
Longest stage:
482 km (300 miles)

Highest point:
Col du Galibier: 2556 m (8386 ft)
Mountain stages: 5

Starters: 120
Finishers: 38

Winning time: 222 h 08' 06"
Average speed:
24.196 kph (15.034 mph)

1. Firmin Lambot (Bel)
2. Jean Alavoine (Fra) at 41' 15"
3. Félix Sellier (Bel) at 42' 02"

Just as it had done since 1913, the Tour continued to follow the same tried and trusted anti-clockwise route from Paris to Le Havre on stage 1, down France's west coast, through the Pyrenees, then the Alps, with a final stage from Dunkirk back to Paris. The drudgery seemed to be amplified by yet another Belgian win – the seventh in succession – this time a second win by 1919 champion Firmin Lambot, now a relic of a man at 36 years, 4 months and 9 days old. He remains the oldest ever winner of the race.

Stage 4, between Brest and Les Sables-d'Olonne, saw some older names come to the fore as Philippe Thys – Tour champ in 1913, 1914 and 1920 – took the stage victory, and perennial nearly-man Eugène Christophe took hold of the yellow jersey.

However, on the Galibier, on stage 11, Christophe – having by then dropped out of overall contention by losing too much time on stage 9 – experienced the misfortune of his forks breaking for a third time at the Tour. Yellow jerseys and stage wins had made him a household name, but luck – or a lack of it – would see to it that he was destined never to win his beloved Tour de France.

While Alpine giants the Col d'Izoard and Col de Vars both made their first Tour appearances – on stage 10 between Nice and Briançon – crowd favourite the Col du Tourmalet, which had appeared in the race every year since 1910, had to be dropped from the route of stage 6 due to snow.

Firmin Lambot and Joseph Muller quench their thirst between Les Sables-d'Olonne and Bayonne

DUNKIRK

340 km · 15

432 km · 14

CHERBOURG

LE HAVRE

364 km · 2 · 388 km

METZ

300 km · 13

405 km · 3

🏁 🏁 PARIS · 1

STRASBOURG

412 km · 4

371 km · 12

LES SABLES-D'OLONNE

GENEVA

482 km · 5

260 km · 11

BRIANÇON

274 km · 10

411 km · 8

284 km · NICE

BAYONNE

9

326 km · 6

323 km · 7

TOULON

LUCHON

PERPIGNAN

55

Ottavio Bottecchia became the first Italian to don the iconic *maillot jaune*

Start: Paris, France, on 24 June
Finish: Paris, France, on 22 July

Total distance:
5396 km (3353 miles)
Longest stage:
482 km (300 miles)

Highest point:
Col du Galibier: 2556 m (8386 ft)
Mountain stages: 5

Starters: 139
Finishers: 48

Winning time: 222 h 15' 30"
Average speed:
24.233 kph (15.057 mph)

1. Henri Pélissier (Fra)
2. Ottavio Bottecchia (Ita)
   at 30' 41"
3. Romain Bellenger (Fra)
   at 1 h 04' 43"

If the previous few editions of the race had become dull and somewhat predictable, national pride was restored when Henri Pélissier became the first French winner since Gustave Garrigou in 1911.

Pélissier's victory came despite organiser Henri Desgrange having opined a couple of years earlier that Pélissier "will never win", threatening he would never put him on the front of his newspaper, *L'Auto*, in retaliation for what he viewed as Pélissier's laziness as a rider.

Pélissier set Desgrange straight all right in 1923, forcing the Tour organiser to print a *L'Auto* cover that went against his earlier wishes as Pélissier crushed his closest rivals by more than half-an-hour overall.

Along the way, runner-up Ottavio Bottecchia became the first Italian to wear the yellow jersey after sprinting to victory on stage 2 from Le Havre to Cherbourg, and proceeded to ride a consistent race, while Pélissier took a beating from compatriot and two-time runner-up Jean Alavoine in the Pyrenees. However, Alavoine crashed on stage 10 and was forced to retire the next day, while Bottecchia was outclassed in the Alps by Pélissier.

In a combination of what Desgrange had done with his race in the past – first basing it on overall time, then on points, and then back to cumulative time – for the first time in 1923, a two-minute time bonus to the winner of each stage was introduced. It was a practice that was to fall in and out of favour over the years.

Pélissier clashed again with Desgrange at the 1924 Tour and, following his retirement from cycling in 1927, Pélissier's life took a turn for the worse. After his wife committed suicide in 1933, he was shot and killed in 1935 by his mistress, who had acted in self-defence.

DUNKIRK

CHERBOURG

LE HAVRE

343 km

15

381 km

1

433 km

14

METZ

300 km

13

371 km

2

PARIS

405 km

3

STRASBOURG

412 km

4

377 km

12

LES SABLES-
D'OLONNE

GENEVA

11

260 km

BRIANÇON

482 km

5

275 km

10

281 km

NICE

427 km

9

BAYONNE

8

TOULON

326 km

6

LUCHON

323 km

7

PERPIGNAN

1924
18th Edition

"One of these days he's going to make us put lead weights in our pockets because he thinks that God made man too light."

1923 Tour champion Henri Pélissier after quitting the 1924 Tour in disgust at what for him were Henri Desgrange's constant efforts to make the race even harder

Start: Paris, France, on 22 June
Finish: Paris, France, on 20 July

Total distance:
5425 km (3371 miles)
Longest stage:
482 km (300 miles)

Highest point:
Col du Galibier: 2556 m (8386 ft)
Mountain stages: 6

Starters: 157
Finishers: 60

Winning time: 226 h 18' 21"
Average speed:
24.250 kph (15.068 mph)

1. Ottavio Bottecchia (Ita)
2. Nicolas Frantz (Lux)
   at 35' 36"
3. Lucien Buysse (Bel)
   at 1 h 32' 13"

With the life of the winner of the 1923 Tour, Henri Pélissier, ending in tragedy, what an ill-fated time it was in the Tour's history, when 1924 and 1925 champion Ottavio Bottecchia was also found dead in mysterious circumstances years later.

Bottecchia was found unconscious at the side of the road in June 1927, close to his home near Udine, in northern Italy, seemingly having crashed on his bike. He had a fractured skull and never regained consciousness, dying twelve days later. Officially, his death was attributed to injuries sustained from the crash. The conspiracy theory, however, is that he was murdered by Mussolini-supporting fascists for voicing his low opinion of the Italian prime minister.

Bottecchia won the first stage of the 1924 Tour – a stage that had become the regular opener, between Paris and Le Havre – and then held on to his lead along each side of 'the hexagon', over fifteen stages, and back to Paris. Bottecchia had become the first Italian to finish on the podium the year before, and stepped up to take cycling's ultimate prize. So pleased was he with his yellow jersey, in fact, that he wore it all the way home to Milan on the train.

With no French rider even on the podium in 1924 – yet another argument between the two Henris, Desgrange and Pélissier, saw the defending champion quit the race early on – this early *mondialisation* of the Tour came at France's expense. Things were really going to change in 1925 – bar Bottecchia winning again.

Ottavio Bottecchia climbs through the crowds on the Col du Tourmalet

DUNKIRK

343 km
15

433 km
14

CHERBOURG

LE HAVRE

371 km
2

381 km
1

METZ

300 km
13

PARIS

405 km
3

STRASBOURG

412 km
4

360 km
12

LES SABLES-
D'OLONNE

GEX

307 km
11

BRIANÇON

482 km
5

275 km
10

427 km
8

280 km
NICE

BAYONNE

9

326 km
6

TOULON

323 km
7

LUCHON

PERPIGNAN

A weary Bartolomeo Aimo struggles up to the Col d'Izoard

Start: Paris, France, on 21 June
Finish: Paris, France, on 19 July

Total distance:
5430 km (3374 miles)
Longest stage:
433 km (269 miles)

Highest point:
Col du Galibier: 2556 m (8386 ft)
Mountain stages: 6

Starters: 130
Finishers: 49

Winning time: 219 h 10' 18"
Average speed:
24.820 kph (15.422 mph)

1. Ottavio Bottecchia (Ita)
2. Lucien Buysse (Bel) at 54' 20"
3. Bartolomeo Aimo (Ita)
   at 56' 37"

While Ottavio Bottecchia again won the Tour de France in 1925, fundamental changes were made by organiser Henri Desgrange to help push his race forward. The Tour increased its number of stages – up to eighteen from the fifteen it had been run over for so long – and the time bonuses for stage wins were done away with, for the time being. Desgrange even went as far as proposing that every rider was to eat the same amount of food, but that idea was dropped after the riders threatened to strike.

The race also started a little further outside Paris, in the suburb of Le Vésinet, while new stage start/finish towns included Mulhouse, near the Swiss border and, a little further south, spa town Évian.

Bottecchia started where he had left off, winning the first stage to Le Havre before losing the jersey two days later to unheralded Belgian Adelin Benoît.

There was to be no repeat of the Italian's 1923 Tour win when he wore the famous golden tunic from start to finish, but Bottecchia was back in yellow after winning the flat stage 7 between Bordeaux and Bayonne.

Benoît then showed the race his climbing legs, winning the tough first day in the Pyrenees and reclaiming the race lead before Bottecchia took control once more the next day – and this time retained yellow all the way to Paris.

It was also Eugène Christophe's last Tour – the unlucky Frenchman whose dreams of winning the race were dashed by broken forks, but who nonetheless would always be remembered as the first ever wearer of the yellow jersey in 1919. Christophe finished a lowly eighteenth overall, almost seven hours down on the Italian winner. In fact, no French rider was even to finish in the top ten; Romain Bellenger was the highest-placed home rider in eleventh.

DUNKIRK

CHERBOURG

LE HAVRE

METZ

PARIS

343 km

18

340 km

1

371 km

2

405 km

3

4

08 km

VANNES

204 km

5

293 km

6

LES SABLES-
D'OLONNE

BORDEAUX

189 km

7

BAYONNE

326 km

8

LUCHON

9

323 km

PERPIGNAN

215 km

10

NÎMES

215 km

11

TOULON

280 km

NICE

12

275 km

13

BRIANÇON

14

303 km

ÉVIAN

373 km

15

MULHOUSE

16

334 km

17

433 km

61

Lucien Buysse powers to victory despite personal tragedy

Start: Évian, France, on 20 June
Finish: Paris, France, on 18 July

Total distance:
5745 km (3570 miles)
Longest stage:
433 km (269 miles)

Highest point:
Col du Galibier: 2556 m (8386 ft)
Mountain stages: 6

Starters: 126
Finishers: 41

Winning time: 238 h 44' 25"
Average speed:
24.273 kph (15.082 mph)

1. Lucien Buysse (Bel)
2. Nicolas Frantz (Lux)
   at 1 h 22' 25"
3. Bartolomeo Aimo (Ita)
   at 1 h 22' 51"

Radical changes the year previously turned yet more radical as the Tour started outside Paris for the first time. Évian, a town that had featured in the race for the first time only the year before – and best known today for its bottled water – was truly put on the map thanks to being used for the race's *Grand Départ*. The race returned to its Paris start in 1927, however, where it remained until 1951, and a start in Metz. Only then did the race start in a different town or city each year, until 2003 when, for one year only, it started again in Paris, on the site of the Au Réveil Matin café, where it had started in 1903, to celebrate 100 years of the race. In a sad footnote, the building was gutted by fire in late 2003, barely two months after the Tour start.

At 5745 km (3570 miles), the 1926 edition was, and remains, the longest-ever Tour de France, although Desgrange dropped the total number of stages down to seventeen from eighteen the year before. He preferred longer, more epic stages, and judged the distances of the 1925 stages to be too short.

Thirty-three-year-old Belgian Lucien Buysse, second to Bottecchia in 1925, won overall in 1926, despite receiving the shocking news on stage 3 that his daughter had died. He only continued in the race after being encouraged to do so by his family.

His younger brother, 24-year-old Jules, had won the opening stage between Évian and Mulhouse by a massive 13-minute margin, and held yellow until stage 3. They became – and remain – the only brothers to wear the yellow jersey in the same edition of the race.

The Tour's globalisation continued, too, when Kisso Kawamura became the first Japanese rider to take part – although he abandoned during the first stage.

DUNKIRK

4 361 km

3 433 km

CHERBOURG

LE HAVRE

5 357 km

METZ

PARIS

17 341 km

2 334 km

6 405 km

MULHOUSE

7 412 km

DIJON

1 373 km

16 321 km

ÉVIAN

LES SABLES-D'OLONNE

8 285 km

15 303 km

BRIANÇON

BORDEAUX

9 189 km

14 275 km

BAYONNE

NICE

12 427 km

13 280 km

10 326 km

TOULON

11 323 km

LUCHON

PERPIGNAN

MANCHE

MER MÉDITERRANÉE

63

André Leducq (left) and Tour champion Nicolas Frantz (right)

Start: Paris, France, on 19 June
Finish: Paris, France, on 17 July

Total distance:
5320 km (3306 miles)
Longest stage:
360 km (224 miles)

Highest point:
Col du Galibier: 2556 m (8386 ft)
Mountain stages: 6

Starters: 142
Finishers: 39

Winning time: 198 h 16' 42"
Average speed:
27.244 kph (16.928 mph)

1. Nicolas Frantz (Lux)
2. Maurice De Waele (Bel)
   at 1 h 48' 21"
3. Julien Vervaecke (Bel)
   at 2 h 25' 06"

Francis Pélissier's older brother, Henri, had done little to impress Tour organiser Henri Desgrange over the years. The two were almost permanently at loggerheads over how tough the race was – Henri the rider believing that it was too hard; organiser Henri always on the hunt for something to make it even harder. Even Henri's 1923 victory displeased the race founder: it meant he had to put Pélissier on the cover of his newspaper.

One can only imagine, then, Desgrange's feelings when Francis Pélissier became the first rider to quit the Tour while clad in the by-now hallowed yellow jersey. He was simply unable to match the speed set by his Dilecta-Wolber team-mates on stage 6 – one of the race's many team time trials – and waved them onwards once it all became too much. It was in fact a good call: his team-mate, Ferdinand Le Drogo, took yellow in Brest that evening, although, by the end of the ninth stage, the whole eight-man team had quit the race.

It's a dubious 'honour' for the young Pélissier to hold. Only fifteen riders have ever abandoned while in the yellow tunic, Britain's Chris Boardman being another, in 1998, with the latest being Michael Rasmussen at the 2007 Tour, thrown out by his Rabobank team for having lied on his UCI 'whereabouts' form about where dope testers would be able to find him. He told them Mexico; he was training in Italy.

Nicolas Frantz became the second rider from Luxembourg to win the race, following in the tyre tracks of 1909 champion François Faber.

Dinan, Vannes, Pontarlier and Charleville were used as stage starts/ finishes for the first time in a race made up of a massive twenty-four stages, with sixteen of those run as team time trials, in which teams started at 15-minute intervals, confusing the spectators immensely. Sponsored teams – usually headlined by bicycle manufacturers – had only just begun to reappear following a number of financially difficult post-war years for the major bike brands, such as Alcyon, Dilecta and JB Louvet.

DUNKIRK

270 km
23

344 km
24

CHARLEVILLE
159 km
22

DIEPPE
2
103 km
METZ
165 km
21

CHERBOURG
140 km
4
LE HAVRE
180 km
1
STRASBOURG

CAEN
3
225 km
145 km
20

199 km
5
BELFORT
119 km
19

206 km
DINAN
6

7
207 km
PONTARLIER
213 km
18

VANNES
ÉVIAN

204 km
8
283 km
17

LES SABLES-
D'OLONNE
BRIANÇON

285 km
9
275 km
16

BORDEAUX
NICE

189 km
10
280 km
15

360 km
13
120 km
BAYONNE
MARSEILLE
14

TOULON

326 km
11
323 km
12
PERPIGNAN

LUCHON

65

1928
22nd Edition

Nicolas Frantz won despite losing 40 minutes due to a mechanical problem

Start: Paris, France, on 17 June
Finish: Paris, France, on 15 July

Total distance:
5475 km (3402 miles)
Longest stage:
387 km (241 miles)

Highest point:
Col du Galibier: 2556 m (8386 ft)
Mountain stages: 6

Starters: 162
Finishers: 41

Winning time: 192 h 48' 58"
Average speed:
28.400 kph (17.646 mph)

1. Nicolas Frantz (Lux)
2. André Leducq (Fra) at 50' 07"
3. Maurice De Waele (Bel)
   at 56' 16"

Nicolas Frantz's convincing 1927 Tour win was repeated in 1928, and this time he became only the second rider to hold the yellow jersey all the way from start to finish. Ottavio Bottecchia had been the first to perform the feat, in 1924, but that was 'only' over fifteen stages. Luxembourger Frantz defended it over twenty-two stages.

It was touch and go as late as stage 19 between Metz and Charleville, however, when a mechanical problem lost Frantz 40 minutes to stage winner Marcel Huot of the Alleluia-Wolber outfit, but by that point in the race, Frantz had enough of a buffer over team-mate André Leducq to ensure that the race was in the bag anyway.

Leducq, having finished fourth overall, and best Frenchman, the year before, held the French end up again, improving this time to finish runner-up to his Alcyon team-mate, the dominant Frantz. The importance of team riding continued to grow – in the Tour's first couple of decades in existence, riders rode very much for themselves – and Desgrange stuck with the team time trial format for most of the race, despite the confusion of the roadside crowds. Of the Tour's twenty-two stages, fifteen were held as team time trials.

One of those teams was the French-sponsored, but green-and-gold-jerseyed, Ravat-Wonder-Dunlop squad, made up of three Australian riders – Ernie Bainbridge, Hubert Opperman (knighted in 1968 for his work as the Maltese High Commissioner) and Perry Osborne – plus a Kiwi, Harry Watson.

MALO-LES-BAINS

234 km
21

271 km
20

CHARLEVILLE

159 km
19

DIEPPE

330 km
22

207 km
1

METZ

165 km
18

CHERBOURG

140 km
2

CAEN

STRASBOURG

145 km
17

199 km
3

DINAN

206 km
4

PARIS

BELFORT

5

119 km
16

208 km

VANNES

PONTARLIER

213 km
15

204 km
6

ÉVIAN

LES SABLES-
D'OLONNE

329 km
14

285 km
7

GRENOBLE

BORDEAUX

333 km
13

225 km
8

363 km
11

NICE

330 km
12

HENDAYE

MARSEILLE

387 km
9

323 km
10

PERPIGNAN

LUCHON

67

"My race has been won by a corpse."
Organiser Henri Desgrange bemoans the ailing Belgian Maurice De Waele
having won the Tour after being helped by his team-mates

Feverish spectators cheer on the peloton between Belfort and Strasbourg

Start: Paris, France, on 30 June
Finish: Paris, France, on 28 July

Total distance:
5256 km (3266 miles)
Longest stage:
366 km (228 miles)

Highest point:
Col du Galibier: 2556 m (8386 ft)
Mountain stages: 6

Starters: 155
Finishers: 60

Winning time: 186 h 39' 15"
Average speed:
28.319 kph (17.596 mph)

1. Maurice De Waele (Bel)
2. Giuseppe Pancera (Ita)
   at 44' 23"
3. Jef Demuysere (Bel) at 57' 10"

Nicolas Frantz and André Leducq had dominated the 1928 Tour as Alcyon team-mates, and that looked set to continue in 1929 when Leducq won the second stage between Caen and Cherbourg, with Frantz following up with victory in Bordeaux on stage 7.

Frantz, Leducq and Elvish-Wolber's Victor Fontan finished that seventh stage sharing the same overall accumulated time, and in first place at that, which, after 1448 km (900 miles) by that point, was more than a little extraordinary. Unable to separate them, all three were awarded a yellow jersey to wear on the next day's stage.

While Belgian rider Gaston Rebry took over the yellow jersey from the trio on the next stage, Fontan again took sole control of the race on stage 9. On stage 10, however, Fontan's forks broke and – after losing too much time – he broke down upon the realisation that his race was over. The Frenchman became the second rider in three years to quit the race while wearing the yellow jersey, after Francis Pélissier in 1927.

Leducq – despite five stage wins in total – and Frantz had fallen out of contention as the race progressed, but their Alcyon team-mate, Maurice De Waele, found himself in a good position to win the race, in second place behind Fontan prior to stage 10. However, De Waele fell ill on that stage and Alcyon's new plan looked set to derail. De Waele struggled through, though, to take the yellow jersey by default, and from that point on, De Waele's Alcyon team-mates somehow managed to shepherd him through the rest of the race to Paris and overall victory.

Henri Desgrange was not happy with what in his eyes was an unworthy winner. The power that he felt the bike-manufacturer-sponsored teams held over his race enraged him. It was soon fixed: the next edition, in 1930, would have the riders competing for national, rather than sponsored, teams.

MALO-LES-BAINS

270 km
20

234 km
21

332 km
22

206 km
1

CHARLEVILLE

159 km
19

METZ

165 km
18

DIEPPE

CHERBOURG

140 km
2

CAEN

199 km
3

206 km
4

DINAN

ST

STRASBOURG

145 km
17

BELFORT

5
208 km

VANNES

204 km
6

283 km
16

ÉVIAN

329 km
15

LES SABLES-
D'OLONNE

285 km
7

GRENOBLE

333 km
14

BORDEAUX

182 km
8

366 km
11

191 km

133 km

NICE
13

12

CANNES

BAYONNE

MARSEILLE

363 km
9

323 km
10

LUCHON

PERPIGNAN

PARIS

Start: Paris, France, on 2 July
Finish: Paris, France, on 27 July

Total distance:
4818 km (2994 miles)
Longest stage:
333 km (207 miles)

Highest point:
Col du Galibier: 2556 m (8386 ft)
Mountain stages: 6

Starters: 100
Finishers: 59

Winning time: 172 h 12' 16"
Average speed:
28.000 kph (17.398 mph)

1. André Leducq (Fra)
2. Learco Guerra (Ita) at 14' 13"
3. Antonin Magne (Fra)
   at 16' 03"

The Tour headed into the fourth decade of the twentieth century with some revolutionary changes. Having become annoyed with the sponsored teams dictating how his race was ridden, Henri Desgrange responded by organising the 1930 edition of the Tour as one for national teams, and it would remain that way until 1962. The sponsors – most of them bicycle manufacturers – were damaged further in 1930 by Desgrange's insistence that all participants rode identical yellow bicycles provided by the race organisers.

The team time trials of the previous few years were gone, too, but the race retained the 'outside circuit' of the country, continuing to avoid central France entirely.

There were some new stage towns on the route, however, and these included Cannes, Montpellier and Pau, with the latter two, in particular, going on to be well used by the race in the future thanks to being large towns with the ability to house the Tour's ever-increasing convoy. In fact, 1930 was the first time that the famous publicity caravan appeared – a cavalcade of floats promoting the race's advertising partners' products.

André Leducq had won five stages in 1929, and although he 'only' won two on his way to his victory in 1930, his team-mate Charles Pélissier – the youngest of the three Pélissier brothers – took eight stages: a record he now shares with Eddy Merckx and Freddy Maertens.

Marcel Bidot, Magne brothers Pierre and Antonin, André Leducq and Charles Pélissier (left to right) pose with matching bikes

MALO-LES-BAINS

271 km
20

300 km
21

CHARLEVILLE
159 km
19

METZ

206 km
1

CAEN

203 km
2

206 km
3

DINAN

223 km
18

210 km
4

VANNES

202 km
5

BELFORT

282 km
17

LES SABLES-D'OLONNE

ÉVIAN

331 km
16

285 km
6

GRENOBLE

BORDEAUX

333 km
15

222 km
7

132 km
NICE
14

209 km
12

181 km
13

MONTPELLIER

CANNES

146 km
8

HENDAYE

PAU

164 km

MARSEILLE

231 km
9

11

LUCHON

322 km
10

PERPIGNAN

PARIS

Charles Pélissier and Antonin Magne recover after the gruelling stage from Nice to Gap

Start: Paris, France, on 30 June
Finish: Paris, France, on 26 July

Total distance:
5095 km (3166 miles)
Longest stage:
338 km (210 miles)

Highest point:
Col du Galibier: 2556 m (8386 ft)
Mountain stages: 9

Starters: 81
Finishers: 35

Winning time: 177 h 10' 03"
Average speed:
28.735 kph (17.885 mph)

1. Antonin Magne (Fra)
2. Jef Demuysere (Bel) at 12' 56"
3. Antonio Pesenti (Ita)
   at 22' 51"

Just as it had with each year that passed, the Tour continued to grow both in prestige and in renown, and there were more 'firsts' as Max Bulla became the first Austrian to wear the yellow jersey, following his win on stage 2 between Caen and Dinan, and the race added Gap, Aix-les-Bains and Colmar as first-time stage hosts – more towns that would later become real regulars on the Tour's route.

Frenchman Antonin Magne gained his first of two Tour victories, taking decisive control of the race once it hit the mountains for the first time on stage 9 between Pau and Luchon, which took the riders over the by now extremely tried and tested Col d'Aubisque and Col du Tourmalet. The yellow jersey then remained safely on Magne's capable shoulders all the way to Paris, where a 'pitch invasion' – or, rather, a track invasion – welcomed him home as the winner once the race reached the velodrome at the Parc des Princes.

If Magne was a great rider, he was an even better *directeur sportif*, going on to manage the mighty mauve Mercier team in the 1950s and 1960s, whose charges included Raymond Poulidor, Jean Stablinski and Britain's Barry Hoban.

MALO-LES-BAINS

271 km
23

313 km
24

CHARLEVILLE

159 km
22

METZ

192 km
21

CAEN

208 km
1

212 km
2

DINAN

206 km
3

ST

4

211 km

VANNES

202 km
5

LES SABLES-
D'OLONNE

338 km
6

BORDEAUX

180 km
7

BAYONNE

106 km
8

PAU

9
231 km

LUCHON

10
322 km

PERPIGNAN

PARIS

COLMAR

209 km
20

BELFORT

282 km
19

ÉVIAN

204 km
18

230 km

AIX-LES-BAINS

17

GRENOBLE

102 km
16

GAP

233 km
15

132 km

NICE
14

181 km
13

CANNES

207 km
12

MONTPELLIER

164 km
11

MARSEILLE

73

A triumphant André Leducq jokes with the media after taking his second Tour de France crown

Start: Paris, France, on 6 July
Finish: Paris, France, on 31 July

Total distance:
4520 km (2809 miles)
Longest stage:
387 km (241 miles)

Highest point:
Col du Galibier: 2556 m (8386 ft)
Mountain stages: 8

Starters: 80
Finishers: 57

Winning time: 154 h 11' 49"
Average speed:
29.214 kph (18.153 mph)

1. André Leducq (Fra)
2. Kurt Stoepel (Ger) at 24' 03"
3. Francesco Camusso (Ita)
   at 26' 21"

André Leducq – winner of the 1930 Tour – was back on form, and firing on all cylinders for the 1932 race. His compatriot, and 1931 champion, Antonin Magne, was a non-starter for the French national squad, and instead Leducq's biggest challenge came from within the German team.

Kurt Stoepel won the sprint for stage 2 between Caen and Nantes from a thirteen-man group that included Leducq. When the Frenchman won stage 3 into Bordeaux, it was game on between the two. Stoepel had become the first German rider to wear the yellow jersey after his stage win, but once the race hit the Pyrenees, Leducq began to stride out and, come the Alps, the French rider held a lead of just over three minutes from his German rival.

Leducq steadily increased his lead over Stoepel on the climbs, winning stage 13 from Grenoble to Aix-les-Bains over some tough climbs including a snow-covered Col du Galibier – consistently the highest mountain scaled by the Tour peloton – which, at 2556 m (8386 ft), was covered in snow despite the high temperatures of a French summer. By the time the race reached Paris – Leducq having also won the last two stages, just for good measure – Stoepel was a massive 24 minutes behind, and it was a third straight victory for a French rider since the introduction of the national-teams format.

MALO-LES-BAINS

271 km
20
212 km
19

CHARLEVILLE

159 km
18

AMIENS

METZ

159 km
21

165 km
17

208 km
1

CAEN

STRASBOURG

PARIS

145 km
16

300 km
2

BELFORT

291 km
15

NANTES

ÉVIAN

204 km
14

230 km
13

AIX-LES-BAINS

387 km
3

GRENOBLE

102 km
12

BORDEAUX

GAP

233 km
11

206 km
4

NICE

132 km
10

MONTPELLIER

206 km
8

191 km
9

CANNES

168 km
7

MARSEILLE

PAU

229 km
5

LUCHON

322 km
6

PERPIGNAN

At last – a clockwise Tour, for the first time since 1912. While the riders could 'unwind' after two decades of dizziness caused by following what had become a very samey anti-clockwise route around the edge of France, the watching public, too, must have appreciated the change of direction.

The dizzy heights of the race's mountain climbs continued to capture the imagination as well, and 1933 was the first year that the organisers introduced an official *grand prix de la montagne* – the climber's prize that would later use that garish white and red polka-dot jersey to identify the leader in the competition. That wouldn't come until 1975.

Vicente Trueba – 'The Torrelavega Flea', hailing from the same Cantabrian town as Óscar Freire, who won Spain's first, and only, green jersey in 2008 – hoovered up the big points available on most of the climbs in both the Alps and then the Pyrenees, including topping the Galibier and the Lautaret on stage 7, the Peyresourde and the Aspin on stage 17, and the Tourmalet and the Aubisque on stage 18, all at the head of the race.

Over in the French camp, both defending champion André Leducq and 1931 winner Antonin Magne were back, helping to make up a very strong team, but it was another member of the squad, 26-year-old Georges Speicher, who came to life in the Alps, winning two stages, and then won a third en route to Marseille to take the yellow jersey, which his team ably helped him defend all the way to Paris.

The race literally had a new direction, the French were still winning, and the race was more popular than ever, continuing to help shift copies of *L'Auto*, as had been the intention since the outset way back in 1903.

Start: Paris, France, on 27 June
Finish: Paris, France, on 23 July

Total distance:
4396 km (2732 miles)
Longest stage:
293 km (182 miles)

Highest point:
Col du Galibier: 2556 m (8386 ft)
Mountain stages: 11

Starters: 80
Finishers: 40

Winning time: 147 h 51' 37"
Average speed:
29.732 kph (18.475 mph)

1. Georges Speicher (Fra)
2. Learco Guerra (Ita) at 4' 01"
3. Giuseppe Martano (Ita)
   at 5' 08"

Mountains: Vicente Trueba (Spa)

Spaniard Vicente Trueba conquered the Alps and Pyrenees, becoming the first rider to claim the *grand prix de la montagne* crown

LILLE

192 km
2

CHARLEVILLE

262 km
1

166 km
3

222 km
23

CAEN

METZ

PARIS

169 km
22

220 km
4

RENNES

BELFORT

266 km
21

293 km
5

ÉVIAN

LA ROCHELLE

207 km
6

229 km
7

AIX-LES-BAINS

183 km
20

GRENOBLE

102 km
8

BORDEAUX

GAP

227 km
9

233 km
19

DIGNE

156 km
10

NICE

MONTPELLIER

168 km

128 km
11

PAU

13

208 km

CANNES

185 km
18

TARBES

MARSEILLE

17

166 km

91 km

165 km
16

14

158 km

LUCHON

AX-LES-THERMES
15

PERPIGNAN

77

*"I thought my Tour was over. But then, suddenly, on one of the corners further down the descent,
I spied Vietto making his way back up to me – in order to give me his bicycle."*

1934 winner Antonin Magne was grateful for the help he received from French national team-mate René Vietto

An altruistic René Vietto (left) aids compatriot Antonin Magne on the Col de Puymorens

Start: Paris, France, on 3 July
Finish: Paris, France, on 29 July

Total distance:
4370 km (2716 miles)
Longest stage:
293 km (182 miles)

Highest point:
Col du Galibier: 2556 m (8386 ft)
Mountain stages: 11

Starters: 60
Finishers: 39

Winning time: 147 h 13' 58"
Average speed:
30.360 kph (18.865 mph)

1. Antonin Magne (Fra)
2. Giuseppe Martano (Ita)
   at 27' 31"
3. Roger Lapébie (Fra) at 52' 15"

Mountains: René Vietto (Fra)

This purple patch of home Tour winners like André Leducq, Antonin Magne and Georges Speicher was all well and good, but what the French public really loved – and still love – is a rider up against it, selfless and emotional.

With former fans' favourite, the hapless Eugène Christophe, having retired in 1926, 20-year-old René Vietto fitted the bill perfectly to become France's new *chouchou*. Riding in the service of defending champions Speicher, Leducq and Magne, Vietto found himself having to help Magne, in particular. On the descent of the Col de Puymorens, on stage 15, Magne damaged his front wheel, and so Vietto stopped and gave him his. Having been in the front group, and perhaps overcome with the frustration of being left behind, Vietto wept at the side of the road while waiting for a new wheel. Pretty endearing. The next day, while descending the Portet d'Aspet, it was deja-vu: this time it was Magne's rear wheel and Vietto was in Magne's group

again. It was some time before he realised there was a problem. Once he did, he rode back up the hill to give Magne his bike so that his French team-mate could continue – and win the Tour de France.

Those tears shed by Vietto would have dried soon enough, though: not only did Vietto come away with four stage victories, but he also won the second edition of the race's official mountains competition, out-climbing inaugural winner Vicente Trueba. He won French hearts, too.

In all, the French won twenty stages out of twenty-four, which in 1934 included the Tour's first ever individual time trial as part of the Tour's first ever 'split stage': stage 21a in the morning – an 81-km (50-mile) road race between La Rochelle and La-Roche-sur-Yon; and stage 21b that afternoon – the 90-km (56-mile) time trial from La-Roche-sur-Yon to Nantes.

For the first time, too, the Tour's average speed crept above the 30 kph (18.6 mph) mark.

LILLE

192 km
2

CHARLEVILLE

262 km

161 km
3

1

METZ

221 km

23

220 km
4

CAEN

PARIS

275 km

22

293 km
5

BELFORT

NANTES

90 km

21B

ÉVIAN

LA ROCHE-SUR-YON

207 km
6

81 km

21A

229 km

LA ROCHELLE

7   AIX-LES-BAINS

183 km

GRENOBLE   102 km

20

8

BORDEAUX

GAP

227 km

215 km

9

DIGNE

19

156 km
10

NICE

126 km

172 km

11

PAU

MONTPELLIER   177 km   172 km   13   CANNES

TARBES

12

18   17   14

91 km   165 km   158 km   MARSEILLE

16   15   PERPIGNAN

LUCHON   AX-LES-THERMES

1935
29th Edition

Start: Paris, France, on 4 July
Finish: Paris, France, on 28 July

Total distance:
4338 km (2696 miles)
Longest stage:
325 km (202 miles)

Highest point:
Col du Galibier: 2556 m (8386 ft)
Mountain stages: 9

Starters: 93
Finishers: 46

Winning time: 141 h 32' 00"
Average speed:
30.650 kph (19.045 mph)

1. Romain Maes (Bel)
2. Ambrogio Morelli (Ita) at 17' 52"
3. Félicien Vervaecke (Bel)
   at 24' 06"

Mountains:
Félicien Vervaecke (Bel)

Romain Maes became the fifth rider – and still the last – to have led the race from the first stage all the way to the finish in Paris. The Belgian escaped the clutches of the peloton on the opening stage, and while he at first appeared to present no real danger to overall contenders such as defending champion Antonin Magne, when Maes slipped through a railway crossing in Haubourdin on the outskirts of Lille just before the gates closed, with a group of chasers hot on his heels, the rest of the race was stopped in its tracks and he was able to hold on to win by a minute.

Maes battled gamely on through the first week in the *maillot jaune*, even finishing the stage 5b time trial between Geneva and Évian in fourth place, while Magne fought hard to steadily close the gap.

However, when Magne was hit by a car in the race convoy on the Col du Télégraphe on stage 7, and had to abandon the race, Maes found himself with a 12-minute lead over the rest. That same stage was also marked by the death of Spain's Francisco Cepeda, who died from his injuries after a crash on the descent of the Col du Galibier.

The race route had taken another step towards resembling modern Tour routes, with shorter stages than ever – interspersed, nevertheless, with a few longer ones too – and three individual time trials, following the success of the race's first one in 1934, as well as three team time trials. It was also at the 1935 Tour that the famous 'red kite', strung over the road to mark each stage's final kilometre, made its first appearance.

Maes finished things off as fabulously as he'd started them: just as he had on the first stage, he escaped the clutches of the main bunch on the final stage, bursting into the Parc des Princes alone in a blur of yellow to win overall by almost 18 minutes.

Romain Maes storms to victory in the Parc des Princes velodrome having led the race from start to finish

LILLE

192 km
2

CHARLEVILLE

262 km
1

161 km
3

METZ

221 km
21

220 km
4

CAEN

55 km
20B

VIRE

20A

BELFORT

262 km
5A

NANTES

95 km
19B

58 km

LA ROCHE-SUR-YON

EVIAN

GENEVA

5B

81 km
19A

LA ROCHELLE

33 km
18B

ROCHEFORT

207 km
6

229 km
7

AIX-LES-BAINS

159 km
18A

GRENOBLE

102 km
8

BORDEAUX

GAP

227 km
9

224 km
17

DIGNE

156 km
10

NICE

NÎMES

56 km
13B

112 km
13A

126 km
11

12

PARIS

MONTPELLIER

195 km

CANNES

103 km
14A

MARSEILLE

PAU

NARBONNE

194 km
16

325 km
15

63 km
14B

LUCHON

PERPIGNAN

81

Yvan Marie, Romain Maes and Félicien Vervaecke squeeze through the crowds on the Col d'Aspin

Start: Paris, France, on 7 July
Finish: Paris, France, on 2 August

Total distance:
4438 km (2758 miles)
Longest stage:
325 km (202 miles)

Highest point:
Col du Galibier: 2556 m (8386 ft)
Mountain stages: 9

Starters: 90
Finishers: 43

Winning time: 142 h 47' 32"
Average speed:
31.045 kph (19,290 mph)

1. Sylvère Maes (Bel)
2. Antonin Magne (Fra)
   at 26' 55"
3. Félicien Vervaecke (Bel)
   at 27' 53"

Mountains:
Julian Berrendero (Spa)

82

If a return to five stages run as team time trials and no individual time trials at all made the 1936 Tour feel like a step back in time, it was but a temporary blip. There was to be a return to what resembles the modern Tour, complete with individual time trials, in 1937, and with it a new era as Henri Desgrange, the founding father and race organiser since the first edition in 1903, stepped aside to let Jacques Goddet, Desgrange's deputy at *L'Auto*, take hold of the reins.

However, having had a prostate operation prior to the 1936 race, and already struggling on stage 1, Desgrange had to abandon his own race, handing over what he hoped was only temporary control of his event to Goddet as early as stage 2.

Defending Tour champion Romain Maes then abandoned on stage 7 – the by-now regular 'queen stage', which included the brutal climbs of the Télégraphe, the Galibier and the Lautaret – and it was his Belgian team-mate, Sylvère Maes, and no relation, who rose to the top in the Alps.

Sylvère left the mountains behind with a 2 minute-48 second lead over another Belgian team-mate, Félicien Vervaecke, who had been third overall and 'king of the mountains' in 1935. Strong riding in the Pyrenees and Maes's Belgian squad finishing best in all but one of the team time trials helped to increase his lead, and Maes arrived in Paris with an almost 27-minute advantage over France's Antonin Magne.

LILLE

192 km
2

CHARLEVILLE

258 km
1

161 km
3

METZ

220 km
4

CAEN

55 km
20B

234 km

21

BELFORT

VIRE

204 km   20A

ANGERS

298 km
5

67 km
19C

PARIS

ÉVIAN

CHOLET

65 km
19B

212 km
6

LA ROCHE-SUR-YON

81 km
19A

230 km
7

AIX-LES-BAINS

LA ROCHELLE

75 km
18B

SAINTES

8

GRENOBLE

117 km
18A

194 km

BRIANÇON

BORDEAUX

9

229 km
17

220 km

DIGNE

156 km
10

NÎMES

52 km
13B

112 km

NICE

126 km
11

PAU

195 km

MONTPELLIER

103 km

13A

12

CANNES

194 km
16

14A

MARSEILLE

NARBONNE

325 km
15

63 km
14B

LUCHON

PERPIGNAN

83

1937
31st Edition

Start: Paris, France, on 30 June
Finish: Paris, France, on 25 July

Total distance:
4415 km (2743 miles)
Longest stage:
263 km (164 miles)

Highest point:
Col du Galibier: 2556 m (8386 ft)
Mountain stages: 9

Starters: 98
Finishers: 46

Winning time: 138 h 58' 31"
Average speed:
31.768 kph (19.740 mph)

1. Roger Lapébie (Fra)
2. Mario Vicini (Ita) at 7' 17"
3. Léo Amberg (Swi) at 26' 13"

Mountains:
Félicien Vervaecke (Bel)

The race route was back down to only two team time trials, and the individual time trial returned, too. This edition was held over twenty race days, much as it is today but, like in 1936, there was a proliferation of 'split stages' – eight in all, with three of those split into three stages in a single day: an 'a', a 'b' and a 'c'.

Thank goodness, then, that derailleur gears were permitted for the first time in the race, giving riders a variety of gear options for the various terrains covered by the Tour.

The 1937 edition also saw the first participation of Italian legend Gino Bartali, who went into the race as the favourite having won the last two editions of the Tour de France's Italian counterpart, the Giro d'Italia.

Everything seemed to be following the script when Bartali won stage 7, which took the field between Aix-les-Bains and Grenoble via the Col du Télégraphe and the Col du Galibier, and took the yellow jersey. Despite a crash, he retained it following the race's third day in the Alps on stage 8, but on stage 9 his injuries caused him to lose touch with the leaders, and the Italian eventually abandoned at the start of stage 12a in Marseille.

The defending champion, Sylvère Maes, had taken over the race lead on stage 9, but he – and the whole Belgian team – quit the race in disgust on stage 16 to Bordeaux after Maes was handed a time penalty for having been paced back into the race after a puncture by two independent Belgian riders who were not competing as part of the national squad. It was the third time that a race leader had left the race while in yellow; France's Roger Lapébie took over the *maillot jaune* from Maes and, having won a stage back in 1932, and taken third overall in 1934, took the top honours in Paris in 1937.

Roger Lapébie claimed his first and only title in 1937

LILLE

192 km

2

CHARLEVILLE

161 km

263 km

3

1

METZ

234 km

20

CAEN

59 km

19B

220 km

4

VIRE

19A

114 km

PARIS

RENNES

172 km

18B

BELFORT

175 km

5A

LA ROCHE-SUR-YON

81 km

34 km

5B

CHAMPAGNOLE

18A

LONS-LE-SAUNIER

LA ROCHELLE

67 km

93 km

5C

GENEVA

17C

37 km

180 km

6

17B

SAINTES

228 km

ROYAN

123 km

7

AIX-LES-BAINS

17A

GRENOBLE

8

194 km

BRIANÇON

BORDEAUX

9

235 km

220 km

16

DIGNE

251 km

10

NÎMES

112 km

51 km

12B

169 km

NICE

MONTPELLIER

12A

103 km

65 km

11A

13A

11B

MARSEILLE

PAU

NARBONNE

194 km

167 km

59 km

TOULON

13B

15

63 km

99 km

PERPIGNAN

LUCHON

14C

14B

AX-LES-THERMES

14A

BOURG-MADAME

85

Italy's Gino Bartali cuts a lonely figure as he rides through the iconic Casse Déserte section of the Col d'Izoard on his way to victory on stage 14, setting himself up for his first Tour title in 1938.

1938
32nd Edition

Antonin Magne and André Leducq bow out of the Tour, finishing arm-in-arm at the Parc des Princes velodrome

Start: Paris, France, on 5 July
Finish: Paris, France, on 31 July

Total distance:
4681 km (2909 miles)
Longest stage:
311 km (193 miles)

Highest point:
Col de l'Iseran: 2770 m (9088 ft)
Mountain stages: 6

Starters: 95
Finishers: 55

Winning time: 148 h 29' 12"
Average speed:
31.565 kph (19.614 mph)

1. Gino Bartali (Ita)
2. Félicien Vervaecke (Bel)
   at 18' 27"
3. Victor Cosson (Fra) at 29' 26"

Mountains: Gino Bartali (Ita)

Even though the number of proper mountain stages was reduced to just six, the 1938 Tour was to be a real battle of the climbers: Italy's Gino Bartali versus Belgium's Félicien Vervaecke.

Bartali felt hard done by to have had to leave the 1937 Tour due to a crash, while Vervaecke, twice a winner of the mountains classification, had also left the race in 1937 in support of his Belgian team leader Sylvère Maes, who quit after being handed a time penalty that he didn't agree with.

The race also saw the first use of the Col de l'Iseran, which, at 2770 m (9088 ft), superseded the Col du Galibier as the highest pass the race had visited. Vervaecke was first to reach the summit of the Iseran on stage 15, but was caught by a yellow-clad Bartali on the descent,

and the two finished together. Bartali had stolen the *maillot jaune* from Vervaecke's shoulders on the previous stage thanks to a solo win in Briançon. Once the yellow jersey was on the Italian's shoulders, that's where it stayed, as Bartali policed Vervaecke's every move, with the final time trial on stage 20b, won by Vervaecke, being the only opportunity for the Belgian to pull back a couple of minutes.

Bartali had nevertheless won comfortably by the time the race finished in Paris, with an 18-minute 27-second buffer over Vervaecke. That final stage was most notable, though, for the arm-in-arm tied win by Antonin Magne and André Leducq – both two-time champions who were also both riding their last Tour.

LILLE
107 km
20C
279 km
21
ST-QUENTIN
20B   42 km
LAON
48 km
20A
REIMS
19   196 km   METZ
186 km
18
STRASBOURG
143 km
17B
BELFORT
89.5 km
17A
BESANÇON
16
284 km
AIX-LES-BAINS
15
311 km
BRIANÇON
14
219 km
DIGNE
13
284 km   CANNES
223 km   199 km
11   12
MARSEILLE

CAEN
215 km
1
237 km
2
ST-BRIEUC
238 km
3
NANTES
62 km
4A
LA ROCHE-SUR-YON
83 km
4B
LA ROCHELLE
83 km
4C
ROYAN
198 km
5
BORDEAUX
ARCACHON
6A
52.5 km
6B
171 km
BAYONNE
115 km   PAU
7
193 km
8
LUCHON
260 km
9
10A   63 km   PERPIGNAN
NARBONNE
10B
27 km   10C
73 km
BÉZIERS
MONTPELLIER

PARIS

"He laughed like you would if you'd just been told you'd won the national lottery."

Henri Desgrange, having retired due to ill health, and at what would be his last Tour, on presenting René Vietto with his first yellow jersey on stage 4.

Having first won the Tour in 1936, Belgian Sylvère Maes was back to his best at the 1939 edition. His namesake, compatriot and 1935 Tour champion Romain Maes – no relation, remember – made the early running, but by the end of the first week, it was René Vietto – the little rider who had won French hearts when he selflessly helped his leader Antonin Magne to Tour victory in 1934 – riding for the French Sud-Est regional team, who had carved out a commanding lead.

On the Col d'Izoard, in the Alps, on stage 15, Sylvère Maes made his move, cracking Belgian team-mate Edward Vissers and Vietto, winning the stage alone in Briançon.

Maes then pummelled Vissers into second place by over four minutes in the Tour's first-ever individual mountain time trial over the Col de l'Iseran, starting midway up from Bonneval-sur-Arc and then plunging over the summit down to Bourg-St-Maurice.

The Iseran is today the highest paved mountain pass in the Alps, but in 1939 such climbs were still stony, unmade roads, although the proliferation of the new derailleur gears at the end of the 1930s made climbing them that little bit easier compared to the two-geared 'flip-flop' rear wheels – wheels that you had to remove and flip back-to-front to use the other gear – that had been used on racing bikes for so long.

The 1939 race also headed into the principality of Monaco for the first time, and in fact remained there for an unprecedented three stages. Annecy and Lorient appeared on the route as stage towns for the first time, too, and would become popular destinations for the Tour in the years to come.

Vietto, despite finishing over half-an-hour down as runner-up to Maes, was left convinced that the 1940 tour could be his. Alas, a month after the finish in Paris, Europe was at war again.

Sylvère Maes takes on the Col de l'Iseran in the Tour's first individual mountain time trial

Start: Paris, France, on 10 July
Finish: Paris, France, on 30 July

Total distance:
4225 km (2625 miles)
Longest stage:
311 km (193 miles)

Highest point:
Col de l'Iseran: 2770 m (9088 ft)
Mountain stages: 7

Starters: 79
Finishers: 49

Winning time: 132 h 03' 17"
Average speed:
31.986 kph (19.875 mph)

1. Sylvère Maes (Bel)
2. René Vietto (Fra) at 30' 38"
3. Lucien Vlaemynck (Bel)
   at 32' 08"

Mountains: Sylvère Maes (Bel)

CAEN
63.5 km
215 km
2A
1
VIRE
119.5 km
2B
244 km
3
174 km
4
RENNES
LORIENT
207 km
5
NANTES
144 km
6A
LA ROCHELLE
107 km
6B
ROYAN
198 km
7
BORDEAUX
210.5 km
8A
68.5 km
SALIES-DE-BÉARN
8B
PAU
311 km
9
TOULOUSE
148.5 km
10A
27 km
10B
NARBONNE
BÉZIERS
10C
70.5 km
MONTPELLIER
11
MARSEILLE
12A
157 km
ST-RAPHAËL
12B
121.5 km
MONACO
14
101.5 km
175 km
DIGNE
212 km
15
219 km
BRIANÇON
126 km
BONNEVAL-SUR-ARC
16A
16B
64.5 km
103.5 km
16C
BOURG-ST-MAURICE
ANNECY
17A
226 km
17B
59 km
DOLE
DIJON
18A
151 km
TROYES
201 km
18B
PARIS

91

 Start: Paris, France, on 25 June
Finish: Paris, France, on 20 July

 Total distance:
4630 km (2877 miles)
Longest stage: 314 km (195 miles)

 Highest point:
Col du Galibier: 2556 m (8386 ft)
Mountain stages: 6

 Starters: 100
Finishers: 53

 Winning time: 148 h 11' 25"
Average speed:
31.412 kph (19.519 mph)

 1. Jean Robic (Fra)
2. Édouard Fachleitner (Fra)
    at 3' 58"
3. Pierre Brambilla (Ita)
    at 10' 07"

 Mountains: Pierre Brambilla (Ita)

Following the war – and after previous efforts to revive the race – the Tour de France proper recommenced in 1947, although without its founding father, Henri Desgranges, who had died in 1940. After the war, a stone monument was erected in his honour atop the Col du Galibier, which is still there today. The newspaper for which the race had been created as publicity, *L'Auto*, was gone too, having been closed down at the end of the war. In its place came new sports newspaper *L'Equipe*, edited by Desgrange's old understudy, Jacques Goddet, who continued his stewardship of the race.

René Vietto, who, after second place in 1939, had talked up his chances of winning the non-existent 1940 Tour, was back eight years later – still with all guns blazing – and took yellow on the second stage from Lille to Brussels, which was the first time that Belgium had hosted a Tour stage. The Frenchman held the lead as the race then visited Luxembourg later in the first week, but would lose it to Italian Aldo Ronconi on stage 7. However, once Vietto reclaimed yellow following his victory on stage 9 in the Alps, it looked as though he was going to be strong enough to hold it all the way to Paris.

Despite two stage victories in the opening week, Jean Robic was a rider Vietto hadn't banked on having to look out for. The diminutive Frenchman had only turned pro in 1943, and was riding his first Tour in 1947 for the Ouest regional squad, while Vietto was on the French national team.

Vietto held a 1-minute 34-second lead over Italian Pierre Brambilla going into stage 19 – the race's only time trial, contested over a massive 139 km (86 miles) between Vannes and St-Brieuc, which remains the record for the longest individual time trial to feature in the Tour. While Belgian Raymond Impanis won the stage, almost five minutes ahead of second-placed Robic, Vietto cracked over such a distance, and finished another ten minutes down again. Ronconi was still in the mix, finishing third, while Brambilla's fifth place gave him the race lead.

Going into the final stage, it looked as though it was going to be an Italian one-two in Paris, but Robic had other ideas, attacking with team-mate Édouard Fachleitner, and tapping out a thirteen-minute advantage over Brambilla, Vietto, Ronconi et al. by the end of the stage – enough for Fachleitner to jump up to second overall and for Robic to win the whole thing, without ever having worn yellow during the race.

ANGLETERRE

LA MANCHE

ÎLES ANGLO-NORMANDES
(rattachées à la Grande-Bretagne)

BRUSSELS

LILLE

2 — 182 km

314 km

3

236 km — 1

LUXEMBOURG

223 km — 4

STRASBOURG

CAEN

21 — 257 km

235 km

20

248 km — 5

ST-BRIEUC

19 — 139 km

VANNES

BESANÇON

236 km — 18

6 — 249 km

PARIS

172 km

LYON

7

LES SABLES-
D'OLONNE

185 km

8

GRENOBLE

272 km — 17

BRIANÇON

9 — 217 km

BORDEAUX

255 km

DIGNE

10

NICE

GOLFE
DE
GASCOGNE

16 — 195 km

165 km

12

MONTPELLIER

11 — 230 km

13 — 172 km

MARSEILLE

PAU

CARCASSONNE

14

15 — 195 km

253 km

LUCHON

GOLFE DU LION

MER MÉDITERRANÉE

ESPAGNE

93

Gino Bartali's ten-year gap between titles is the longest in Tour history

Start: Paris, France, on 30 June
Finish: Paris, France, on 25 July

Total distance:
4922 km (3058 miles)
Longest stage:
286 km (178 miles)

Highest point:
Col du Galibier: 2556 m (8386 ft)
Mountain stages: 7

Starters: 120
Finishers: 44

Winning time: 147 h 10' 36"
Average speed:
33.443 kph (20.781 mph)

1. Gino Bartali (Ita)
2. Briek Schotte (Bel) at 26' 16"
3. Guy Lapébie (Fra) at 28' 48"

Mountains: Gino Bartali (Ita)

An extraordinary ten years after winning his first Tour, Italy's Gino Bartali returned to the Tour de France to win a second title. An equally extraordinary seven stage wins along the way, as well as the mountains title, cemented him as one of the race's legends. Later, his battles with Fausto Coppi at the Giro d'Italia would make the fellow countrymen icons of the sport, but the younger Coppi wouldn't appear at the Tour until 1949.

As it had done in 1947, the 1948 Tour again visited Belgium, but also added forays into Switzerland – where the riders tackled the Col de la Forclaz for the first time – and, appropriately enough, Italy. An Italian team hadn't participated in the race since 1938 – the year Bartali had won – while it wasn't until 1955 that German riders

returned, and even then it was as part of a mixed team with Luxembourg.

It was also the first time that the mountains were classified according to their difficulty, with points attributed accordingly, which remains the case today. But while in today's Tours they range from the easier fourth-category, to first-category, to *hors-catégorie* ('beyond classification' for the very toughest climbs), in 1948 they were categorised as either A or B, or *hors GPM* – the latter for those climbs not considered tough enough to count for the mountains competition, or *grand prix de la montagne*.

The 1948 Tour also added an interesting rule whereby the last-placed man on the general classification following both stage 3 and stage 18 was eliminated – a sure-fire way to keep riders on their toes.

ANGLETERRE

LA MANCHE

ÎLES ANGLO-NORMANDES
(rattachées à la Grande-Bretagne)

ALLEMAGNE

SUISSE

GOLFE
DE
GASCOGNE

ESPAGNE

MER MÉDITERRANÉE

ROUBAIX

LIÈGE

228 km
20

249 km
19

METZ

286 km
21

237 km
1

TROUVILLE

259 km
2

DINARD

251 km
3

NANTES

166 km
4

LA ROCHELLE

262 km
5

BORDEAUX

244 km
6

BIARRITZ

219 km
7

LOURDES

261 km
8

PARIS

195 km
18

STRASBOURG

120 km
17

MULHOUSE

243 km
16

LAUSANNE

256 km
15

AIX-LES-BAINS

263 km
14

BRIANÇON

274 km
13

SAN REMO

170 km
12

CANNES

245 km
11

248 km
10

MONTPELLIER

MARSEILLE

246 km
9

TOULOUSE

GOLFE DU LION

Gino Bartali and Fausto Coppi share a drink between Pau and Luchon

Start: Paris, France, on 30 June
Finish: Paris, France, on 24 July

Total distance:
4810 km (2989 miles)
Longest stage:
340 km (211 miles)

Highest point:
Col de l'Iseran: 2770 m (9088 ft)
Mountain stages: 6

Starters: 120
Finishers: 55

Winning time: 149 h 40' 49"
Average speed:
32.121 kph (19.959 mph)

1. Fausto Coppi (Ita)
2. Gino Bartali (Ita) at 10' 55"
3. Jacques Marinelli (Fra)
   at 25' 13"

Mountains: Fausto Coppi (Ita)

Gino Bartali's great Italian rival, Fausto Coppi – who had won the 1940 Giro, and then both the 1947 and 1949 editions – came to his first Tour in 1949, and promptly won. Coppi had returned to his cycling career from a POW camp in northern Africa, where he'd worked as a barber for the British soldiers until the end of the war, but once he was back on his bike, he proved that he could still cut it.

Of course, while the two Italian riders rode for their respective trade teams during the 1949 season – Coppi for Bianchi and Bartali for his own Bartali-Gardiol squad – at the Tour they were thrown together on the same Italian team, and were forced to work together against what was a strong French squad.

Coppi won the stage-7 time trial, and then began to turn the screw once the race reached the Pyrenees, where it also made its first visit to Spain, visiting San Sebastián. Bartali then joined up with Coppi in the Alps, and on stage 16, between Cannes and Briançon, which took the riders over the Col d'Izoard, the pair attacked together and finished together – Bartali taking the stage and the yellow jersey – with France's Jean Robic, the 1947 Tour winner, over five minutes down in third place.

On stage 17 – between Briançon and Aosta in their native Italy – they did it again, but after Bartali punctured with less than 50 km to go, Coppi pushed on alone to win the stage by almost five minutes over his compatriot – taking the yellow jersey in the process – leaving Robic again bringing home the best of the rest another five minutes behind.

ANGLETERRE

LA MANCHE

ÎLES ANGLO-NORMANDES
(rattachées à la Grande-Bretagne)

BRUSSELS

BOULOGNE-SUR-MER

211 km
3

185 km
4

273 km
2

ROUEN

REIMS

182 km
1

340 km
21
NANCY

137 km
20

ST-MALO

PARIS

293 km
5

COLMAR

283 km
19

305 km
6

LAUSANNE

LES SABLES-
D'OLONNE

92 km
7

265 km
18
AOSTA

LA ROCHELLE

262 km
8

257 km
17

BORDEAUX

BRIANÇON

228 km
9

275 km
16

NÎMES

199 km
14

215 km
15

192 km
10

SAN
SEBASTIÁN

PAU

193 km
11

TOULOUSE

289 km
13

CANNES

134 km
12

MARSEILLE

GOLFE
DE
GASCOGNE

GOLFE DU LION

LUCHON

ESPAGNE

MER MÉDITERRANÉE

1950
37th Edition

Start: Paris, France, on 13 July
Finish: Paris, France, on 7 August

Total distance:
4774 km (2967 miles)
Longest stage:
316 km (196 miles)

Highest point:
Col d'Izoard: 2360 m (7743 ft)
Mountain stages: 7

Starters: 116
Finishers: 51

Winning time: 145 h 36' 56"
Average speed:
32.718 kph (20.330 mph)

1. Ferdi Kübler (Swi)
2. Stan Ockers (Bel) at 9' 30"
3. Louison Bobet (Fra) at 22' 19"

Mountains: Louison Bobet (Fra)

There was no defending champion at the 1950 Tour; Fausto Coppi had broken his pelvis in a crash at the Giro d'Italia, seemingly opening the way for compatriot and rival Gino Bartali to take an easy third Tour victory.

But the French spectators, it would seem, were not prepared for that to happen. It appeared that they had had enough of the Italians' winning ways in the past couple of years at 'their' race, and it didn't help that there was strong evidence that the *Cadets Italiens* squad – an additional Italian team made up of younger riders – was colluding with the senior Italian team. Bartali complained of being jeered at, of being called names, and even of some spectators trying to push him off his bike.

Enough was enough for Bartali and, being the elder statesman at 36 years of age, he pulled both Italian squads out of the race on the morning of stage 12 – despite his Italian team-mate, Fiorenzo Magni, at that point being in the yellow jersey. Magni wasn't happy, of course, but bowed to his boss's wishes.

That left Ferdi Kübler to assume the race lead, which he held all the way to Paris, becoming the race's first Swiss winner, despite fans' hopes that rising French stars Louison Bobet or Raphaël Géminiani would be able to step up to the plate.

The 1950 Tour also saw a continued globalisation of the race, with a North African team made up of four Algerians and two Moroccans taking part, and Algerian Marcel Molinès even winning a stage – stage 13 between Perpignan and Nîmes – giving him the honour of being the first African rider to do so.

Marcel Molinès rode himself into the history books when he won stage 13 between Perpignan and Nîmes

ANGLETERRE

SOMERSET

DEVON

LA MANCHE

ILES ANGLO-NORMANDES
(rattachées à la Grande-Bretagne)

232.5 km
3
Bruxelles
LIÈGE

231 km
4
LILLE
241 km
2
METZ

307 km
1

ROUEN

78 km
6
DINARD
316 km
5
PARIS

ST-BRIEUC

248 km
7

314 km
22

ANGERS
DIJON

181 km
8
233 km
21

NIORT
98 km
20
LYON

206 km
9
ST-ÉTIENNE
291 km
19
BRIANÇON

BORDEAUX
165 km
18
GAP

229 km
17
MENTON

202 km
10
NÎMES
222 km
14
16
NICE
96 km
15
205.5 km

PAU
230 km
11
ST-GAUDENS
13
215 km
233 km
12
TOULON

PERPIGNAN

MER MÉDITERRANÉE

GOLFE DU LION

GOLFE DE GASCOGNE

ESPAGNE

99

The Tour tackles the 'moonscape' of Mont Ventoux in Provence for the first time, in 1951.

1951
38th Edition

"I wanted to go left, but I went straight on…"

Wim van Est gives his take on misjudging the bend on the descent of the
Col d'Aubisque that saw him plunge 70 metres down into the ravine below

The steep, arid Mont Ventoux makes its first appearance at the Tour

Start: Metz, France, on 4 July
Finish: Paris, France, on 29 July

Total distance:
4692 km (2915 miles)
Longest stage:
322 km (200 miles)

Highest point:
Col d'Izoard: 2360 m (7743 ft)
Mountain stages: 10

Starters: 123
Finishers: 66

Winning time: 142 h 20' 14"
Average speed:
32.964 kph (20.483 mph)

1. Hugo Koblet (Swi)
2. Raphaël Géminiani (Fra)
   at 22' 00"
3. Lucien Lazaridès (Fra)
   at 24' 16"

Mountains:
Raphaël Géminiani (Fra)

The 1951 Tour's start in Metz was the first time that the race had started outside Paris since 1926 – the only other time that it had – when it started in Évian. But from 1951 onwards, the Tour would always start somewhere other than Paris – save for in 2003 – while the French capital continued to remain the race's final destination.

Having missed the 1950 race because of injury, Fausto Coppi was back, but arguably shouldn't have been there at all due to the distress of having lost his brother, Serse, to a fatal accident at the Giro del Piemonte, just five days before the start of the Tour. Coppi nevertheless finished tenth overall in Paris, as well as winning stage 20, between Gap and Briançon – alone, by almost four minutes.

Just as there had been in 1950, there was more drama when Dutchman Wim Van Est – leading the race, and the first rider from the Netherlands to

do so – crashed on the descent of the Col d'Aubisque on stage 13, plunging off the edge of the mountain and down a 70-metre-deep ravine, requiring his team to string together a number of inner tubes to pull him back up to safety.

Luckily, Van Est was not badly hurt, but he was taken to hospital and wasn't able to continue in the race. Instead, after just one day in yellow for France's Gilbert Bauvin, Switzerland's Hugo Koblet assumed the race lead, just as his compatriot Ferdi Kübler had done the year before thanks to the race leader pulling out and, again like his countryman, Koblet then held it all the way to Paris.

Also making its first appearance on the Tour route in 1951 was the infamous climb of Mont Ventoux – set to bring so much heartache and controversy in the years to come.

ANGLETERRE

GHENT

LE TRÉPORT

219 km

228 km

3

2

188 km

REIMS

185 km

4

1

METZ

CAEN

215 km

5

PARIS

182 km

6

322 km

24

RENNES

85 km

LA GUERCHE

7

DIJON

ANGERS

197 km

23

241 km

8

GENEVA

97 km

236 km

22

9

CLERMONT-FERRAND

AIX-LES-BAINS

LIMOGES

10

216 km

201 km

21

BRIVE-LA-GAILLARDE

BRIANÇON

165 km

20

GAP

177 km

11

208 km

AGEN

AVIGNON

224 km

173 km

19

12

185 km

17

18

DAX

MONTPELLIER

201 km

MARSEILLE

13

TARBES

192 km

142 km

CARCASSONNE

16

14

15

213 km

LUCHON

GOLFE DU LION

ESPAGNE

MER MÉDITERRAN

Jean Robic leads Italy's Fausto Coppi on Alpe d'Huez in 1952, the year the climb was featured on the Tour route for the first time. Coppi reeled the Frenchman back in with 6 km to go, taking the stage win and sealing his second and last Tour overall victory.

Fausto Coppi wins at Alpe d'Huez, claiming the second of five stage wins en route to overall glory

Start: Brest, France, on 25 June
Finish: Paris, France, on 19 July

Total distance:
4827 km (2999 miles)
Longest stage:
354 km (220 miles)

Highest point:
Col du Galibier: 2556 m (8386 ft)
Mountain stages: 9

Starters: 122
Finishers: 78

Winning time: 151 h 57' 20"
Average speed:
31.739 kph (19.722 mph)

1. Fausto Coppi (Ita)
2. Stan Ockers (Bel) at 28' 17"
3. Bernardo Ruiz (Spa) at 34' 38"

Mountains: Fausto Coppi (Ita)

With Mont Ventoux having first appeared in the 1951 Tour, in 1952 it was the turn of the equally famous Alpe d'Huez to make its first appearance.

The Ventoux was there again, too – later, the Tour tended to favour one or the other, although they are also both on the 2013 Tour route – and together with the Galibier, the Tourmalet, the Aubisque, Sestriere in Italy, and the Puy de Dôme in the Massif Central, which was also on the Tour route for the first time, this was a climber's Tour of epic proportions.

Fausto Coppi was back, and back to his very best at that. He was the first to the top of Alpe d'Huez, which put him in yellow, while French rival Jean Robic was first over the Ventoux, and won in Avignon that day.

Stan Ockers proved that his second place at the 1950 Tour was no fluke, netting himself the runner-up spot again through clever, consistent riding, although without any stage wins. No one could touch Coppi, though, who finished almost half-an-hour ahead of the Belgian overall.

The Luxembourg team fielded two Australians in its ranks, one of whom – Edward Smith – was a non-starter, while John Beasley finished outside the time limit on stage 2 and was eliminated. The English speakers' dominance of the Tour was still a long way off; for the time being, approaching fifty years since the race was first run, it was the Italians, the French, the Swiss and the Belgians who ruled the roost.

ANGLETERRE

LA MANCHE

ÎLES ANGLO-NORMANDES
(rattachées à la Grande-Bretagne)

BELGIQUE

ROUBAIX

NAMUR

5 197 km

4 232 km

6 228 km

LUXEMBOURG

ALLEMAGNE

ROUEN

METZ

3 189 km

7 60 km

PARIS

NANCY

2 181 km

ST

RENNES

LE MANS

8 252 km

1 246 km

MULHOUSE

354 km

23

9 238 km

SUISSE

LAUSANNE

22 63 km

VICHY

10 266 km

245 km

21

LIMOGES

PUY DE DÔME

CLERMONT-FERRAND

L'ALPE-D'HUEZ

SESTRIERE

228 km

LE BOURG-D'OISANS

11

20

182 km

BORDEAUX

251 km

12

195 km

19

AVIGNON

178 km

14

GOLFE
DE
GASCOGNE

TOULOUSE

275 km

15

AIX-EN-PROVENCE

MONACO

13 214 km

ESPAGNE

PAU

BAGNÈRES-
DE-BIGORRE

17

149 km

18

204 km

16

200 km

PERPIGNAN

MER MÉDITERRANÉE

GOLFE DU LION

107

A rampant Louison Bobet makes his way up the Col d'Izoard to claim the stage and the yellow jersey

Start: Strasbourg, France, on 3 July
Finish: Paris, France, on 26 July

Total distance: 4479 km (2783 miles)
Longest stage: 345 km (214 miles)

Highest point:
Col d'Izoard: 2360 m (7743 ft)
Mountain stages: 8

Starters: 119
Finishers: 76

Winning time: 129 h 23' 25"
Average speed: 34.596 kph (21.497 mph)

1. Louison Bobet (Fra)
2. Jean Malléjac (Fra) at 14' 18"
3. Giancarlo Astrua (Ita) at 15' 02"

Points: Fritz Schär (Swi)
Mountains: Jesús Loroño (Spa)

It seemed only right, with the Tour celebrating its fiftieth anniversary (but only its fortieth edition due to two interruptions for war), that a Frenchman should win the race overall in 1953. That man was Louison Bobet. Despite third place overall at the 1950 Tour, no one could have foreseen him winning three Tour titles on the trot, making him one of France's greatest-ever riders.

After winning stage 11 in the Pyrenees by a minute-and-a-half from compatriot Bobet, it was 1947 Tour winner Jean Robic who was looking like the man most likely to bring home the bacon for France for the first time since his victory six years previously. However, Robic was riding for the Ouest regional team, while Bobet was on the French national team.

Stage 12 between Luchon and Albi proved to be the one and only day that Robic would wear the yellow jersey in his career, having only won the Tour on the last day in 1947. Robic crashed on the road to Albi, but the race lead passed to his 22-year-old Ouest team-mate François Mahé. It was also to be a short-lived tenure in yellow for the young Frenchman, however, as another Ouest rider, Jean Malléjac, assumed the lead the next day.

Rather than for his stage win earlier in the 1953 Tour and his five stages in yellow, Malléjac is probably best remembered for collapsing on Mont Ventoux during the 1955 Tour, which ended with him in hospital. Drugs were suspected by the race doctor as the cause of his collapse, although Malléjac always denied it.

Bobet took control of the 1953 race on stage 18 with a magisterial display of climbing through the Casse Déserte on the climb of the Izoard, winning the stage by 5 minutes 23 seconds over Holland's Jan Nolten. Malléjac was well over ten minutes off the pace, and Bobet sewed up his first Tour title with victory in the final time trial.

The green points jersey also arrived, with Switzerland's Fritz Schär proving to be the most consistent finisher at the 1953 Tour.

ANGLETERRE

LA MANCHE

ÎLES ANGLO-NORMANDES
(rattachées à la Grande-Bretagne)

LILLE
188 km
4
DIEPPE
3
221 km
LIÈGE
227 km
2
METZ
195 km
1
STRASBOURG
5 200 km
CAEN
PARIS
206 km
6
LE MANS
7 181 km
328 km
22
NANTES
345 km
8
MONTLUÇON
210 km
21
LYON
20
70 km
ST-ÉTIENNE
227 km
19
BRIANÇON
165 km
18
GAP
BORDEAUX
197 km
9
261 km
17
ALBI
228 km
12
189 km
13
214 km
14
NÎMES
173 km
15
236 km
16
MONACO
PAU
103 km
10
115 km
11
BÉZIERS
MARSEILLE
CAUTERETS
LUCHON

GOLFE DE GASCOGNE

ALLEMAGNE

SUISSE

ESPAGNE

GOLFE DU LION

MER MÉDITERRANÉE

In 1954 the Tour set off from outside France for the first time

Start: Amsterdam, Netherlands, on 8 July
Finish: Paris, France, on 1 August

Total distance:
4865.4 km (3023 miles)
Longest stage:
343 km (213 miles)

Highest point:
Col du Galibier: 2556 m (8386 ft)
Mountain stages: 9

Starters: 110
Finishers: 69

Winning time: 140 h 06' 05"
Average speed:
34.742 kph (21.588 mph)

1. Louison Bobet (Fra)
2. Ferdi Kübler (Swi) at 15' 49"
3. Fritz Schär (Swi) at 21' 46"

Points: Ferdi Kübler (Swi)
Mountains:
Federico Bahamontes (Spa)

In 1954, the Tour went Dutch, starting for the first time outside France, in Amsterdam. Having started in Paris each year (bar 1926) until 1951, it was quite an escalation to go from starting in the French capital, to starting in other French towns like Metz, Brest and Strasbourg, to starting abroad in such a short space of time.

Thousands of Dutch fans turned out to watch the opening stage, and it was one of their own, Wout Wagtmans, who sprinted to victory and the race's first yellow jersey in Brasschaat, just over the border in Belgium.

For the second year in a row, French hero Louison Bobet took the final applause in Paris. As soon as stage 4a – the return to the race of a team time trial – Bobet was in yellow, even though the Swiss team, which included Messrs Kübler and Koblet, beat the French squad to the stage win.

Despite pressure from the two Swiss riders (although 1951 Tour winner Koblet – nicknamed 'Le Pédaleur du Charme', as he always carried a comb in his jersey pocket – would pull out after a crash on stage 12), Bobet soared to his second straight win thanks once again to a dominating ride through the Casse Déserte on the relentless southern slopes of the Col d'Izoard, on stage 18, beating Kübler to the finish in Briançon by almost two minutes.

Spain's Federico Bahamontes, competing in the Tour for the first time, won the mountains competition – a sign of things to come.

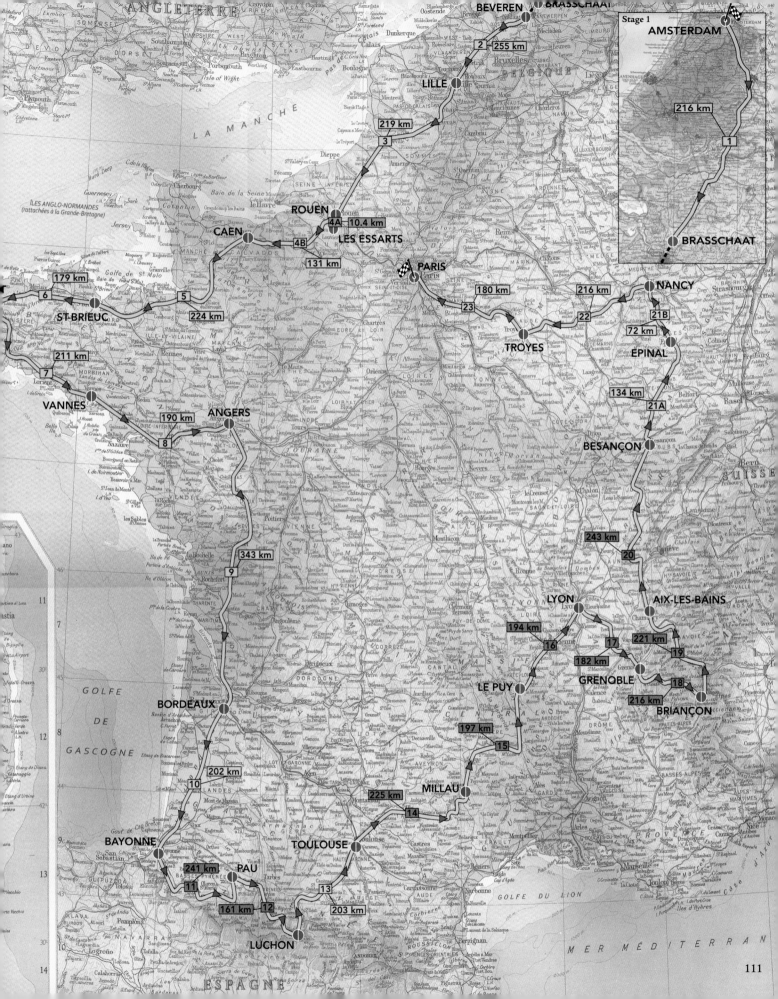

ANGLETERRE

LA MANCHE

ÎLES ANGLO-NORMANDES
(rattachées à la Grande-Bretagne)

ESPAGNE

MER MÉDITERRANÉE

GOLFE DE GASCOGNE

GOLFE DU LION

Stage 1

AMSTERDAM

216 km

1

BRASSCHAAT

BEVEREN

255 km

2

LILLE

219 km

3

ROUEN

4A 10.4 km

4B

LES ESSARTS

131 km

CAEN

5

224 km

ST-BRIEUC

6

179 km

211 km

7

VANNES

8

190 km

ANGERS

9

343 km

BORDEAUX

10

202 km

BAYONNE

11

241 km

PAU

12

161 km

13

203 km

LUCHON

TOULOUSE

14

225 km

MILLAU

15

197 km

LE PUY

16

194 km

LYON

17

182 km

GRENOBLE

18

216 km

BRIANÇON

19

221 km

AIX-LES-BAINS

20

243 km

21A

134 km

BESANÇON

21B

72 km

EPINAL

22

216 km

NANCY

23

180 km

PARIS

TROYES

111

In 1920, Belgium's Philippe Thys became the first rider to win three Tours de France, adding to his titles in 1913 and 1914. In 1955, however, France's Louison Bobet became the first rider to win three consecutive Tours – a huge achievement.

The French public, of course, was ecstatic, but Bobet was equally as ecstatic to be able to climb off his bike. He had struggled with a serious saddle sore for much of the race, and had barely been able to sit down. It was a malady that blighted him throughout his career as a professional cyclist, but achieving three Tour wins in a row must have helped to numb it just a little.

The opening stage – stage 1a, between Le Havre and Dieppe – was won by Miguel Poblet, who became the first Spanish rider to wear the yellow jersey. He still held it following the team time trial stage that afternoon, despite a less-than-stellar performance against the clock by his national team.

By the following day, the jersey was firmly on the shoulders of the Netherlands' Wout Wagtmans – the rider who had worn the first yellow jersey the year before.

Bobet waited until stage 17 and the Pyrenees to make his decisive move, having trailed Frenchman Antonin Rolland by nearly five minutes that morning. Luxemborg's pint-sized climber Charly Gaul stole the show across the Col d'Aspin and the Col de Peyresourde, and beat Bobet to the stage victory in St-Gaudens by 1-minute 24-seconds, but Bobet's reward was yellow.

The 1955 Tour also heralded the return of the first German riders since the war, albeit only two of them as part of the Luxembourg mixed team, sharing squad space with an Austrian and two Australians – John Beasley and Russell Mockridge – with riders from Luxembourg making up the rest of the ten-man team. A ten-man Great Britain team took part, too, although only two of them – Brian Robinson and Tony Hoar – would make it to Paris, in turn becoming the first British riders to finish the race. Robinson would also become Britain's first Tour stage winner, in 1958.

Lousion Bobet celebrates his third successive Tour victory

Start: Le Havre, France, on 7 July
Finish: Paris, France, on 30 July

Total distance:
4476.1 km (2781 miles)
Longest stage:
275 km (171 miles)

Highest point:
Col du Galibier: 2556 m (8386 ft)
Mountain stages: 7

Starters: 130
Finishers: 69

Winning time: 130 h 29' 26"
Average speed:
34.446 kph (21.404 mph)

1. Louison Bobet (Fra)
2. Jean Brankart (Bel) at 4' 53"
3. Charly Gaul (Lux) at 11' 30"

Points: Stan Ockers (Bel)
Mountains: Charly Gaul (Lux)

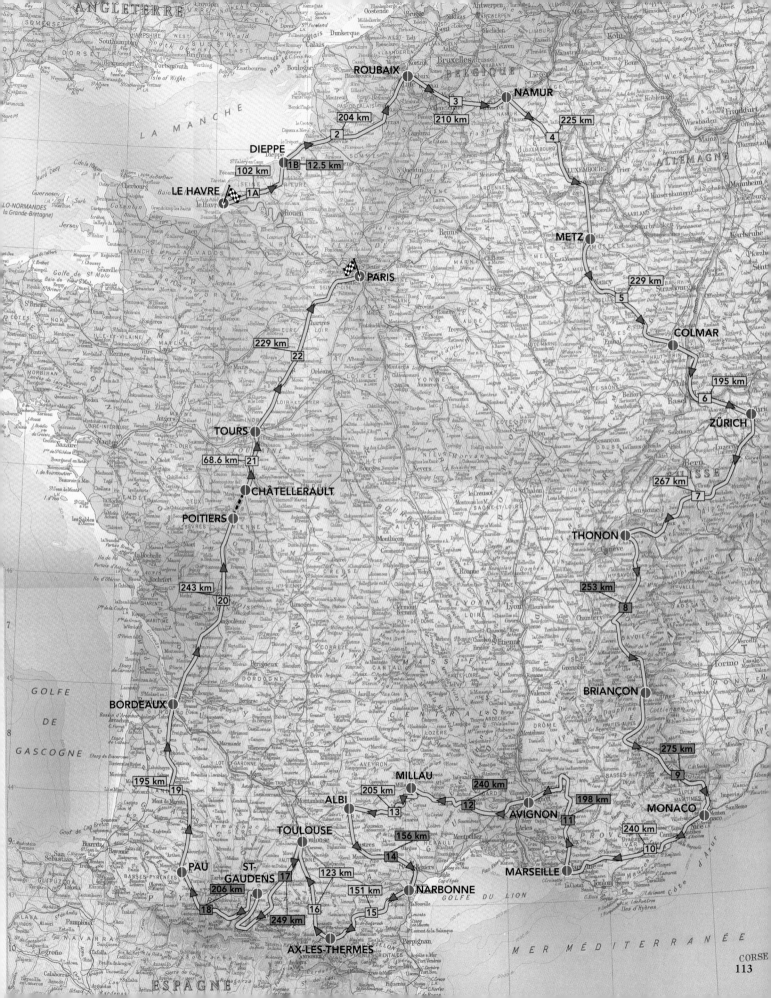

ANGLETERRE

LA MANCHE

ROUBAIX

NAMUR

204 km
2

210 km
3

225 km
4

DIEPPE

1B 12.5 km

102 km

LE HAVRE 1A

METZ

229 km
5

COLMAR

195 km
6

ZÜRICH

267 km
7

PARIS

229 km
22

TOURS

68.6 km 21

CHÂTELLERAULT

POITIERS

THONON

253 km
8

243 km
20

BRIANÇON

275 km
9

BORDEAUX

GOLFE
DE
GASCOGNE

MILLAU

195 km
19

ALBI

205 km
13

240 km
12

AVIGNON

198 km
11

MONACO

240 km
10

156 km
14

TOULOUSE

MARSEILLE

PAU

ST-
GAUDENS 17

206 km
18

123 km
16

151 km
15

NARBONNE

249 km

AX-LES-THERMES

ESPAGNE

MER MÉDITERRANÉE

CORSE

113

1956
43rd Edition

 Start: Reims, France, on 5 July
Finish: Paris, France, on 28 July

 Total distance:
4527.1 km (2813 miles)
Longest stage:
331 km (206 miles)

 Highest point:
Col d'Izoard: 2360 m (7743 ft)
Mountain stages: 8

 Starters: 120
Finishers: 88

 Winning time: 124 h 01' 16"
Average speed:
36.268 kph (22.536 mph)

 1. Roger Walkowiak (Fra)
2. Gilbert Bauvin (Fra) at 1' 25"
3. Jan Adriaenssens (Bel) at 3' 44"

 Points: Stan Ockers (Bel)
Mountains: Charly Gaul (Lux)

After surgery during the 1955–1956 off-season on what was a serious saddle boil, Louison Bobet won the 1956 edition of Paris-Roubaix, despite not being at the height of fitness. Struggling to get into form, however, Bobet decided to skip the 1956 Tour – leaving the door wide open for new favourites such as Luxembourg's Charly Gaul and Spanish climbing sensation Federico Bahamontes.

The final podium positions in Paris, however, ended up being quite a surprise. The relatively unknown Belgian, Jan Adriaenssens, took third place, while runner-up Gilbert Bauvin, of France, had worn the yellow jersey before – in 1951 and in 1954, when he'd also won two stages and finished tenth overall.

At the top of the podium in Paris stood France's Roger Walkowiak. Other than second place at the 1955 Dauphiné Libéré, Walkowiak had shown little sign of ever being a Tour contender, and that remained the case at the 1956 Tour – until he was part of a thirty-one-man breakaway group that finished stage 7 between Lorient and Angers almost nineteen minutes ahead of the peloton. Bauvin and Adriaenssens were in it, too, and although Walkowiak only finished nineteenth on the stage, it was enough to give him the yellow jersey, which he then surprised everyone by defending. Poor Walkowiak was not a popular winner, however; the general consensus was that he wasn't good enough, and so didn't deserve, to win.

With no Great Britain team taking part in 1956, Brian Robinson was the sole British participant as part of the motley crew that was the Luxembourg mixed squad, which also included an Italian and a Portuguese rider. Robinson finished third on the opening stage, and went on to finish fourteenth overall in only his second Tour.

Roger Walkowiak was deemed an unworthy winner

ANGLETERRE

SOMERSET
DORSET

LA MANCHE

ÎLES ANGLO-NORMANDES
(rattachées à la Grande-Bretagne)

ESPAGNE

LILLE
217 km — 2
225 km
3
223 km
1
LIÈGE
REIMS

ROUEN
4A — 15.1 km
125 km
4B
CAEN
189 km
PARIS
5 ST-MALO
192 km
6
LORIENT
244 km
7
ANGERS
331 km
22
180 km
8
MONTLUÇON
237 km
21
LA ROCHELLE
LYON
73 km — 20
173 km
219 km
9
ST-ÉTIENNE
19
GRENOBLE
250 km
18
TURIN
BORDEAUX
234 km
17
GAP
201 km
10
203 km
16
204 km
15
TOULOUSE
231 km
MONTPELLIER
AIX-EN-PROVENCE
176 km
14
BAYONNE
255 km
PAU
11
130 km
13
12
LUCHON

GOLFE
DE
GASCOGNE

ALLEMAGNE
SUISSE
GOLFE DU LION
MER MÉDITERRANÉE

115

Sprinter André Darrigade, famous for winning the opening stage of the Tour five times between 1956 and 1961, wins the final stage of the 1957 Tour at the Parc des Princes velodrome. The velodrome hosted the finish of the Tour from 1903 to 1967.

Debutant Jacques Anquetil was an instant success on and off the bike

Start: Nantes, France, on 27 June
Finish: Paris, France, on 20 July

Total distance:
4683.8 km (2910 miles)
Longest stage:
317 km (197 miles)

Highest point:
Col du Galibier: 2556 m (8386 ft)
Mountain stages: 7

Starters: 120
Finishers: 56

Winning time: 135 h 44' 42"
Average speed:
34.250 kph (21.282 mph)

1. Jacques Anquetil (Fra)
2. Marcel Janssens (Bel)
   at 14' 56"
3. Adolf Christian (Aut)
   at 17' 20"

Points: Jean Forestier (Fra)
Mountains: Gastone Nencini (Ita)

The 1957 Tour saw the emergence of Jacques Anquetil – a talented 23-year-old Frenchman who seemed more than happy to take up where Louison Bobet had left off, while Bobet – now 32 – relatively happily stepped aside to allow the new generation in.

Anquetil was at his first Tour, and certainly not a natural climber. He had to learn on his feet how best to ride the race – which turned out to be with a mixture of calculation and intelligence. While limiting his losses in the Alps and the Pyrenees, it was in time trials that Anquetil truly dominated his rivals, and in that respect he was one of the pioneers of modern-day racing: follow the competition in the mountains and then annihilate them against the clock, à la Miguel Indurain, Cadel Evans or Bradley Wiggins.

Anquetil's French team-mate, André Darrigade, had again won the first stage and so the race's first yellow jersey, just as he had done in 1956. Darrigade was very much a French precursor to Mark Cavendish today: Darrigade sprinted to twenty-two Tour stage wins in his career, and won the race's first yellow jersey – i.e. the Tour's opening stage – an astonishing five times between 1956 and 1961.

The 1957 Tour also dipped into Spain, with Barcelona hosting the finish of stage 15a before an afternoon individual time trial up the climb of Montjuich – won by Anquetil.

Once more there was no British team taking part, but again it was the Luxembourg mixed team who hosted Brian Robinson as the only British participant. He came to the Tour off the back of a stunning third place at Milan-San Remo, but crashed out on the cobbles of stage 5 between Roubaix and Charleroi.

ANGLETERRE

LA MANCHE

ÎLES ANGLO-NORMANDES
(rattachées à la Grande-Bretagne)

ROUBAIX

CHARLEROI

5   170 km

232 km

4

6   248 km

METZ

ROUEN

134 km

CAEN

223 km

226 km

3A   3B

7

2   CIRCUIT
         DE LA PRAIRIE

COLMAR

GRANVILLE

15 km

192 km

PARIS

8

204 km

1

227 km   BESANÇON

22

188 km

9

TOURS

THONON

317 km

21

247 km

10

LIBOURNE   BRIANÇON

66 km

20

BORDEAUX

286 km

11

GOLFE

DE

GASCOGNE

ALÈS

194 km

19   160 km

13   CANNES

age 15A, 15B and 16

PERPIGNAN

246 km   239 km

AX-LES-
THERMES   PAU   14   12

197 km

0 km   ST-GAUDENS   236 km   MARSEILLE

16   15A

207 km

15B   18   17   PERPIGNAN

9.8 km

BARCELONA   AX-LES-THERMES

GOLFE DU LION   MER MÉDITERRAN

ESPAGNE

BELGIQUE

ALLEMAGNE

SUISSE

André Darrigade, bandaged after his collision with an official, congratulates Charly Gaul

Start: Brussels, Belgium, on 26 June
Finish: Paris, France, on 19 July

Total distance:
4319.5 km (2684 miles)
Longest stage:
320 km (199 miles)

Highest point:
Col d'Izoard: 2360 m (7743 ft)
Mountain stages: 8

Starters: 120
Finishers: 78

Winning time: 116 h 59' 05"
Average speed:
36.919 kph (22.940 mph)

1. Charly Gaul (Lux)
2. Vito Favero (Ita) at 3' 10"
3. Raphaël Géminiani (Fra)
   at 3' 41"

Points: Jean Graczyk (Fra)
Mountains:
Federico Bahamontes (Spa)

At last, Charly Gaul got the Tour win he deserved. It was defending champion Jacques Anquetil, of course, who posed the biggest threat to the man from Luxembourg, but the Frenchman, ill, was not at his best, and it was is team-mate, Raphaël Géminiani, and Italian Vito Favero who revealed themselves to be Gaul's biggest threats.

Gaul waited until stage 21 to make his move, dropping Federico Bahamontes on the Col de Luitel before pushing clear of the few riders who remained at the front of the race on the Col de Porte in apocalyptic weather, winning alone in Aix-les-Bains, more than ten minutes ahead of Favero and nearly fifteen minutes ahead of Géminiani. The Italian nevertheless retained the lead, but, in Anquetil's absence, Gaul proved to be the race's best time triallist, and on the Tour's penultimate stage pulled back the time he needed to put himself in yellow.

For the third time in a row, French sprinter André Darrigade had won the Tour's opening stage and the yellow jersey, but it was to be an horrific end to the race in Paris when Darrigade crashed into an official, Constant Wouters, who had stepped onto the track at the Parc des Princes. Wouters died from his injuries two weeks later, while Darrigade, despite broken ribs and a fractured skull, was able to make a full recovery.

Brian Robinson won stage 7 between St-Brieuc and Brest to become the first British Tour stage winner, competing as part of a special international team made up of Danes, Britons, Austrians and Portuguese riders.

Also in that same international team was Ireland's Shay Elliott, riding his first Tour. Elliott would go on to become the first Irishman to wear the yellow jersey, in 1963.

1959
46th Edition

Spanish climber Federico Bahamontes (right) sealed his only Tour victory in 1959

Start: Mulhouse, France,
on 25 June
Finish: Paris, France, on 18 July

Total distance:
4358 km (2708 miles)
Longest stage:
331 km (206 miles)

Highest point:
Col de l'Iseran: 2770 m (9088 ft)
Mountain stages: 8

Starters: 120
Finishers: 65

Winning time: 123 h 46' 45"
Average speed:
35.183 kph (21.862 mph)

1. Federico Bahamontes (Spa)
2. Henry Anglade (Fra) at 4' 01"
3. Jacques Anquetil (Fra)
   at 5' 05"

Points: André Darrigade (Fra)
Mountains:
Federico Bahamontes (Spa)

Spain's Federico Bahamontes had been threatening to win the Tour since bursting onto the scene and winning the 'king of the mountains' title in 1954. However, many said that his Tour win – the first by a Spanish rider – was down less to his ability (although a fantastic climber, his descending skills were rudimentary, and that's being kind) and more to the fact that he had benefited from unrest among the French camp.

The French 'dream team' national squad – which included Louison Bobet, Jacques Anquetil and Raphaël Géminiani – was barely firing on one cylinder between them, let alone all of them, but they were nevertheless alleged to have worked as a unit to ensure that if one of their own couldn't win, then at least their compatriot on the Centre-Midi regional team, Henry Anglade, wouldn't either.

Anglade – a stroppy rider, by all accounts, who wasn't well liked – had won the Dauphiné Libéré stage race in the build-up to the Tour, as well as the French national championships. Thanks to warring French rider agents – keen to get their riders the best start money in the lucrative post-Tour criterium races – Anglade didn't stand a chance against the more established stars hoping for the biggest pay days after the race.

122

ANGLETERRE

LA MANCHE

ROUBAIX

NAMUR
3
217 km

230 km
4

240 km
2

ROUEN

METZ

238 km
1

331 km
22

PARIS

MULHOUSE

286 km
5

RENNES

DIJON
21   69.2 km

BLAIN
6   45.3 km
NANTES

SEURRE

CHALON-SUR-SAÔNE

190 km
7

202 km
20

251 km
19

ST-
VINCENT

LA ROCHELLE

ANNECY

201 km

12.5 km   210 km

8

PUY DE DÔME
15
16

243 km

197 km
17

CLERMONT-
FERRAND

231 km

ST-ÉTIENNE

GRENOBLE
18

14

AURILLAC

BORDEAUX

219 km

207 km
9

13

ALBI

184 km

BAYONNE
235 km
12

10

BAGNÈRES-DE-
BIGORRE

ST-GAUDENS

11

119 km

ESPAGNE

GOLFE
DE
GASCOGNE

GOLFE DU LION

MER MÉDITERRAN

1960

47th Edition

Roger Rivière's race ended in tragedy, plunging into a ravine on stage 14

Start: Lille, France, on 26 June
Finish: Paris, France, on 17 July

Total distance:
4171.8 km (2592 miles)
Longest stage:
244 km (152 miles)

Highest point:
Col d'Izoard: 2360 m (7743 ft)
Mountain stages: 8

Starters: 128
Finishers: 81

Winning time: 112 h 08' 42"
Average speed:
37.210 kph (23.121 mph)

1. Gastone Nencini (Ita)
2. Graziano Battistini (Ita)
   at 5' 02"
3. Jan Adriaenssens (Bel)
   at 10' 24"

Points: Jean Graczyk (Fra)
Mountains:
Imerio Massignan (Ita)

The 1960 Tour de France was infamously marked by French rider Roger Rivière's crash on the descent of the Col de Perjuret on stage 14. The 24-year-old time-trial star – Rivière had broken the Hour record in 1957, and then broke his own record in 1959 – survived the fall, but never raced again, his injuries confining him as they did to a wheelchair for the rest of his life. He died aged 40, of throat cancer.

In Jacques Anquetil's absence – the French star was exhausted after putting everything into winning the 1960 Giro d'Italia – Rivière had been France's main hope for the overall victory, despite the elevation of unpopular 1959 runner-up Henry Anglade to the French national team.

Rivière's prowess against the clock led many to believe that, having won the race's first time trial on stage 1b, he'd easily be able to overcome Italy's Gastone Nencini, who took the race lead on that same first time-trial stage, in the final 83-km (52-mile) test between Pontarlier and Besançon on stage 19. Alas, Rivière's tragic accident put paid to French hopes, and Nencini led home an Italian one-two ahead of team-mate Graziano Battistini, and Italy's success was added to by Imerio Massignan's victory in the mountains competition. Belgium's Jan Adriaenssens took third overall in the race, just as he had in 1956.

The 1960 Tour also featured the first major transfer of the Tour's participants en masse – by train from the stage finish in Bordeaux on stage 9 to the start of stage 10 at Mont-de-Marsan. Usually, the race had finished and then started the next day in the same town, although there had been a few exceptions over the years.

There was a Great Britain team taking part in the 1960 Tour, too, led by the very able Brian Robinson, who had won stages in both 1958 and 1959. The eight-man squad also featured a young second-year pro called Tom Simpson, riding his first Tour, who rode for the French Rapha-Gitane outfit when not on national duty. Along with Robinson, he was the only British finisher in 1960.

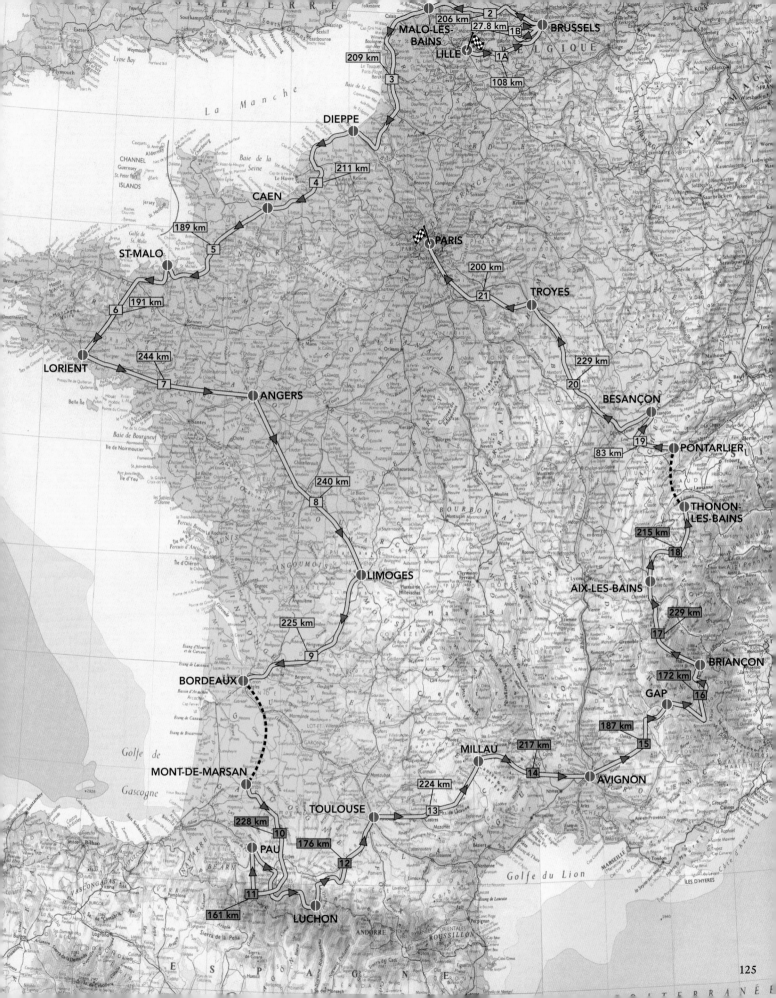

MALO-LES-BAINS

BRUSSELS

206 km
2
27.8 km
1B

LILLE
1A

209 km
3

108 km

DIEPPE

211 km
4

CAEN

189 km
5

ST-MALO

191 km
6

LORIENT

244 km
7

ANGERS

240 km
8

LIMOGES

225 km
9

BORDEAUX

MONT-DE-MARSAN

228 km
10

PAU

176 km

161 km
11

LUCHON

12

TOULOUSE

13

224 km

MILLAU

217 km
14

AVIGNON

187 km
15

GAP

16

172 km

BRIANCON

17

229 km

AIX-LES-BAINS

18

215 km

THONON-LES-BAINS

19

83 km

PONTARLIER

BESANÇON

20

229 km

TROYES

21

200 km

PARIS

Jacques Anquetil and team-mate André Darrigade lead an early breakaway on the opening stage

Start: Rouen, France, on 25 June
Finish: Paris, France, on 16 July

Total distance:
4397.5 km (2732 miles)
Longest stage:
309.5 km (192.3 miles)

Highest point:
Col du Tourmalet:
2115 m (6939 ft)
Mountain stages: 9

Starters: 132
Finishers: 72

Winning time: 122 h 01' 33"
Average speed:
36.033 kph (22.390 mph)

1. Jacques Anquetil (Fra)
2. Guido Carlesi (Ita) at 12' 14"
3. Charly Gaul (Lux) at 12' 16"

Points: André Darrigade (Fra)
Mountains: Imerio Massignan (Ita)

It had been four years since Jacques Anquetil's first Tour victory – and what a way for him to score his second. The 1957 winner almost – *almost* – led the 1961 edition from start to finish, having been part of a fifteen-man breakaway that got away on the opening stage – stage 1a, between Rouen and Versailles. It was that man again, André Darrigade, Anquetil's French team-mate, who had the fastest sprint that day, winning his fifth Tour opening stage in six years – taking with it the yellow jersey each time, too, of course.

Romain Maes, in 1935, had been – and remains – the last rider to wear the Tour's yellow jersey all the way from beginning to end, although Anquetil did take the jersey from his compatriot Darrigade in the afternoon of the Tour's first day in 1961. The 28.5-km (18-mile) time trial saw Anquetil dominate; no one got

within two-and-a-half minutes of the Frenchman's winning time, and he was already almost five minutes up on his nearest rival overall at the end of day one.

Superbagnères – the tough climb that towers over the town of Bagnères-de-Luchon in the Pyrenees – made its first appearance at the Tour, where, appropriately enough, the mountains jersey winner in both 1960 and 1961, Italian rider Imerio Massignan, took the victory on stage 16.

The Tour also made a relatively deep sortie into Italy to Turin for the finish of stage 10 and the start of stage 11, the latter stage finishing in another new stage town, the beautifully named Antibes suburb of Juan-les-Pins.

ROUBAIX

BELGIQUE

230.5 km

3

237.5 km

197.5 km

CHARLEROI

2

4

METZ

ROUEN

PONTOISE

221 km

136.5 km

PARIS

5

1A

STRASBOURG

VERSAILLES

28.5 km

180.5 km

6

1B

252.5 km

BELFORT

21

214.5 km

7

TOURS

CHALON-SUR-SAÔNE

309.5 km

20

240.5 km

8

250.5 km

ST-ÉTIENNE

TURIN

PÉRIGUEUX

74.5 km

9

GRENOBLE

19

230 km

10

BORDEAUX

225 km

BERGERAC

11

207 km

18

177.5 km

ANTIBES

TOULOUSE

MONTPELLIER

199 km

16

13

174 km

AIX-EN-

PROVENCE

12

PAU

208 km

14

206 km

LUCHON

15

17

197 km

SUPERBAGNÈRES

PERPIGNAN

ESPAGNE

127

MER MÉDITERRANÉE

1962
49th Edition

Riders cross the Col de la Bonette en route to the Tour's highest ever point – the Cime de la Bonette-Restefond

Start: Nancy, France, on 24 June
Finish: Paris, France, on 15 July

Total distance:
4273.5 km (2656 miles)
Longest stage:
271 km (168 miles)

Highest point:
Cime de la Bonette-Restefond:
2802 m (9193 ft)
Mountain stages: 5

Starters: 149
Finishers: 94

Winning time: 114 h 31' 54"
Average speed:
37.306 kph (23.181 mph)

1. Jacques Anquetil (Fra)
2. Joseph Planckaert (Bel)
   at 4' 59"
3. Raymond Poulidor (Fra)
   at 10' 24"

Points: Rudi Altig (Ger)
Mountains:
Federico Bahamontes (Spa)

For the first time since 1929, sponsored 'trade' teams contested the Tour, and fifteen squads of ten riders lined up in Nancy on 24 June. Save for two later years – 1967 and 1968 – the Tour has continued with the sponsored-teams format ever since.

Tour director Jacques Goddet had been infuriated by what he saw as a lack of ambition by the other riders to challenge Jacques Anquetil for the win in 1961, and there wasn't better news in 1962: the Frenchman, riding for the St Raphaël-Helyett team, managed by the recently retired Raphaël Géminiani, faced little competition and won overall in Paris by one second shy of five minutes from Belgium's Joseph (better known as Jef) Planckaert. In third place was a 26-year-old French rider named Raymond Poulidor. 'Poupou' would become Anquetil's greatest rival in the years to come, although would never beat him at the Tour, earning him the rather unfair nickname 'The Eternal Second'.

Great Britain's Tom Simpson, riding his third Tour, became the first Briton – and in fact the first rider from an English-speaking nation – to wear the yellow jersey when he finished in a front group of eighteen riders that included Poulidor, Anquetil and Planckaert on the tough twelfth stage that took the race over the Tourmalet, the Aspin and the Peyresourde. Simpson lost it on stage 13 to Federico Bahamontes, but finished sixth overall in Paris.

The 1962 Tour also reached the highest point it ever had, and still ever can: 2802 m (9193 ft) above sea level at the Cime de la Bonette-Restefond – the highest paved road in Europe. Reached via the Col de la Bonette – a 2715-metre-high (8907-ft) pass – the Cime de la Bonette is an additional, higher road loop at the top of the Bonette. The Col de l'Iseran – also frequently used by the Tour de France – remains the highest paved pass proper at 2770 m (9088 ft).

BRUSSELS

SPA

147 km

210 km

3

AMIENS

196.5 km

4

LE HAVRE

PONT-
L'ÉVÊQUE

215 km

5

ST-
MALO

DINARD

235.5 km

6

IMPER

7

201 km

ST-NAZAIRE

8A

155 km

LUÇON

43 km

8B

LA ROCHELLE

214 km

9

BORDEAUX

184.5 km

10

BAYONNE

155.5 km

11

PAU

207.5 km ST-GAUDENS

12

LUCHON

18.5 km

13   SUPERBAGNÈRES

14

215 km

CARCASSONNE

15

196.5 km

MONTPELLIER

16

185 km

AIX-EN-
PROVENCE

17

201 km

ANTIBES

18

241.5 km

BRIANÇON

19

204.5 km

AIX-LES-BAINS

68 km

20

BOURGOIN

LYON

21

232 km

NEVERS

22

271km

PARIS

253 km

1

NANCY

23 km   Stage 2A and B

HERENTALS

2B

2A

147 km

147 km

BRUSSELS

La Manche

129

1963
50th Edition

Start: Nogent-sur-Marne (Paris), on 23 June
Finish: Paris, France, on 14 July

Total distance:
4140.6 km (2573 miles)
Longest stage:
285 km (177 miles)

Highest point:
Col de l'Iseran: 2770 m (9088 ft)
Mountain stages: 7

Starters: 130
Finishers: 76

Winning time: 113 h 30' 05"
Average speed:
37.092 kph (23.048 mph)

1. Jacques Anquetil (Fra)
2. Federico Bahamontes (Spa)
   at 3' 35"
3. José Pérez-Francés (Spa)
   at 10' 14"

Points: Rik Van Looy (Bel)
Mountains:
Federico Bahamontes (Spa)

The 1963 race started in the eastern-Paris suburb of Nogent-sur-Marne. In order to try to placate the French public, who had booed in Paris on the occasion of Jacques Anquetil's third, and second consecutive, Tour triumph in 1962, race organiser Jacques Goddet decided to reduce the number of kilometres against the clock and increase the amount of climbing in the 1963 edition of the Tour in the hope of evening things out a little.

Anquetil still won both individual time trials – by 45 seconds over compatriot Raymond Poulidor in the first one, and by over a minute from Belgium's Ferdinand Bracke in the second – and easily kept pace with Poulidor and Federico Bahamontes in the mountains to finish 3 minutes 35 seconds ahead of the Spaniard at the Parc des Princes in Paris. This time it was Poulidor who was on the receiving end of the crowd's whistles for having only managed eighth overall.

After Great Britain's Tom Simpson had become the first English-speaking rider to wear the yellow jersey at the 1962 Tour, in 1963 it was Ireland's turn. Seamus 'Shay' Elliott – who rode for Anquetil's St Raphaël-Gitane team – took the jersey on stage 3 between Jambes, in Belgium, and Roubaix. Elliott attacked from a group that included his team-mate Jean Stablinski and soloed to the stage victory in Roubaix's famous velodrome. He kept the jersey all the way to stage 6b – the race's first individual time trial, won by Anquetil – after which the *maillot jaune* passed to the shoulders of Gilbert Desmet of the Belgian Wiel's-Groene Leeuw team. Anquetil wouldn't take it until stage 17, but then held it all the way to Paris.

Shay Elliott celebrates his stage win in Roubaix, becoming Ireland's first yellow jersey weare

ROUBAIX

JAMBES

21.6 km

2B

223.5 km

3

185.5 km

2A

235.5 km

4

REIMS

152.5 km

ÉPERNAY

1

ROUEN

PARIS

21

TROYES

185.5 km

233.5 km

20

BESANÇON

54.5 km

19

ARBOIS

285 km

5

RENNES

118.5 km

6A

24.5 km

6B

ANGERS

7

LONS-LE-SAUNIER

225 km

18

CHAMONIX

227.5 km

17

VAL
D'ISÈRE

236 km

LIMOGES

236.5 km

14

ST-ÉTIENNE

15

174 km

GRENOBLE

16

202 km

231.5 km

8

BORDEAUX

AURILLAC

202 km

9

13

234 km

TOULOUSE

PAU

BAGNÈRES-
DE-BIGORRE

12

172.5 km

10

148.5 km

11

131 km

LUCHON

131

1964
51st Edition

The enduring image of the 1964 Tour – helped, no doubt, by the iconic black-and-white photograph – is of eventual winner Jacques Anquetil and rival Raymond Poulidor locking horns on the lower slopes of the Puy de Dôme – a dormant volcano in the Massif Central. Neither was in the frame for the stage victory, which went to Spain's Julio Jiménez, but higher up the climb it was Poulidor who got the better of the reigning Tour champ, putting 42 seconds into Anquetil to close the gap between them to just 14 seconds overall with just three stages of the race left.

The final stage, however, was a 27.5-km (17-mile) time trial between Versailles and Paris's Parc des Princes, which gave Anquetil the opportunity to increase his narrow lead over Poulidor. Anquetil won the stage, and finished atop the podium in Paris with a margin of just 55 seconds back to 'Poupou' – the closest yet anyone had come to deposing Anquetil, but who nevertheless took his fifth Tour victory.

The excitement and closeness of racing on the narrow road up the Puy de Dôme puts the climb close to the top of many people's wish lists as a venue for future Tour routes, but the problem the organisers face today is that the Tour's infrastructure is now so large that it would be a struggle to fit everyone and everything into the car park at the summit – much as they'd like to return for the first time since 1988.

After its start in Rennes, in Brittany, the 1964 Tour visited Belgium, Germany, Monaco and Andorra, and this international route certainly helped contribute to it being one of the most entertaining Tours in years.

An exciting Tour was marred, however, by tragedy on stage 19 between Bordeaux and Brive. Ahead of the peloton's arrival at Port-de-Couze, near Bergerac in the Dordogne, a lorry driver lost control of his vehicle, which plunged into the crowd of waiting spectators on a narrow bridge and on down into the canal below. Eight people were killed, and many more injured, in what was the worst accident to ever befall the Tour.

Raymond Poulidor drops Jacques Anquetil at the top of the Puy de Dôme

Start: Rennes, France, on 22 June
Finish: Paris, France, on 14 July

Total distance:
4503.7 km (2799 miles)
Longest stage:
311 km (193 miles)

Highest point:
Cime de la Bonette-Restefond:
2802 m (9193 ft)
Mountain stages: 7

Starters: 132
Finishers: 81

Winning time: 127 h 09' 44"
Average speed:
35.420 kph (22.009 mph)

1. Jacques Anquetil (Fra)
2. Raymond Poulidor (Fra)
   at 0' 55"
3. Federico Bahamontes (Spa)
   at 4' 44"

Points: Jan Janssen (Hol)
Mountains:
Federico Bahamontes (Spa)

FOREST

21.3 km

196.5 km

3B

3A

291.5 km

4

AMIENS

208 km

METZ

2

LISIEUX

27.5 km

215 km

22B

PARIS

1

VERSAILLES

LUNÉVILLE

5

RENNES

22A

161.5 km

FREIBURG IM BREISGAU

118.5 km

200 km

ORLÉANS

6

BESANÇON

311 km

CHAMPAGNOLE

21

THONON-LES-BAINS

7

195 km

248.5 km

8

PUY DE DÔME

CLERMONT-FERRAND

237 km

20

BRIANÇON

215.5 km

239 km

19

BRIVE-LA-GAILLARDE

9

BORDEAUX

187 km

250 km

18

MONACO

187.5 km

BAYONNE

PEYREHORADE

10A

17

PAU

42.6 km

TOULOUSE

174 km

11

20.8 km

203 km

186 km

MONTPELLIER

10B

15

12

TOULON

14

170 km

HYÈRES

16

13

LUCHON

197 km

ANDORRA

PERPIGNAN

133

Cologne was the first German city to host the *Grand Dépar*

Start: Cologne, Germany,
on 22 June
Finish: Paris, France, on 14 July

Total distance:
4176.9 km (2595 miles)
Longest stage:
298.5 km (185.5 miles)

Highest point:
Col d'Izoard: 2360 m (7743 ft)
Mountain stages: 9

Starters: 130
Finishers: 96

Winning time: 116 h 42' 06"
Average speed:
35.886 kph (22.299 mph)

1. Felice Gimondi (Ita)
2. Raymond Poulidor (Fra)
   at 2' 40"
3. Gianni Motta (Ita) at 9' 18"

Points: Jan Janssen (Hol)
Mountains: Julio Jiménez (Spa)

By rights, in the absence of Jacques Anquetil, who decided to sit out the 1965 Tour having already taken five Tour titles, this should have been Raymond Poulidor's Tour. Instead, the race saw the emergence of 23-year-old Italian Felice Gimondi – a late selection for his Salvarani team's Tour roster – and poor Poulidor's 'Eternal Second' nickname was cemented. The Frenchman finished 2 minutes 40 seconds down on the young Italian in Paris after Gimondi had proved himself the better man against the clock in the race's two later time trials, despite Poulidor having bettered the Italian in 'the race of truth' on stage 5b.

Gimondi had already put 30 seconds into the main field, including Poulidor, as early as stage 3, on the flat run between Roubaix and Rouen, which was also enough to take the yellow jersey.

Poulidor subsequently came alive on stage 14, which finished at the top of

Mont Ventoux, taking over a minute-and-a-half out of Gimondi, but the Italian still retained a 34-second lead, and just seemed to get stronger as the race went on.

For the first time, the Tour also climbed Mont Revard, in the Alps, which will also feature in the penultimate stage of the 2013 Tour.

As in 1964, the route of the 1965 Tour visited a number of countries en route to Paris, starting in Germany, in Cologne, before heading into Belgium, with stage 11 finishing in Barcelona, where the race took a rest day before leaving Spain again on stage 12.

Also like 1964, the race finished with a time trial between Versailles and Paris, during which a yellow-clad Gimondi proved that he really was the best rider by winning the stage.

ROUBAIX

22.5 km 1B

1A COLOGNE

LIÈGE

149 km

2

200.5 km

240 km

3

ROUEN

CAEN

37.8 km

22

Paris

VERSAILLES

147 km

227 km

4

ST-BRIEUC

5A

EAULIN

5B

26.7 km

UIMPER

6

210.5 km

LA BAULE

219 km

7

LA ROCHELLE

8

197.5 km

BORDEAUX

DAX

9

226.5 km

BAGNÈRES-
DE-BIGORRE

222.5 km

10

AX-LES-
THERMES

11

240.5 km

12

219 km

PERPIGNAN

164 km

13

MONTPELLIER

14

173 km

CARPENTRAS

15

MONT
VENTOUX

167.5 km

177 km

GAP

16

BRIANÇON

17

193.5 km

18

MONT
REVARD

26.9 km

AIX-LES-
BAINS

19

165 km

LYON

20

298.5 km

AUXERRE

21

225.5 km

Stage 11 and 12

11

240.5 km

12

219 km

BARCELONA

135

"If anyone wants to accuse me of doping, it's not exactly difficult. You only have to look at my backside: it's like a sieve."

Jacques Anquetil was never in the business of denying that he injected performance-enhancing drugs

The Ford France-Hutchinson team were integral to Lucien Aimar's success

Start: Nancy, France, on 21 June
Finish: Paris, France, on 14 July

Total distance:
4329.1 km (2690 miles)
Longest stage:
264.5 km (164.5 miles)

Highest point:
Col du Galibier: 2556 m (8386 ft)
Mountain stages: 8

Starters: 130
Finishers: 82

Winning time: 117 h 34' 21"
Average speed:
36.760 kph (22.842 mph)

1. Lucien Aimar (Fra)
2. Jan Janssen (Hol) at 1' 07"
3. Raymond Poulidor (Fra)
   at 2' 02"

Points: Willy Planckaert (Bel)
Mountains: Julio Jiménez (Spa)

After a couple of very 'international' Tours, during which the race made multiple visits into other countries, the 1966 edition made only a brief stop in Italy: for the finish of stage 17 in Turin, and the start of stage 18 in Ivrea.

Five-time champion Jacques Anquetil was back, but Gimondi was a non-starter, and so the Anquetil-Gimondi duel that had been hoped for wasn't going to happen. However, the Anquetil-Poulidor battle was on.

Raymond Poulidor fought hard, and got the better of Anquetil to win the individual time trial at Vals-les-Bains on stage 14b, while they matched each other pedal stroke for pedal stroke over the Croix de Fer, Télégraphe and Galibier between Bourg d'Oisans and Briançon on stage 16.

When Anquetil's Ford France-Hutchinson team-mate Lucien Aimar – who had been riding well all race – was part of a breakaway on stage 17 between Briançon and Turin, which gave the 26-year-old the yellow jersey, Anquetil shifted focus and chose to put both himself and his team to work to help their young team-mate win the entire race. It was to be Anquetil's last Tour, and, unwell, he retired on stage 19.

Jan Janssen, a formidable sprinter who had won the green jersey the previous two years, found his climbing legs during the 1966 Tour and finished second overall to Aimar in Paris by just 1 minute 7 seconds, while Poulidor finished less than a minute further back in third.

DUNKIRK 131.5 km 3A 20.8 km
3B
205 km 4 TOURNAI
2
198 km
DIEPPE CHARLEVILLE 1
178.5 km 208.5 km
5
51.3 km NANCY
CAEN PARIS
216.5 km 22B
6 RAMBOUILLET
22A
111 km
ORLÉANS
ANGERS 232.5 km
21
252.5 km 7
MONTLUÇON
223.5 km
20 CHAMONIX 188 km
ROYAN 264.5 km 18
137.5 km 19 IVREA
8 ST-ÉTIENNE 160 km
17
LE BOURG-D'OISANS 16 TURIN
BORDEAUX 15 PRIVAS BRIANÇON
VALS-LES-BAINS 148.5 km
201 km 20 km 14B
9 AUBENAS
144 km 203.5 km
14A
BAYONNE
234.5 km MONTPELLIER
10 REVEL SÈTE
PAU 188 km
11 12 13
191.5 km
218.5 km
LUCHON

137

Tour doctor Pierre Dumas (in shorts) helps to load Tom Simpson into the helicopter that would take him off Mont Ventoux and out of the 1967 Tour, to hospital in Avignon, where he was declared dead.

A minute's silence is held prior to the start of stage 14 following the tragic death of Tom Simpson

Start: Angers, France, on 29 June
Finish: Paris, France, on 23 July

Total distance:
4780.4 km (2970 miles)
Longest stage:
359 km (223 miles)

Highest point:
Col du Galibier: 2556 m (8386 ft)
Mountain stages: 9

Starters: 130
Finishers: 88

Winning time: 136 h 53' 50"
Average speed:
35.018 kph (21.759 mph)

1. Roger Pingeon (Fra)
2. Julio Jiménez (Spa) at 3' 40"
3. Franco Balmamion (Ita)
   at 7' 23"

Points: Jan Janssen (Hol)
Mountains: Julio Jiménez (Spa)

The 1967 Tour de France saw a return to national teams – for both the 1967 and 1968 editions as an experiment by the organisers – while it was also the end of an era in that the Tour finished at the Parc des Princes for the last time. Later that year, the velodrome was demolished in order to rebuild the venue as the home of Paris Saint-Germain football club, as well as the home of the French national football and rugby teams. However, the building of the Stade de France for the 1998 World Cup saw the national sides decamp, while the Parc des Princes remains the home of PSG today.

If some had been teary-eyed at the nostalgia of leaving behind the venue that had hosted the finish of the Tour since its inception in 1903, it was overshadowed by a far more tragic incident during that year's race: the death of Britain's Tom Simpson on

Mont Ventoux on stage 13. The mountain went from simple legendary status to being infamous when Simpson, riding for the British national team, collapsed on the climb and, following attempts on the scree slopes next to the road to resuscitate him, was airlifted to hospital in Avignon, where he died, aged 29.

The race – which was the first to commence with a short, 'prologue' time trial (still called stage 1a in 1967) – nevertheless continued, although on the day following Simpson's death his GB team-mate Barry Hoban was allowed to win the stage in his compatriot's honour.

France's Roger Pingeon, riding only his third Tour, was the winner in Paris, where fellow countryman Raymond Poulidor had the honour of being the last rider to win a bike race in the Parc des Princes by taking victory in the final-stage time trial.

ROUBAIX

17 km

5B

JAMBES

238 km

5A

172 km

4

191 km

AMIENS

248 km

3

CAEN

46.6 km

22B

Paris

205.5 km

METZ

180 km

VERSAILLES

FONTAINEBLEAU

22A

STRASBOURG

2

ST-MALO

104 km

7

215 km

8

BALLON D'ALSACE

185.5 km

1

BELFORT

21

P ANGERS

359 km

238.5 km

5.8 km

9

DIVONNE-LES-BAINS

222 km

243 km

20

10

LIMOGES

CLERMONT-FERRAND

PUY DE DÔME

217 km

BRIANÇON

19

BORDEAUX

197 km

11

206.5 km

DIGNE

18

CARPENTRAS

201.5 km

13

TOULOUSE

14

211.5 km

207.5 km

PAU

188 km

12

16

15

SÈTE MARSEILLE

17

Golfe du Lion

250 km

LUCHON

MER MÉDITERRANÉE

Dutchman Jan Janssen remained cool under pressure, securing the yellow jersey on the final stage between Melun and Paris

Start: Vittel, France, on 27 June
Finish: Paris, France, on 21 July

Total distance:
4684.8 km (2911 miles)
Longest stage:
250.5 km (155.5 miles)

Highest point:
Port d'Envalira: 2408 m (7900 ft)
Mountain stages: 7

Starters: 110
Finishers: 63

Winning time: 133 h 49' 42"
Average speed:
34.894 kph (21.682 mph)

1. Jan Janssen (Hol)
2. Herman Van Springel (Bel)
 at 0' 38"
3. Ferdinand Bracke (Bel)
 at 3' 03"

Points: Franco Bitossi (Ita)
Mountains:
Aurelio González (Spa)

Dutchman Jan Janssen – a very real contender for the title of coolest rider ever thanks to his penchant for achingly hip sunglasses – finally topped the podium in Paris in 1968 to take the Netherlands' first Tour title.

Although not a natural climber in the mould of contemporaries Raymond Poulidor, Franco Bitossi or Julio Jiménez, Janssen's metronomic consistency throughout the Tour's three weeks – the same consistency that had seen him win three points-jersey competitions prior to 1968 – resulted in him being able to take the yellow jersey for the first time in the race when it mattered most: on the very last stage when he won the individual time trial between Melun and Paris's Bois de Vincennes, giving him the overall victory by just 38 seconds from Belgium's Herman Van Springel.

With the Paris finish no longer in the Parc des Princes, which saw its last Tour in 1967, the Cipale velodrome – a shortening of *municipale*, and today called the Vélodrome Jacques Anquetil – stepped in as the new finish in 1968, and continued to host the Tour until 1975 when the Tour chose the Champs-Élysées for the race's *arrivée*, which remains the case today.

Britain's Barry Hoban, having been given the honour of winning the stage following the death of countryman Tom Simpson during the 1967 Tour, proved he could win on his own merit by breaking away on the Col des Aravis on stage 19 and leading the race over the Colombière and to the top of the Cordon to win alone in Sallanches by over four minutes from second-placed Bitossi of Italy.

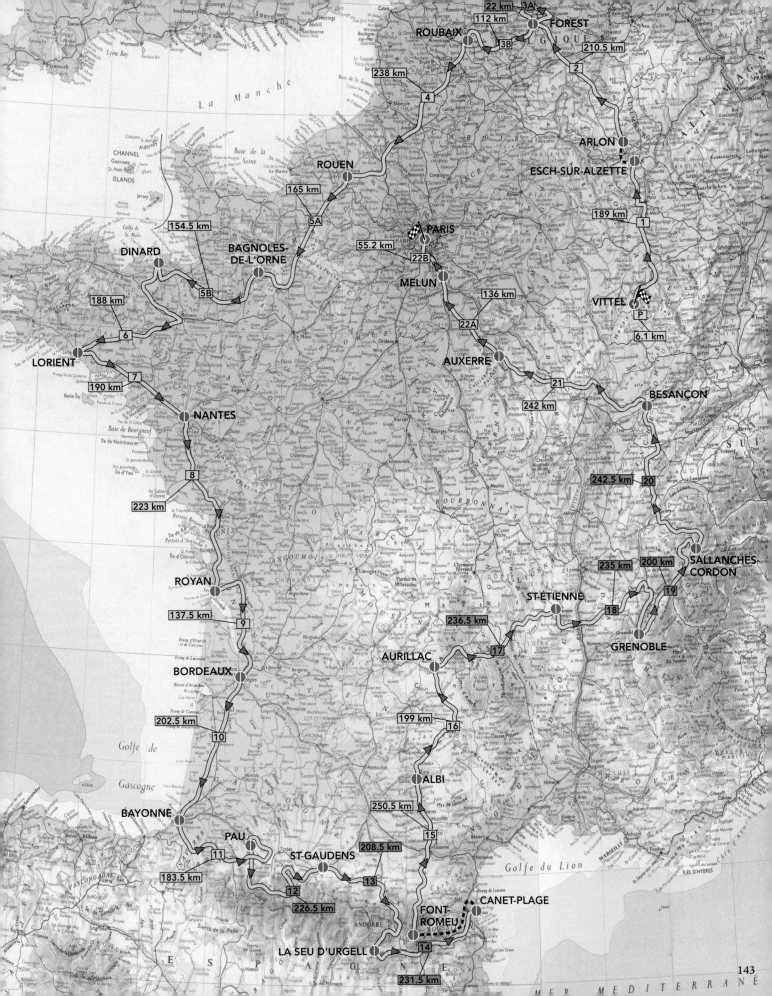

ROUBAIX

FOREST

22 km · 3A
112 km
3B
210.5 km
2

238 km
4

ARLON

ESCH-SUR-ALZETTE

ROUEN

189 km
1

165 km
5A

154.5 km

5B

PARIS

55.2 km
22B

VITTEL
P

6.1 km

DINARD

BAGNOLES-
DE-L'ORNE

MELUN

136 km
22A

188 km

6

LORIENT

7

190 km

NANTES

AUXERRE

21

242 km

BESANÇON

242.5 km
20

8

223 km

SALLANCHES-
CORDON

235 km   200 km

19

ROYAN

ST-ÉTIENNE

18

137.5 km
9

236.5 km

GRENOBLE

BORDEAUX

AURILLAC

17

202.5 km

10

199 km
16

ALBI

BAYONNE

250.5 km

15

PAU

208.5 km

11

ST-GAUDENS

183.5 km

12

13

226.5 km

CANET-PLAGE

FONT-
ROMEU

LA SEU D'URGELL   14

231.5 km

143

1969
56th Edition

Start: Roubaix, France, on 28 June
Finish: Paris, France, on 20 July

Total distance:
4117.6 km (2559 miles)
Longest stage:
329.5 km (204.5 miles)

Highest point:
Col du Galibier: 2556 m (8386 ft)
Mountain stages: 11

Starters: 130
Finishers: 86

Winning time: 116 h 16' 02"
Average speed:
35.409 kph (22.002 mph)

1. Eddy Merckx (Bel)
2. Roger Pingeon (Fra) at 17' 54"
3. Raymond Poulidor (Fra)
   at 22' 13"

Points: Eddy Merckx (Bel)
Mountains: Eddy Merckx (Bel)

The team sponsors were back in 1969, and have remained since; the 1968 Tour was the last to be contested by national teams, which are today only formed for the annual world championships and for the Olympics on the road.

The 1969 Tour continued a true golden age for cycling in what was a short space of time: first came the emergence of Louison Bobet and Jacques Anquetil for France, contributing greatly to giving the home nation eleven Tour wins in the space of fifteen years between 1953 and 1967. Then, in 1969, came arguably the biggest legend of them all – although, unluckily for French fans, he was Belgian.

That man, of course, was Eddy Merckx, and he was to dominate the Tour de France, and professional cycling in general, for the best part of ten years.

Right from the off, in the prologue time trial in Roubaix, the young Merckx signalled his intent with second place, 7 seconds down on stage winner Rudi Altig of Germany. Merckx's Faema team's win in the team time trial on stage 1b gave the Belgian his first yellow jersey on home turf in Woluwe-St-Pierre on the outskirts of Brussels, but Merckx then lost the jersey to Belgian team-mate Julien Stevens the next day when the race continued through the Netherlands.

However, Merckx's crushing defeat of the rest of the field on stage 6 to the top of the Ballon d'Alsace to take back the *maillot jaune* set the agenda for the rest of the race, and the next few years. The Belgian went on to win another five stages in the 1969 Tour – three of them individual time trials – finishing in Paris not only having won the leader's jersey, but also the points and mountains jerseys, which was unprecedented at the Tour, although

Merckx had pulled off the same feat of winning all three competitions at the 196[ ] Giro d'Italia. Despite it being achieved at both the 1993 and 1995 editions of the Tour of Spain – through Tony Rominger and Laurent Jalabert, respectively – no one has repeated Merckx's 'three-jersey' achievements at the Giro or the Tour.

Eddy Merckx got off to an explosive start in Roubaix

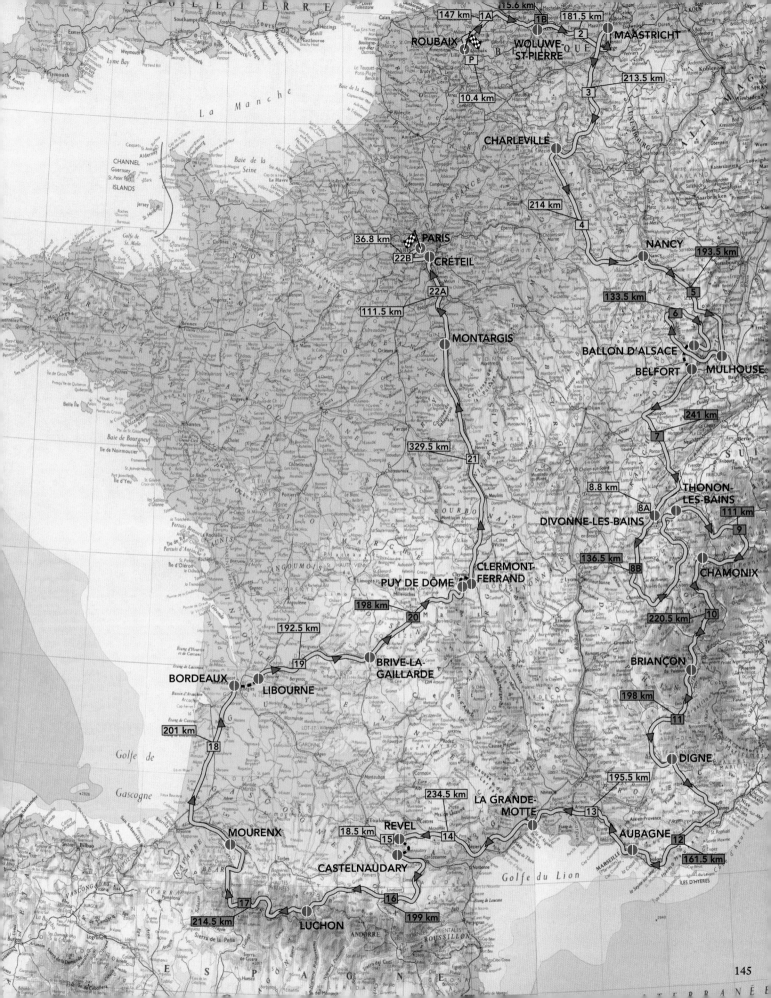

147 km — 1A
115.6 km
1B
181.5 km
2
ROUBAIX
P
WOLUWE-ST-PIERRE
MAASTRICHT
213.5 km
3
10.4 km
CHARLEVILLE
214 km
4
NANCY
193.5 km
5
133.5 km
6
36.8 km
PARIS
22B
CRÉTEIL
22A
111.5 km
BALLON D'ALSACE
BELFORT
MULHOUSE
MONTARGIS
241 km
7
329.5 km
21
8.8 km
8A
THONON-LES-BAINS
DIVONNE-LES-BAINS
111 km
9
136.5 km
8B
CHAMONIX
CLERMONT-FERRAND
PUY DE DÔME
198 km
20
220.5 km
10
192.5 km
19
BRIVE-LA-GAILLARDE
BRIANÇON
BORDEAUX
LIBOURNE
198 km
11
201 km
18
DIGNE
195.5 km
13
234.5 km
LA GRANDE-MOTTE
MOURENX
REVEL
AUBAGNE
18.5 km
15
14
12
CASTELNAUDARY
161.5 km
17
16
214.5 km
199 km
LUCHON

145

Eddy Merckx and Joaquim Agostinho climb the lower slopes of Mont Ventou

Start: Limoges, France, on 26 June
Finish: Paris, France, on 19 July

Total distance: 4370.8 km (2713 miles)
Longest stage: 269.5 km (167.5 miles)

Highest point: Col du Tourmalet: 2115 m (6939 ft)
Mountain stages: 8

Starters: 150
Finishers: 100

Winning time: 119 h 31' 49"
Average speed: 35.589 kph (22.114 mph)

1. Eddy Merckx (Bel)
2. Joop Zoetemelk (Hol) at 12' 41"
3. Gösta Pettersson (Swe) at 15' 54"

Points: Walter Godefroot (Bel)
Mountains: Eddy Merckx (Bel)

146

Belgium's Eddy Merckx proved his diversity once again by coming to the 1970 Tour having already won the Paris-Nice stage race, the Paris-Roubaix one-day Classic and the overall classification at the Giro d'Italia that season.

Just as he did in 1969, Merckx took the 1970 Tour by the scruff of the neck, winning all but one of the five individual time trials, while his Faema-Faemino team won the team time trial in Angers on stage 3a.

But Merckx wasn't going to be happy with 'just' time-trial wins. He won the flat stage 7a between Valenciennes and Forest, and then the *moyenne montagne* ('medium mountain') tenth stage, both while clad in yellow, and then attacked in yellow again – which was to become his trademark – on the terrible slopes of

Mont Ventoux to win stage 14, always keen for more stage wins, even when leading the race overall. Merckx won eight stages, plus the team time trial.

In second place overall in Paris, a huge 12 minutes 41 seconds down on Merckx, was 23-year-old Joop Zoetemelk. The Dutch rider was to finish runner-up at the Tour an incredible six times – twice as many second places as France's 'Eternal Second' Raymond Poulidor, who also finished third five times, but never won. Zoetemelk, however, did eventually win the Tour – ten years after his first second place, aged 33 in 1980.

Gösta Pettersson, a 29-year-old Swedish first-year professional with the Italian Ferretti team, became the first Swedish rider, and Scandinavian, to stand on the Tour's final podium.

FOREST **7.2 km** **7B**

VALENCIENNES **7A** **120 km** CINEY

135.5 km **6**

AMIENS **8** **232.5 km**

5B SAARLOUIS

113 km FELSBERG

94.5 km ROUEN **269.5 km**

5A LISIEUX **9**

Paris

VERSAILLES **54 km**

23 MULHOUSE

229 km BELFORT

4

238.5 km

22

RENNES

241 km

140 km **3B** **10**

10.7 km **8.8 km**

ANGERS **3A** TOURS DIVONNE-LES-BAINES **11A** THONON-LES-BAINS

2 **21**

200 km **191.5 km** **11B**

224.5 km **139.5 km**

LA ROCHELLE **12** **194 km**

1

RUFFEC

P LIMOGES GRENOBLE

7.4 km **195.5 km** **13** GAP

MONT **14**

VENTOUX **170 km**

BORDEAUX **20B** **144.5 km** CARPENTRAS

8.2 km **15**

231 km MONTPELLIER

20A **190 km** TOULOUSE **259.5 km**

MOURENX **17**

BAGNÈRES- **16**

DE-BIGORRE

185.5 km **19**

LA **18** ST-GAUDENS

MONGIE **135.5 km**

1971
58th Edition

Luis Ocaña was on course to finish on top of the podium before his untimely exit

Start: Mulhouse, France, on 26 June
Finish: Paris, France, on 18 July

Total distance: 3584.2 km (2227 miles)
Longest stage: 257.5 km (160 miles)

Highest point: Col du Tourmalet: 2115 m (6939 ft)
Mountain stages: 11

Starters: 130
Finishers: 94

Winning time: 96 h 45' 14"
Average speed: 36.925 kph (22.944 mph)

1. Eddy Merckx (Bel)
2. Joop Zoetemelk (Hol) at 9' 51"
3. Lucien Van Impe (Bel) at 11' 06"

Points: Eddy Merckx (Bel)
Mountains: Lucien Van Impe (Bel)

There were shades of the Jacques Anquetil years a decade earlier when, for the 1971 Tour, the organisers drastically altered the format in the hope of derailing Eddy Merckx's dominance. Jacques Goddet had been joined at the helm of the Tour by Félix Lévitan, and it was he who knocked the number of individual time trials at the 1971 Tour down to two, from five the year before.

However, Merckx's Molteni squad easily won the prologue, run as a team time trial, to put the Belgian into yellow from the off, and it looked as though it was going to be business as usual – until stage 11 when Spanish climber Luis Ocaña stormed the stage, finishing alone at the Orcières-Merlette ski station to take almost nine minutes out of Merckx, and lead the general classification by 8 minutes 43 seconds from Joop Zoetemelk, with the defending champion left languishing way down in fifth place overall, 9 minutes 46 seconds behind Ocaña.

Merckx replied by taking two minutes back the next day, and then a few more seconds in the time trial the following day, but was still trailing the Spaniard by 7 minutes 23 seconds going into the very lumpy stage 14 between Revel and Luchon, which crossed the Pyrenean climbs of the Portet d'Aspet, the Col de Mente and the Col du Portillon.

In pouring rain, Ocaña crashed heavily on the descent of the Col de Mente, and then had to suffer the ignominy, not to mention the pain, of Zoetemelk losing control and piling straight in to him while he was down. The Spanish rider's race was over, and Merckx refused to wear the yellow jersey on the following day's stage out of respect for his rival. Merckx went on to easily win the race by nearly ten minutes from Zoetemelk, but, as the Belgian said himself, it was the most disappointing of his Tour wins due to the absence of Ocaña, who would have surely beaten him.

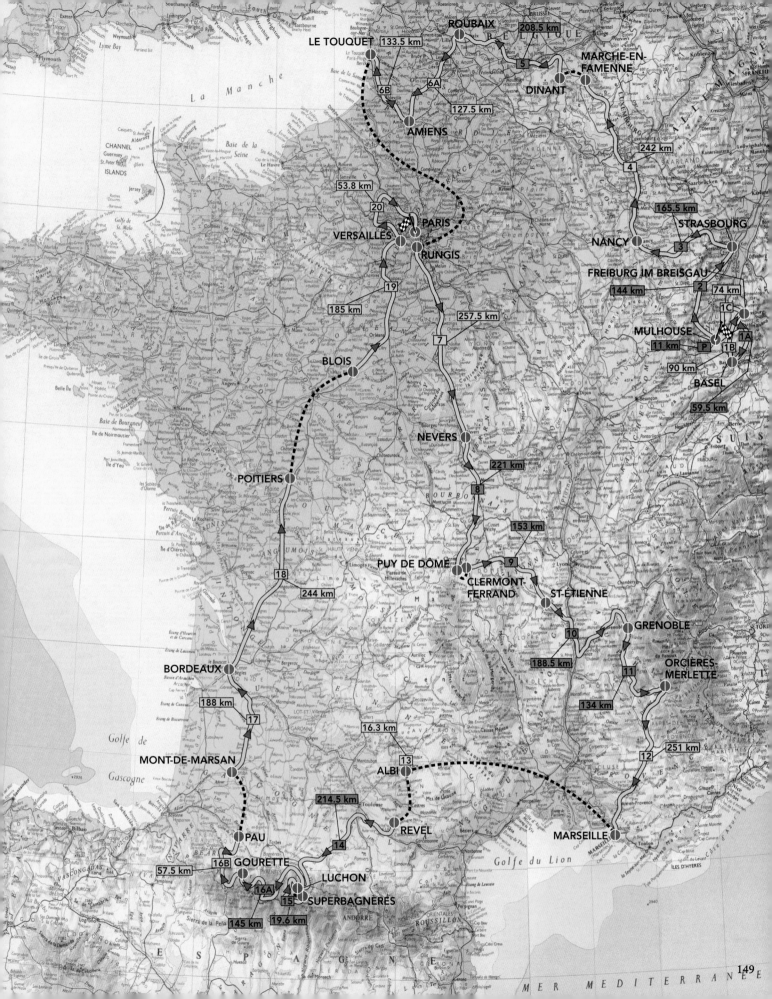

ROUBAIX

LE TOUQUET 133.5 km

208.5 km

5

MARCHE-EN-FAMENNE

6A

DINANT

6B

127.5 km

AMIENS

242 km

4

53.8 km

165.5 km

20

STRASBOURG

Paris

NANCY

3

VERSAILLES

FREIBURG IM BREISGAU

Rungis

144 km

2

74 km

19

1C

185 km

257.5 km

MULHOUSE

1A

7

11 km

P

1B

BLOIS

90 km

BASEL

59.5 km

POITIERS

NEVERS

221 km

8

153 km

18

PUY DE DÔME

9

244 km

CLERMONT-FERRAND

ST-ÉTIENNE

GRENOBLE

10

ORCIÈRES-MERLETTE

188.5 km

BORDEAUX

11

134 km

188 km

17

12

251 km

MONT-DE-MARSAN

16.3 km

13

ALBI

214.5 km

REVEL

PAU

14

MARSEILLE

57.5 km

16B

GOURETTE

LUCHON

16A

SUPERBAGNÈRES

15

145 km

19.6 km

1972
59th Edition

"Ocaña talks too much. I've won the Tour three times, whereas he's never had the yellow jersey in Paris... He's also abandoned twice in the three times that he's ridden it. With a record like that, he shouldn't be saying anything."

Eddy Merckx responds to Luis Ocaña's trash talk prior to the Tour
Merckx won easily after the Spaniard crashed out for the second year in a row

Start: Angers, France, on 1 July
Finish: Paris, France, on 23 July

Total distance:
3846.6 km (2388 miles)
Longest stage:
257.5 km (160 miles)

Highest point:
Col du Galibier: 2556m (8386ft)
Mountain stages: 8

Starters: 132
Finishers: 88

Winning time: 108 h 17' 18"
Average speed:
35.371 kph (21.965 mph)

1. Eddy Merckx (Bel)
2. Felice Gimondi (Ita) at 10' 41"
3. Raymond Poulidor (Fra) at 11' 34"

Points: Eddy Merckx (Bel)
Mountains:
Lucien Van Impe (Bel)

Following Luis Ocaña's terrible accident at the 1971 Tour, which forced him out of the race while in yellow, the 1972 edition was being billed as the grand rematch between the Spaniard and defending champion Eddy Merckx.

It was a slightly unorthodox route that the 1972 Tour followed in that it remained entirely within France – for the first time since the 1947 edition – and also never went any further north than Paris, concentrating heavily instead on the Alps and the Pyrenees, even more so than usual.

The two mountain ranges were, of course, set to be Merckx and Ocaña's playground – or perhaps 'battleground' is a better word. However, in an extraordinary piece of bad luck, Ocaña found himself the victim of another crash on a slippery, wet descent, this time on his way down the Aubisque on stage 7, and he quit the race with a chest infection following stage 14.

The mountain stages were nonetheless animated by Belgium's Lucien Van Impe, who had finished third overall and won the mountains competition in 1971, by 24-year-old Frenchman Bernard Thévenet – who won stages on both Mont Ventoux and the Ballon d'Alsace – and by his 25-year-old compatriot Cyrille Guimard, although he, too, succumbed to the relentlessness of the Tour with a knee injury and quit on stage 18, having won four stages.

Was it becoming a younger man's game? Merckx certainly didn't think so, despatching his rivals with the kind of consummate ease that helped him to live up to his nickname of 'The Cannibal'. Second-placed Felice Gimondi – the 30-year-old winner of the 1965 Tour – didn't think so, either, and neither did 36-year-old Raymond Poulidor, who took the sixth of what would eventually be eight podium spots at the Tour.

Eddy Merckx celebrates winning stage 13 in Briançon

ST-BRIEUC

235.5 km
[1]

[2]
206.5 km

161 km

LA BAULE
[3A]
PORNICHET

ST-JEAN-DE-MONTS
[3B]
16.2 km
MERLIN-PLAGE

236 km
[4]

ROYAN
133.5 km
[5A]

12.7 km
[5B]
BORDEAUX

205 km
[6]

BAYONNE
PAU
[7]
220.5 km
[8]
163.5 km
[9]
179 km
LUCHON

VERSAILLES   PARIS
42 km
[20A]
[20B]
89 km

230 km
[19]

257.5 km
BALLON
D'ALSACE
[18]
VESOUL
AUXERRE
213 km
[17]

PONTARLIER

[16]
198.5 km

28 km
[15]
AIX-LES-BAINS   MONT REVARD
151 km
[14B]
VALLOIRE
[14A]
51 km
BRIANÇON

ORCIÈRES-MERLETTE
192 km
[13]   201 km
[12]

207 km
MONT VENTOUX
[11]   CARPENTRAS

210 km
LA GRANDE-MOTTE
COLOMIERS   CASTRES
[10]
CARNON-PLAGE

P
ANGERS
7.2 km

151

1973
60th Edition

Start: Scheveningen, Netherlands, on 30 June
Finish: Paris, France, on 22 July

Total distance:
4150.2 km (2579 miles)
Longest stage:
248 km (154 miles)

Highest point:
Col du Galibier: 2556 m (8386 ft)
Mountain stages: 11

Starters: 132
Finishers: 87

Winning time: 122 h 25' 34"
Average speed:
33.407 kph (20.746 mph)

1. Luis Ocaña (Spa)
2. Bernard Thévenet (Fra)
   at 15' 51"
3. José-Manuel Fuente (Spa)
   at 17' 15"

Points:
Herman Van Springel (Bel)
Mountains: Pedro Torres (Spa)

Eddy Merckx, having ridden both the Giro d'Italia and the Vuelta a España – both of which he won – was a non-starter in Scheveningen in the Netherlands, and Raymond Poulidor, Luis Ocaña, Joop Zoetemelk and Bernard Thévenet lined up all with a very realistic hope of taking their first Tour de France victory.

When a 37-year-old Poulidor crashed on the dangerous descent of the Portet d'Aspet on stage 13, he must have been beginning to fear that he would never win the Tour – which would, unfortunately for him, prove to be the case. Despite three second places and five third places overall between 1962 and 1976, 'Poupou' didn't ever get to wear the *maillot jaune* – and remains to this day a true people's hero as a result.

Despite Zoetemelk's home win in the prologue, it was Ocaña who emerged from the Merckx-less mêlée to win the Tour in Paris – and at a canter at that, winning six stages along the way and finishing more than fifteen minutes in front of runner-up Thévenet. Ocaña's compatriot José-Manuel Fuente took the final spot on the podium.

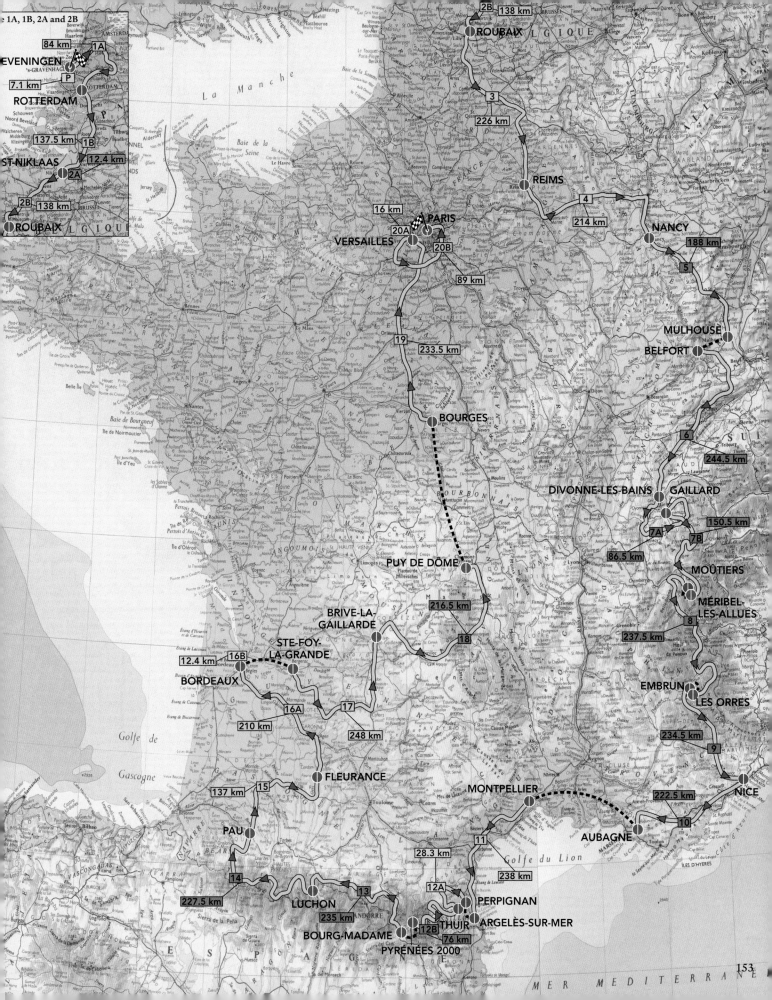

Stage 1A, 1B, 2A and 2B

SCHEVENINGEN   1A
84 km

P

7.1 km
ROTTERDAM

137.5 km
1B

ST-NIKLAAS   12.4 km
2A

2B   138 km
ROUBAIX

2B   138 km
ROUBAIX

3
226 km

REIMS

4
214 km

NANCY

188 km
5

MULHOUSE
BELFORT

6
244.5 km

DIVONNE-LES-BAINS   GAILLARD

7A   150.5 km
7B

86.5 km

MOÛTIERS

MÉRIBEL-LES-ALLUES

8
237.5 km

EMBRUN
LES ORRES

234.5 km
9

NICE

222.5 km
10

AUBAGNE

16 km
20A
PARIS
VERSAILLES   20B

89 km

19
233.5 km

BOURGES

PUY DE DÔME

216.5 km

BRIVE-LA-GAILLARDE

18

STE-FOY-LA-GRANDE

16B   12.4 km
BORDEAUX
16A
210 km   17

248 km

FLEURANCE

137 km   15

PAU

14
227.5 km

LUCHON

13
235 km

MONTPELLIER

11
28.3 km

238 km
12A

PERPIGNAN

BOURG-MADAME   12B   76 km
PYRÉNÉES 2000   THUIR   ARGELÈS-SUR-MER

153

The Tour crossed the Channel for an outing in Plymouth, the first ever British stage

Start: Brest, France, on 27 June
Finish: Paris, France, on 21 July

Total distance:
4104.2 km (2550 miles)
Longest stage:
248.5 km (155 miles)

Highest point:
Col du Galibier: 2556 m (8386 ft)
Mountain stages: 8

Starters: 130
Finishers: 105

Winning time: 116 h 16' 58"
Average speed:
35.241 kph (21.885 mph)

1. Eddy Merckx (Bel)
2. Raymond Poulidor (Fra)
   at 8' 04"
3. Vicente López Carril (Spa)
   at 8' 09"

Points: Patrick Sercu (Bel)
Mountains:
Domingo Perurena (Spa)

Luis Ocaña had finally got his Tour win in 1973 thanks, at least in part, to Eddy Merckx's absence, but in 1974 it was the non-appearance of Ocaña that went some way to helping Merckx take his fifth (and final, as it turned out) Tour victory. Ocaña had crashed at the Midi Libre stage race earlier in the season, while Dutchman Joop Zoetemelk was also a non-starter.

French hope Bernard Thévenet did start, but was a long way from Tour form due to injuries sustained at the Tour of Spain. Instead, it was left to 38-year-old Raymond Poulidor to keep hopes alive of a home winner for the first time since Roger Pingeon in 1967.

Merckx dominated, but perhaps showed a chink in the armour when he was beaten by a second-year pro – 22-year-old Michel Pollentier – in the final time trial. Still, it didn't worry Merckx too much, who equalled Jacques Anquetil's record of five Tour victories by beating Poulidor – who had tried his best to unseat Merckx in the Pyrenees – by just over eight minutes.

For the first time, the Tour cavalcade boarded a ferry to take the race to the UK for stage 2, although it wasn't exactly glamorous: the peloton raced up and down the Plympton bypass in front of a smattering of spectators, with the stage unsurprisingly ending in a bunch sprint, won by Dutch fastman Henk Poppe of the Frisol team. After such a damp squib, Poulidor's Gan team-mate Barry Hoban helped hold the British end up by winning stage 13 between Avignon and Montpellier, while the Tour's return to British shores in 1994 and 2007 would provide much happier memories.

.7 km

2

OUTH

190 km

3

ST-POL-
DE-LÉON

MORLAIX

1

144 km

P
1

184.5 km

4

ST-MALO

CAEN

5

165 km

DIEPPE

239 km

6A

HARELBEKE

6B

9 km

MONS

221.5 km

7

CHÂLONS-SUR-MARNE

8A

136 km

CHAUMONT

152 km

8B

BESANÇON

241 km

9

GAILLARD

131.5 km

10

AIX-LES-BAINS

199 km

11

SERRE-
CHEVALIER

SAVINES-
LE-LAC

231 km

12

ORANGE

AVIGNON

13

126 km

MONTPELLIER

LODÈVE

248.5 km

14

225 km

15

PARIS

146 km

22

37.5 km

21B

112.5 km

ORLÉANS

21A

VOUVRAY

NANTES

20

117 km

ST-GILLES-
CROIX-DE-VIE

12.4 km

19B

BORDEAUX

195.5 km

19A

COLOMIERS

PAU

141.5 km

18

BAGNÈRES-DE-
BIGORRE

LE TOURMALET

17

119 km

ST-LARY-
SOULAN

16

209 km

LA SEU D'URGELL

Eddy Merckx leads the peloton onto the
cobbles of the Champs-Élysées in Paris
for the first time in 1975. The race has
finished on the iconic boulevard ever since.

1975
62nd Edition

The Champs-Élysées has hosted the finish of the Tour since 197[...]

Start: Charleroi, Belgium,
on 26 June
Finish: Paris, France, on 20 July

Total distance:
3999.2 km (2484 miles)
Longest stage:
260 km (161 miles)

Highest point:
Col d'Izoard: 2361 m (7746 ft)
Mountain stages: 8

Starters: 140
Finishers: 86

Winning time: 114 h 35' 31"
Average speed:
34.906 kph (21.677 mph)

1. Bernard Thévenet (Fra)
2. Eddy Merckx (Bel) at 2' 47"
3. Lucien Van Impe (Bel) at 5' 01"

Points: Rik Van Linden (Bel)
Mountains:
Lucien Van Impe (Bel)
Young rider:
Francesco Moser (Ita)

The 1975 Tour was the first to finish on Paris's fabled Champs-Élysées, and has continued to finish there ever since. It was of course a departure from the velodromes the race had always finished at before, but multiple laps up and down the capital's grand boulevard made it an even bigger show, and its central Paris location allowed even more spectators to come and enjoy what had become a French institution.

Eddy Merckx was there again at the start in Charleroi, aiming at an unprecedented sixth Tour victory, but he was to be beaten to the finish in Paris by a Frenchman scoring a long overdue French win. Bernard Thévenet was flying in 1975 and, helped somewhat by Merckx getting punched in the kidneys by a spectator while climbing the Puy de Dôme, arrived in Paris with a 2-minute 47-second lead over Merckx.

Lucien Van Impe finished third, and won the 'king of the mountains' title. Although the prize had been awarded since 1933, the 1975 Tour was the first in which a white jersey with red polka-dots was given to the leader in that competition, marking out the lead rider in the same way as the yellow and green jerseys did.

Although a white jersey had previously been given to the leader of the best placed rider in all three competitions – mountains, points and overall – the 1975 Tour saw the introduction of a 'best young rider' prize, with a white jersey being used to distinguish them. From its introduction in 1975 until 1982, the white jersey was awarded after each stage to the rider in the first three years of their pro career who placed highest in the Tour's general classification. For the 1983 Tour, the rules changed so that the white jersey was awarded to the highest placed rider in their first Tour, and then there was yet another rule change in 1987, whereby it was awarded to the best-placed rider overall aged 25 years or younger during the year of the Tour, which remains the case today. A jersey wasn't awarded from 1989 to 1999, although the title was.

La Manche

CHANNEL ISLANDS

Baie de la Seine

Golfe de Gascogne

MOLENBEEK

108.5 km

ROUBAIX

1B

1A

CHARLEROI

P

94 km

6.25 km

121.5 km

2

AMIENS

169.5 km

3

SENLIS

220.5 km

21

VERSAILLES

PARIS

22

MELUN

163.5 km

256 km

20

LE MANS

4

223 km

SABLÉ

222.5 km

POUILLY-EN-AUXOIS

16 km

5

6

MERLIN-PLAGE

CHALON-SUR-SAÔNE

ST-GILLES-
CROIX-DE-VIE

THONON-LES-BAINS

19

229 km

18

CHÂTEL

7

MORZINE-
AVORIAZ

40 km

235.5 km

17

225 km

ANGOULÊME

PUY DE DÔME

173.5 km

14

VALLOIRE

8

134 km

SUPER-LIORAN

107 km

SERRE-CHEVALIER

16

AURILLAC

BORDEAUX

260 km

BARCELONNETTE

LANGON

13

PRA-LOUP

131 km

15

9A

37.4 km

217.5 km

FLEURANCE

ALBI

AUCH

9B

NICE

206 km

10

12

PAU

242 km

TARBES

11

160 km

ST-LARY-SOULAN

Golfe du Lion

MER MÉDITERRANÉE

159

1976
63rd Edition

Belgian fans had nothing to fear, with Lucien Van Impe and Freddy Maertens making up for the missing Merck

Start: St-Jean-de-Monts, France, on 24 June
Finish: Paris, France, on 18 July

Total distance:
4023.3 km (2500 miles)
Longest stage:
258 km (160 miles)

Highest point:
Col d'Izoard: 2361 m (7746 ft)
Mountain stages: 8

Starters: 130
Finishers: 87

Winning time: 116 h 22' 23"
Average speed:
34.518 kph (21.436 mph)

1. Lucien Van Impe (Bel)
2. Joop Zoetemelk (Hol)
   at 4' 14"
3. Raymond Poulidor (Fra)
   at 12' 08"

Points: Freddy Maertens (Bel)
Mountains: Giancarlo Bellini (Ita)
Young rider:
Enrique Martínez (Spa)

The 1976 race started in the Vendée seaside town of St-Jean-de-Monts, and headed northeast to Caen before a transfer to Le Touquet for the stage-3 time trial. Freddy Maertens won it, having already won the prologue time trial, plus stage 1, giving him victory in three out of the first four stages.

In Eddy Merckx's absence – he only rode the Tour one more time, in 1977 when he finished sixth – the Belgian fans and media had been concerned about how they would fare against the other nations, but the reality was that it couldn't have gone much better for them. Maertens – one of their own – won an extraordinary eight stages in all, which unsurprisingly won him the green points jersey, while Lucien Van Impe – already a winner of the 'king of the mountains' title three

times between 1971 and 1975 – went one better and put his climbing skills to good use to win the whole race thanks to the guidance of pro-turned-team-manager Cyrille Guimard, heading up the French Gitane-Campagnolo squad.

Despite his domination of the race, it was as good as it got for Van Impe, who was unable to repeat his performance, although he did win the polka-dot jersey another three times in his career.

From a French perspective – Guimard's management skills aside – the highs of Bernard Thévenet's victory just a year earlier seemed like a long time ago, and the defending champion was not in the same form as before. Raymond Poulidor, riding his last Tour at 40 years old, nevertheless managed to creep onto the podium in third place.

258 km
BORNEM LEUVEN
4
5A **5B**
4.3 km
VERVIERS
144 km
BASTOGNE
209 km
6
NANCY
205.5 km
7
MULHOUSE
220.5 km
VALENTIGNEY
8
DIVONNE-LES-BAINS
258 km **9**
166 km
10
L'ALPE-D'HUEZ
LE BOURG-D'OISANS
MONTGENÈVRE
224 km
11
MANOSQUE
PORT-BARCARÈS

LE TOUQUET
3
37 km

CAEN
258 km

PARIS
VERSAILLES
22B
22A
6 km **90.7 km**
21
2
236.5 km
145.5 km
MONTARGIS

ANGERS
8 km
1
ST-JEAN-DE-MONTS
P
173 km

PUY DE DÔME
TULLE
219.5 km
123 km
LACANAU
18B
19
BORDEAUX
20
70.5 km
18C
STE-FOY-LA-GRANDE
220 km
LANGON
18A
86 km
FLEURANCE
152 km
16
AUCH
17
38.75 km
PAU
139 km
195 km
ST-GAUDENS
15
14
188 km
ST-LARY-SOULAN
13
FONT-ROMEU-ODEILLO-VIA
12
PYRÉNÉES 2000
205.5 km

161

1977
64th Edition

The Peugeot team parade along the Champs-Élysées with Bernard Thévenet and Jacques Esclass…

Start: Fleurance, France, on 30 June
Finish: Paris, France, on 24 July

Total distance:
4098.6 km (2547 miles)
Longest stage:
256 km (159 miles)

Highest point:
Col du Tourmalet:
2115 m (6939 ft)
Mountain stages: 11

Starters: 100
Finishers: 53

Winning time: 115 h 38' 30"
Average speed:
35.419 kph (21.995 mph)

1. Bernard Thévenet (Fra)
2. Hennie Kuiper (Hol) at 0' 48"
3. Lucien Van Impe (Bel) at 3' 32"

Points: Jacques Esclassan (Fra)
Mountains: Lucien Van Impe (Bel)
Young rider: Dietrich Thurau (Ger)

Bernard Thévenet's 1975 Tour win might have come as a surprise to some people, especially when it came at Eddy Merckx's expense. The Frenchman's 1977 win, however, confirmed him as a Tour legend – especially in French fans' eyes – but it didn't exactly come easy: Thévenet's winning margin over the Netherlands' Hennie Kuiper was just 48 seconds, although defending champion Lucien Van Impe was well off the pace in third, 3 minutes 32 seconds down on Thévenet.

The race had more of a time-trial, rather than climbing, focus to it, with six stages against the clock, including the prologue and a team time trial. It suited Thévenet down to the ground, whereas Van Impe had to try to gap his opponents when he could on the climbs, and succeeded in taking 20 seconds out of Thévenet on the mountain time trial up to the Avoriaz ski station in the Alps.

Arguably the revelation of the race was 22-year-old German rider Dietrich 'Didi' Thurau who won the prologue to take the first yellow jersey, which he held for three-quarters of the race, as well as winning four other stages. He finished the race fifth overall – a place ahead of Merckx – which was enough to win the white jersey as the race's best young rider

ROUBAIX

CHARLEROI

242.5 km

11

12

192.5 km

FREIBURG
IM BREISGAU

ROUEN

174 km

46 km

10

13A

BAGNOLES-
DE-L'ORNE

PARIS

22B

VERSAILLES

22A

50 km

159.5 km

187 km

6 km

90.7 km

20

13B

9

21

MONTEREAU-
FAULT-YONNE

ALTKIRCH

RENNES

141.5 km

DIJON

BESANÇON

4 km

LORIENT

ANGERS

7B

230 km

8

139.5 km

14

246.5 km

7A

THONON-
LES-BAINS

19

14 km

JAUNAY-CLAN

171.5 km

15B

MORZINE-
AVORIAZ

105 km

15A

LIMOGES

ST-TRIVIER

16

CHAMONIX

225.5 km

121 km

30.2 km

6

ST-ÉTIENNE

VOIRON

5B

17

184.5 km

BORDEAUX

18

L'ALPE-
D'HUEZ

138.5 km

199.5 km

5A

237 km

MORCENX

1

SEIGNOSSE

FLEURANCE

256 km

P

253 km

AUCH

5 km

PAU

4

2

VITORIA

OLORON-
STE-MARIE

3

248.2 km

163

1978
65th Edition

Bernard Hinault climbs through the crowds as he heads towards the Puy de Dôm

Start: Leiden, Netherlands, on 29 June
Finish: Paris, France, on 23 July

Total distance:
3924 km (2438 miles)
Longest stage:
244 km (152miles)

Highest point:
Col du Tourmalet:
2115 m (6939 ft)
Mountain stages: 4

Starters: 110
Finishers: 78

Winning time: 108 h 18' 02"
Average speed:
36.084 kph (22.408 mph)

1. Bernard Hinault (Fra)
2. Joop Zoetemelk (Hol) at 3' 58"
3. Joaquim Agostinho (Por) at 6' 54"

Points: Freddy Maertens (Bel)
Mountains: Mariano Martínez (Fra)
Young rider: Henk Lubberding (Hol)

Defending champion Bernard Thévenet arrived at the 1978 Tour not in the best shape, but his failings were more than made up for by the emergence of another French talent named Bernard Hinault. While Thévenet quit the race on stage 11, the 23-year-old Hinault – having already won the stage-8 time trial at Ste-Foy-la-Grande – circled his rivals, waiting for the moment to strike. When the Breton was well beaten by the Netherlands' Joop Zoetemelk and Belgian Michel Pollentier on the mountain time trial up the savage slopes of the Puy de Dôme, it looked as though the old guard were going to have their day once more.

However, Pollentier, the winner of stage 16 to Alpe d'Huez, tried to trick a dope test following the stage by using a hidden tube attached to a pouch under his armpit to give a sample of someone else's urine and was thrown out of the Tour, having taken the yellow jersey that day. Hinault then annihilated the opposition to win the final time trial stage in Nancy and take the yellow jersey for himself, just two days before the race reached Paris.

Hinault won his first Tour by just under four minutes from Zoetemelk, while 36-year-old Joaquim Agostinho, riding for the Belgian Flandria-Velda-Lano squad, became the first Portuguese rider to make it onto the Tour podium in Paris.

La Manche

CHANNEL ISLANDS

5.2 km

LEIDEN
P

ST-WILLEBRORD

135 km

1A

100 km

1B

199 km   2   BRUSSELS

ST-AMAND-LES-EAUX

207.5 km

243.5 km

3

21

ÉPERNAY

METZ

20   72 km

NANCY

CAEN   4   EVREUX

153 km

SENLIS

PARIS

ST-GERMAIN-EN-LAYE

22   161.8 km

BELFORT

181.5 km

244 km   5

19

LAUSANNE

137.5 km

MAZÉ-MONTGEOFFROY

18

MORZINE

166.2 km

6

POITIERS

17   225 km

7

PUY DE DÔME   ST-DIER-D'AUVERGNE

52.5 km

14

242 km

BESSE-EN-CHANDESSE

ST-ÉTIENNE

GRENOBLE   L'ALPE-D'HUEZ

SUPERBESSE

59.3 km

8

221 km   13

15

BORDEAUX

16   240.5 km

196 km

ST-ÉMILION   STE-FOY-LA-GRANDE

FIGEAC

233 km

9

VALENCE-D'AGEN

(Stage 12A annulled due to strike)

12B

96 km

TOULOUSE

BIARRITZ

PAU

TARBES

10

191.5 km

11

161 km   ST-LARY-SOULAN

Golfe de Gascogne

Golfe du Lion

MÉDITERRANÉE

ESPAGNE   ANDORRE

165

Start: Fleurance, France,
on 27 June
Finish: Paris, France, on 22 July

Total distance:
3720.4 km (2312 miles)
Longest stage:
248.2 km (154 miles)

Highest point:
Col du Galibier: 2645 m (8678 ft)
Mountain stages: 7

Starters: 150
Finishers: 89

Winning time: 103 h 06' 50"
Average speed:
36.513 kph (22.675 mph)

1. Bernard Hinault (Fra)
2. Joop Zoetemelk (Hol)
    at 13' 07"
3. Joaquim Agostinho (Por)
    at 26' 53"

Points: Bernard Hinault (Fra)
Mountains:
Giovanni Battaglin (Ita)
Young rider:
Jean-René Bernaudeau (Fra)

For the second time in three years, the Tour departed from Fleurance in the southwest of France, while for the third time in three years a Frenchman finished at the top of the pile in Paris. For the second year in a row, that was Bernard Hinault. Bernard Thévenet's best days were over, and the 1977 Tour winner retired following the 1981 season. Hinault was French cycling's new hero, and would spend close to a decade at the top of his game, matching compatriot Jacques Anquetil's five Tour victories by 1985 – although astonishingly that is the last time a French rider has won the Tour.

Hinault's second win came at the expense of Holland's Joop Zoetemelk, who was still searching for his first win despite having finished second four times prior to the 1979 race. So it was that he finished runner-up again, more than thirteen minutes down on Hinault. Just as he had done in 1978, Portugal's Joaquim Agostinho finished third.

A pattern had emerged at the Tour, and still remains today, more or less, whereby the riders would be 'eased' into the Tour in the first week, when the sprinters got their chance on flatter stages, before heading into the mountains in the second week. The 1979 edition differed in that the race plunged headlong into the Pyrenees as early as stage 1, which meant that Dutch rider Gerrie Knetemann, despite being an accomplished all-rounder who had won the prologue time trial, lost his yellow jersey to French climber Jean-René Bernaudeau – a name many will recognise as the manager of the Europcar pro team today. Bernaudeau would only have the lead for one day; Hinault won the time trial on stage 2,

taking the yellow jersey, and from then on it was a two-man battle as the Frenchman and Zoetemelk waged war on the road to Paris.

Bernard Hinault cruised to victory, finishing thirteen minutes ahead of closest rival Joop Zoetemelk

166

201.2 km
9
ROUBAIX
33.4 km
11
BRUSSELS
10
124 km
ROCHEFORT
12
193 km
METZ
202 km
13
AMIENS
LE HAVRE
8
90.2 km
DEAUVILLE
158.2 km
7
PARIS
LE PERREUX-
SUR-MARNE
NOGENT-
SUR-MARNE
180.3 km
24
23
205 km
BALLON
D'ALSACE
48.8 km
BELFORT
ST-BRIEUC
ST-HILAIRE-
DU-HARCOUËT
238.5 km
6
AUXERRE
21
22
189 km
DIJON
248.2 km
14
ANGERS
145.5 km
5
20
EVIAN
15
54.2 km
MORZINE-
AVORIAZ
NEUVILLE-DE-POITOU
239.6 km
16
201.3 km
ST-PRIEST
LES
MENUIRES
L'ALPE-
D'HUEZ
19
162 km
LE BOURG-
D'OISANS
17
166.5 km
BORDEAUX
86.6 km
4
CAPTIEUX
5 km
P
FLEURANCE
18
118.5 km
PAU
1
225 km
LUCHON
3
180.5 km
23.9 km
2
SUPERBAGNÈRES

1980
67th Edition

Joop Zoetemelk's Tour crown was ten years in the makin[g]

Start: Frankfurt, Germany, on 26 June
Finish: Paris, France, on 20 July

Total distance:
3987.9 km (2478 miles)
Longest stage:
282.5 km (175 miles)

Highest point:
Col du Galibier: 2645 m (8678 ft)
Mountain stages: 4

Starters: 130
Finishers: 85

Winning time: 109 h 19' 14"
Average speed:
35.144 kph (21.824 mph)

1. Joop Zoetemelk (Hol)
2. Hennie Kuiper (Hol) at 6' 55"
3. Raymond Martin (Fra) at 7' 56"

Points: Rudy Pevenage (Bel)
Mountains:
Raymond Martin (Fra)
Young rider:
Johan van der Velde (Hol)

Aged 33, after having come second in his first Tour way back in 1970, and having taken another four second places along the way, Joop Zoetemelk – finally! – could call himself a Tour de France winner in 1980.

Because of this longevity, he's often credited with being the oldest winner of the Tour, but he is in fact nowhere near: 2011 Tour winner Cadel Evans was 34, as was Gino Bartali when he won his second Tour in 1948, and Henri Pélissier was 34, too, when he won in 1923. The crown for the oldest winner, though, goes to the winner of the Tour the year before Pélissier in 1922: Firmin Lambot was a veritably ancient 36-year-old Tour champion.

It had been looking very much as though France's Bernard Hinault was going to take his third Tour victory in a row after setting out his stall by winning the prologue in Frankfurt, Germany, before winning the stage-4 time trial and then stage 5 the next day between Liège, in Belgium, and Lille.

However the wheels came off Hinault's campaign when he started to experience trouble with his knee, and on the night following the twelfth stage, between Agen and Pau, while leading Zoetemelk by 21 seconds overall, Hinault crept out the back door – literally, through the kitchen of his Pau hotel in order to avoid the media.

As has become customary at the Tour when a rider has to quit while in the lead, Zoetemelk opted not to wear the yellow jersey on the next stage between Pau and Luchon. As of stage 14, though, the jersey was firmly on the Dutchman's back, and he shouldered it all the way to Paris to take a second Tour win for the Netherlands after Jan Janssen in 1968.

168

LONDON

ROYAUME-UNI

BELGIQUE

ALLEMAGNE

BRUXELLES 249.6 km 5

LILLE

LIÈGE 34.6 km
SPA-FRANCORCHAMPS 4
3
282.5 km
276 km 2
METZ

65 km
92 km 6 215.8 km
7A
ROUEN 7B
BEAUVAIS COMPIÈGNE
FONTENAY-SOUS-BOIS
PARIS

Stage 1A, 1B and 2
FRANKFURT 1A
133 km
WIESBADEN 1B
45.8 km 7.6 km P
2 276 km
ALLEMAGNE

FLERS
8 164.2 km
ST-MALO
186.1 km
22
208 km
21
AUXERRE

205.3 km
9

FRANCE

SUISSE
BERN

NANTES

MORZINE
198.8 km
18
34.5 km
20 139.7 km
19
17 242 km

ROCHEFORT

ST-ÉTIENNE
VOREPPE
PRAPOUTEL
SERRE-CHEVALIER

203 km
10

ITALIE

BORDEAUX

PRA-LOUP

51.8 km 11 AGEN
DAMAZAN

LAPLUME 194.1 km
12 189.5 km
14 MONTPELLIER
15

OCÉAN ATLANTIQUE

PAU
LÉZIGNAN-CORBIÈRES
MARTIGUES
160 km
TRETS
16
208.6 km

13 200.4 km
LUCHON

ESPAGNE

MER MÉDITERRANÉE

169

Phil Anderson chases Bernard Hinault on the Col de Peyresourd

Start: Nice, France, on 25 June
Finish: Paris, France, on 19 July

Total distance:
3756.1 km (2334 miles)
Longest stage:
264 km (164 miles)

Highest point:
Col de la Madeleine:
2000 m (6562 ft)
Mountain stages: 4

Starters: 150
Finishers: 121

Winning time: 96 h 19' 38"
Average speed:
38.96 kph (24.194 mph)

1. Bernard Hinault (Fra)
2. Lucien Van Impe (Bel)
    at 14' 34"
3. Robert Alban (Fra) at 17' 04"

Points: Freddy Maertens (Bel)
Mountains:
Lucien Van Impe (Bel)
Young rider: Peter Winnen (Hol)

From an English-speaking perspective, this was a Tour of firsts. Jonathan Boyer, riding for Bernard Hinault's Renault-Elf team, was the first American to ride the Tour – and to finish it, too, in thirty-second place overall.

The two Britons riding the 1981 Tour, La Redoute's Paul Sherwen – today a well-known cycling commentator – and Peugeot's Graham Jones, had mixed fortunes, with Sherwen eliminated after finishing outside the time limit on stage 15 and Jones finishing in twentieth place overall.

The most successful English speaker at that year's race, however, was Phil Anderson, who had won the 1978 Commonwealth Games road race. He became the first Australian – and in fact the first non-European – to wear the famous yellow jersey after the race's sole

stage in the Pyrenees, stage 5, between St-Gaudens and St-Lary-Soulan, which took the riders over the Peyresourde and Pla d'Adet. Anderson managed to stick with Hinault during the stage, although it was Lucien Van Impe who crossed the finishing line in first place. Anderson lost the yellow jersey the next day to Hinault in the time trial, but the Australian surprised many to battle on as the Frenchman's main challenger for the 1981 title, only truly dropping out of contention on stage 17 to Alpe d'Huez by which time the race had really begun to take its toll, losing more than seventeen minutes.

Hinault won his third Tour by nearly fifteen minutes from 1976 champion Van Impe, while Anderson had done enough to finish tenth overall.

ROYAUME-UNI

LONDON

BELGIQUE

ALLEMAGNE

BRUSSELS

BERINGEN
ZOLDER
HASSELT

ROUBAIX

107.3 km

12B

137.8 km

12A

13

246 km

11

157 km

LUXEMBOURG

COMPIÈGNE

NORMANDIE

AULNAY-SOUS-BOIS
PARIS

FONTENAY-SOUS-BOIS

22

186.8 km

21

207 km

MULHOUSE

38.5 km

14

LE MANS

10

196.5 km

9

264 km

AUXERRE

BESANÇON

231 km

15

NANTES

BRETAGNE

FRANCE

SUISSE

182 km

8

THONON-
LES-BAINS
MORZINE

ROCHEFORT

OCÉAN
ATLANTIQUE

46.5 km

16

199.5 km

LE PLEYNET

20

17

230.5 km

ST-PRIEST

VEUREY

L'ALPE-D'HUEZ

19

117.5 km

18

131 km

ITALIE

BORDEAUX

GUYENNE

7

227 km

232 km

3

40 km

1B

254 km

77.2 km

CARCASSONNE

MARTIGUES

2

1A

PAU

NAY

ST-GAUDENS

NARBONNE

5.8 km

P NICE

6

5

117.5 km

NARBONNE-PLAGE

4

97 km

26.7 km

ST-LARY
SOULAN

ESPAGNE

MER MÉDITERRANÉE

171

1982
69th Edition

Bernard Hinault's dominance continued, bagging four stages as well as his fourth Tour tit[...]

Start: Basel, Switzerland, on 2 July
Finish: Paris, France, on 25 July

Total distance:
3512 km (2182 miles)
Longest stage: 251 km (156 miles)

Highest point:
L'Alpe-d'Huez: 1860 m (6102 ft)
Mountain stages: 5

Starters: 170
Finishers: 125

Winning time: 92 h 08' 46"
Average speed:
38.059 kph (23.635 mph)

1. Bernard Hinault (Fra)
2. Joop Zoetemelk (Hol) at 6' 21"
3. Johan van der Velde (Hol)
   at 8' 59"

Points: Sean Kelly (Ire)
Mountains: Bernard Vallet (Fra)
Young rider: Phil Anderson (Aus)

Basel, Switzerland, was the start point of the 1982 Tour de France, with French superstar Bernard Hinault going for a fourth title.

The runner-up in 1981, Lucien Van Impe, was not present after his Metauro team didn't receive an invite from the Tour organisers. That should have helped Hinault's chances – and it did; 1982 was arguably Hinault's most straightforward Tour victory.

Joop Zoetemelk – the Dutch rider who had ridden the Tour every year since 1970, scoring consistently high results each year, finally winning the race in 1980 – was the best of the rest once the race reached the Champs-Élysées, where Hinault, in yellow, won both the overall title and the stage – just as he had in 1979 – rubbing the other riders', not least the sprinters', noses in it and proving that he was the best rider no matter what the terrain.

Compared to the year before, Australia's Phil Anderson went one better – or five,

or eight, depending on how you look at it – with a nine-day spell in the yellow jersey this time, and a fifth-place finish overall, up from tenth overall the previous year.

While the racing was 'straightforward' enough at the 1982 Tour, for the organisers it was anything but behind the scenes on stage five, which was eventually cancelled out of fear for the riders' safety after a strike by disgruntled steel workers on the road between Orchies and Fontaine-au-Pire blocked the route. The team-time-trial stage was instead re-run as stage 9a between Lorient and Plumele[...] crowbarred in to the itinerary in the morning ahead of stage 9 (re-named 9b).

It was further proof, if proof were needed, of just how political and mainstream the Tour had become: France's people using 'their' event to get wider attention for their cause.

1983
70th Edition

Debutant Laurent Fignon wi

Start: Fontenay-sous-Bois, France, on 1 July
Finish: Paris, France, on 24 July

Total distance:
3860.1 km (2399 miles)
Longest stage:
300 km (186 miles)

Highest point:
Col du Tourmalet:
2115 m (6939 ft)
Mountain stages: 4

Starters: 140
Finishers: 88

Winning time: 105 h 07' 52"
Average speed:
36.23 kph (22.499 mph)

1. Laurent Fignon (Fra)
2. Angel Arroyo (Spa) at 4' 04"
3. Peter Winnen (Hol) at 4' 09"

Points: Sean Kelly (Ire)
Mountains: Lucien Van Impe (Bel)
Young rider: Laurent Fignon (Fra)

Despite Bernard Hinault's absence – the Renault-Elf team leader had had an operation on his knee following his victory at the 1983 Tour of Spain – French fans were still able to enjoy a win by one of their own after a bookish-looking 22-year-old from Paris was called up to ride the race instead of Hinault, and promptly won.

Laurent Fignon had been instrumental in Hinault's win in Spain, but Renault *directeur* Cyrille Guimard was loath to let his young charge ride a second 'grand tour' in the same season. Still, Hinault's inability to ride left Guimard with a hole to fill – and his protégé didn't disappoint. It was Fignon's first Tour, and the team had hoped that he might be able to go after the white young rider's jersey, or perhaps some stage wins, but it didn't take anyone long to realise that Fignon was in fact in it to win.

However, another Frenchman, Peugeot's Pascal Simon, looked like being the man most likely to bring home the *jambon* for the home nation when he took the lead on stage 10 – the first mountain stage of that year's race, won by Scotland's Robert Millar.

Simon had a comfortable 4-minute 22-second lead over his compatriot Fignon, but a crash on his first day in yellow resulted in a fractured shoulder blade and, despite struggling gallantly on, the pain eventually became too much, and Simon quit during stage 17.

It was Fignon's Tour for the taking then, and he took it with aplomb, winning the final time trial to beat Spain Angel Arroyo by just over four minutes, with Dutchman Peter Winnen in third.

The 1983 Tour also saw the first Colombian team take part – the Colombia-Varta squad – who managed to place Edgar Corredor in sixteenth plac overall, albeit twenty-six minutes down on Fignon.

174

LONDON

ROYAUME-UNI

La Manche

OCÉAN ATLANTIQUE

BELGIQUE

BRUXELLES

ALLEMAGNE

LUXEMBOURG

SUISSE

ITALIE

ESPAGNE

FRANCE

ROUBAIX

VALENCIENNES

152 km
3

300 km
4

FONTAINE-AU-PIRE

100 km
2

SOISSONS

LE HAVRE

5

257 km

FONTENAY-SOUS-BOIS
5.5 km
P

NOGENT-SUR-MARNE
CRÉTEIL
PARIS
195 km
22

163 km
1

50 km
21
DIJON

291 km
20

15 km
19
MORZINE-AVORIAZ

ALFORTVILLE

LE MANS

CHÂTEAUBRIANT
58.5 km
6

NANTES

216 km
7

LA ROCHELLE

ÎLE D'OLÉRON

222 km
8

CLERMONT-FERRAND
PUY DE DÔME
15.6 km
15
ISSOIRE
16
144.5 km

ST-ÉTIENNE
223 km
17
LA TOUR-DU-PIN

247 km
18
L'ALPE-D'HUEZ
LE BOURG-D'OISANS

14
149 km

AURILLAC

210 km
13

BORDEAUX

207 km
9

FLEURANCE
12
261 km

177 km
11

ROQUEFORT-SUR-SOULZON

PAU

201 km
10
LUCHON

175

Laurent Fignon wins his second consecutive To[...]

Start: Montreuil, France,
on 29 June
Finish: Paris, France, on 22 July

Total distance:
4020.9 km (2497 miles)
Longest stage:
338 km (210 miles)

Highest point:
Col du Galibier: 2645 m (8678 ft)
Mountain stages: 5

Starters: 170
Finishers: 124

Winning time: 112 h 03' 40"
Average speed:
35.882 kph (22.283 mph)

1. Laurent Fignon (Fra)
2. Bernard Hinault (Fra)
    at 10' 32"
3. Greg LeMond (USA) at 11' 46"

Points: Frank Hoste (Bel)
Mountains: Robert Millar (GBr)
Young rider: Greg LeMond (USA)

If there had been any nagging doubt about Laurent Fignon's pedigree when he'd taken the race lead, and with it the race itself, from an injured Pascal Simon in 1983, in 1984 Fignon showed everyone a clean pair of heels – including his former team leader Bernard Hinault, who was back, but at the head of new French super-squad La Vie Claire, owned by French businessman and politician, and later Marseille football club president, Bernard Tapie.

But Fignon beat his former team-mate at his own game, first by winning the team time trial on stage 3 as part of the Renault-Elf team – while La Vie Claire languished in seventh place, almost a minute down – and then by beating time-trial specialist Hinault in the three individual time trials on stages 7, 16 and 22, as well as winning alone on the mountain stages to La Plagne and Crans-Montana in Switzerland on stages 18 and 20, respectively.

Fignon's American team-mate, Greg LeMond, riding his first Tour, finished third overall, which also gave him the white jersey as best young rider, and the two Renault-Elf team-mates sandwiched their former leader Hinault, who was well beaten by Fignon in to second place, 10 minutes 32 seconds down.

Britain's Robert Millar, riding for French outfit Peugeot, rode to a superb fourth place overall – the highest ever finish for a Briton at the time – and also took Great Britain's first, and still only, 'king of the mountains' title. There was also a first, and prestigious, Colombian stage win through Luis 'Lucho' Herrera at Alpe d'Huez, whose Colombia-Varta team had brought the first Colombian participants to the Tour in 1983.

LONDON

ROYAUME-UNI

BELGIQUE

ALLEMAGNE

83 km
4
BÉTHUNE
VALENCIÈNNES
3
LOUVROIL
51 km
207 km
5
2
249.5 km
ST-DENIS
BOBIGNY
CERGY-PONTOISE
BONDY
PANTIN
NOISY-LE-SEC
202 km
P
6
5.4 km
PARIS
1
148.5 km
23
196.5 km
MONTREUIL
ALENÇON
67 km   7
LE MANS
192 km
8
NANTES

NORMANDIE

BRETAGNE

FRANCE

CRANS-MONTANA
20   140.5 km
VILLIÉ-MORGON
320.5 km
51 km
22
21
MORZINE
186 km
19
LA RUCHÈRE
338 km
9
VILLEFRANCHE-SUR-SAÔNE
22 km   16
L'ALPE-D'HUEZ
LA PLAGNE
LES ÉCHELLES
17
18   185 km
GRENOBLE
LE BOURG-D'OISANS
151 km
SUISSE
ITALIE
227.5 km
15
241.5 km

BORDEAUX
14
LANGON
DOMAINE DU ROURET
220.5 km
RODEZ
198 km
10
13
BLAGNAC
111 km   12
PAU
ST-GIRONS
11
GUZET-NEIGE
226.5 km

OCÉAN ATLANTIQUE

ESPAGNE

MER MÉDITERRANÉE

1985
72nd Edition

Start: Plumelec, France, on 28 June
Finish: Paris, France, on 21 July

Total distance:
4113.5 km (2556 miles)
Longest stage:
269 km (167 miles)

Highest point:
Col du Tourmalet: 2115 m (6939 ft)
Mountain stages: 5

Starters: 180
Finishers: 144

Winning time: 113 h 24' 23"
Average speed:
36.232 kph (22.500 mph)

1. Bernard Hinault (Fra)
2. Greg LeMond (USA) at 1' 42"
3. Stephen Roche (Ire) at 4' 29"

Points: Sean Kelly (Ire)
Mountains: Luis Herrera (Col)
Young rider: Fabio Parra (Col)

Bernard Hinault arrived at the start of the 1985 Tour in Plumelec, in his native Brittany, with a steely determination to win his fifth title and a La Vie Claire team ready to support him and make it happen. Ironically, given that Hinault had missed the 1983 Tour due to a knee injury, Laurent Fignon, the winner that year and in 1984, was unable to defend his title for the same reason.

Greg LeMond, the American revelation who had finished third in 1984, had moved to Hinault's La Vie Claire outfit during the winter, and in Fignon's absence went one better by finishing second overall to his team leader. In return for the American's help and cooperation – many thought that LeMond was more than capable of winning the Tour himself – Hinault told LeMond that he would help him to win the 1986 Tour.

LeMond's time trial victory at Lac de Vassivière, 5 seconds ahead of Hinault, was perhaps a gauge of who the better rider really was in 1985. However, LeMond was happy enough to play second fiddle to his team leader for now, and that stage win was the first ever by an American.

In third place overall in Paris was Ireland's Stephen Roche, riding for the French La Redoute team. His achievement was the first Tour podium place for an Irish rider. Despite Hinault's victory, was mainland Europe losing its grip? It seemed so.

What's hardest to believe, however, is that after thirty-six Tour de France wins by French riders since the race's inception in 1903 – way ahead of the second most successful nation, Belgium, and its eighteen Tour wins – 1985 remains the last time that a French rider won the Tour.

Bernard Hinault's La Vie Claire team win the team time trial to Fougèr

ROYAUME-UNI

LONDON

BELGIQUE

ALLEMAGNE

LA MANCHE

ROUBAIX
Lille
224 km
5
6
221.5 km

NEUFCHÂTEL-EN-BRAY

REIMS
217.5 km
7

PONT-AUDEMER
239 km
4

SARREBOURG
75 km
8

NANCY
173.5 km
9
STRASBOURG

73 km
3
FOUGÈRES

ÉPINAL

Paris
22
196 km

256 km
1
6.8 km
PLUMELEC
P
ANESTER
2
VITRÉ
242 km
LORIENT
VANNES

ORLÉANS

204.5 km
10

PONTARLIER
195 km
11

OCÉAN ATLANTIQUE

FRANCE

SUISSE

BERN

MORZINE-AVORIAZ

LIMOGES
225 km
20
LAC DE VASSIVIÈRE
21
45.7 km

12
269 km

AUTRANS
179 km
14
ST-ÉTIENNE
LANS-EN-VERCORS
VILLARD-DE-LANS
13
38 km

BORDEAUX
MONTPON-MÉNESTÉROL
AURILLAC
15
237.5 km

ITALIE

247 km
16

TOULOUSE

203 km
19

PAU
83.5 km
18B
18A
LARUNS
COL D'AUBISQUE
LUZ-ARDIDEN
LUZ-ST-SAUVEUR
52.5 km
17
209.5 km

ESPAGNE

MER MÉDITERRANÉE

Start: Boulogne-Billancourt,
France, on 4 July
Finish: Paris, France, on 27 July

Total distance:
4093.4 km (2542 miles)
Longest stage:
258.3 km (160 miles)

Highest point:
Col du Galibier: 2645 m (8678 ft)
Mountain stages: 5

Starters: 210
Finishers: 132

Winning time: 110 h 35' 19"
Average speed:
37.020 kph (22.989 mph)

1. Greg LeMond (USA)
2. Bernard Hinault (Fra) at 3' 10"
3. Urs Zimmermann (Swi) at 10' 54"

Points: Eric Vanderaerden (Bel)
Mountains: Bernard Hinault (Fra)
Young rider:
Andrew Hampsten (USA)

Despite his 1985 promise to help his younger team-mate, Bernard Hinault went on the offensive as early as the first Pyrenean mountain stage between Bayonne and Pau, capturing the yellow jersey and putting enough time into Greg LeMond that the two team-mates were separated by a huge 5 minutes 25 seconds.

It looked very much as though the Frenchman was going to take an unprecedented six Tour wins; he'd already matched Jacques Anquetil and Eddy Merckx's five.

On an equally mountainous stage the next day, however, Hinault paid for his efforts, and LeMond danced to a fine solo win on Superbagnères, beating second-placed Robert Millar, of Scotland, by well over a minute. Hinault finished eleventh, 4 minutes 39 seconds down on LeMond, and although the Frenchman kept the race lead, the deficit was down to just 40 seconds.

Stage 17 – an Alpine stage between Gap and Serre-Chevalier, going over such climbs as the Col de Vars, the Col d'Izoard and the Col du Granon – proved to be another turning point. While Teka's Eduardo Chozas took a lone win for Spain, LeMond kept pace with Switzerland's Urs Zimmermann, while Hinault, in the company of Millar, among others, lost three-and-a-half minutes – and with it the race lead – to LeMond.

On stage 18, finishing on Alpe d'Huez, a truce was called. The two men proved that they were the best two riders in the race by breaking away together, and then, after a brief discussion, the iconic image of them crossing the finish line together hand-in-hand – Hinault slightly in front to get the stage win, in fact –

sealed LeMond's first Tour victory and signalled the end of Hinault's reign.

After such a fine spell of French winners at the Tour – nine winners in eleven years – something had to give, and it gave to an American.

Cycling's globalisation continued to ramp up: not only did the 1986 Tour have the first American winner, but it was also the first to feature an American team – 7-Eleven. Their sprinter, Davis Phinney, won stage 3, which came after the team's Canadian rider, Alex Stieda, had become the first Canadian rider to wear the yellow jersey, for a day on stage 2, after having finished as part of a breakaway on stage 1.

Another American rider, LeMond and Hinault's La Vie Claire team-mate Andy Hampsten, finished fourth overall. The Americans were coming – and in fact were already here.

Greg LeMond became the first American to win the Tour following a truce with Bernard Hinault on Alpe d'Huez

LONDON

ROYAUME-UNI

Southampton
Exeter
Poole
Portsmouth
Brighton
Eastbourne
Pas de Calais

Lyme Bay
Bournemouth

La Manche

BELGIQUE
BRUXELLES

ALLEMAGNE

Cap de la Hague
ST PETER PORT
Guernsey

CHERBOURG
200 km

ST HELIER
Jersey

Îles Normandes

VILLERS-SUR-MER
124.5 km

7

201 km

6

ÉVREUX
BOULOGNE-BILLANCOURT

NANTERRE
4.6 km

P

LEVALLOIS-PERRET

PARIS
MEUDON

1

85 km

ST-QUENTIN-EN-YVELINES

2

SCEAUX

56 km

243 km

4

214 km

3

LIÉVIN

PICARDIE

ST-HILAIRE-DU-HARCOUËT

204 km

8

BRETAGNE

NANTES

61.5 km

9

183 km

10

FUTUROSCOPE

POITOU

11

258.3 km

OCÉAN ATLANTIQUE

FRANCE

BERRY

23

255 km

COSNE-SUR-LOIRE

NEVERS

194 km

22

BOURBONNAIS

MARCHE

LIMOUSIN

BORDEAUX

CLERMONT-FERRAND
PUY DE DÔME

ST-ÉTIENNE

21

190 km

20

58 km

179.5 km

19

162.5 km

18

SERRE-CHEVALIER

Massif Central

AUVERGNE

VILLARD-DE-LANS

L'ALPE-D'HUEZ

BRIANÇON

17

190 km

GAP

16

246.5 km

225.5 km

15

NÎMES

ITALIE

Torino

GUYENNE

AQUITAINE

Golfe du Gascogne

BAYONNE

PAU

154 km

14

BLAGNAC

CARCASSONNE

12

217.5 km

13

186 km

SUPERBAGNÈRES

ESPAGNE

PROVENCE

CAMARGUE

Marseille

MER MÉDITERRANÉE

Golfe du Lion

ANDORRE

SUISSE

BERN

Colombian Luis Herrera poses next to the Berlin Wall at the start of the 1987 Tour, which spent three days in a still-divided Germany.

1987
74th Edition

Down but not out, an exhausted Stephen Roche put up a lung-busting fight to clinch his tit...

Start: Berlin, Germany, on 1 July
Finish: Paris, France, on 26 July

Total distance:
4231.6 km (2627 miles)
Longest stage:
260 km (161 miles)

Highest point:
Col du Galibier: 2645 m (8678 ft)
Mountain stages: 7

Starters: 207
Finishers: 135

Winning time: 115 h 27' 42"
Average speed:
36.645 kph (22.757 mph)

1. Stephen Roche (Ire)
2. Pedro Delgado (Spa) at 0' 40"
3. Jean-François Bernard (Fra)
   at 2' 13"

Points: Jean-Paul van Poppel (Hol)
Mountains: Luis Herrera (Col)
Young rider: Raúl Alcalá (Mex)

Two years before the wall came down, Berlin hosted the 1987 Tour's *Grand Départ*. After stage 1, starting and finishing in West Berlin, Lech Piasecki became the first Polish rider to wear the yellow jersey.

It would be fair to say Greg LeMond getting shot by his brother-in-law while turkey hunting in California in April 1987 put somewhat of a spanner in the works when it came to the American's preparations to defend his Tour crown.

LeMond survived, but was forced to watch from the sidelines as Ireland's Stephen Roche and Spain's Pedro Delgado did battle on the roads of France that summer.

Bernard Hinault had retired at the end of the 1986 season, so in the absence of the two riders who had beaten him the previous year, the right man – Roche – certainly won. He was pushed close by

Delgado, though, and was pushed close to his own limits, too. Who can forget cycling commentator Phil Liggett's excited commentary at the finish on La Plagne on stage 21 when Roche dug deep to limit his losses to Delgado?

Roche had looked dead in the water when the Spaniard had dropped him on the slopes of La Plagne. However, a monumental effort to bring Delgado back prompted Liggett's breathless speech – "That looks like Roche! It's Stephen Roche!" – and, despite the oxygen mask strapped to the Irishman's face at the finish, his thumbs-up to the TV camera let everyone know that he was ready to overturn his 39-second deficit to Delgado.

That's exactly what he did on the race's penultimate stage – a 38-km (23.5-mile) time trial around Dijon. Roche's winning margin in Paris was just 40 seconds.

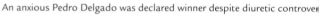

An anxious Pedro Delgado was declared winner despite diuretic controver[sy]

Start: Pornichet, France, on 3 July
Finish: Paris, France, on 24 July

Total distance:
3285 km (2041 miles)
Longest stage:
232 km (144 miles)

Highest point:
Col du Tourmalet:
2115 m (6939 ft)
Mountain stages: 4

Starters: 198
Finishers: 151

Winning time: 84 h 27' 53"
Average speed:
38.909 kph (24.162 mph)

1. Pedro Delgado (Spa)
2. Steven Rooks (Hol) at 7' 13"
3. Fabio Parra (Col) at 9' 58"

Points: Eddy Planckaert (Bel)
Mountains: Steven Rooks (Hol)
Young rider: Erik Breukink (Hol)

A recurrent knee injury meant Stephen Roche was a non-starter, so with neither the 1987 champion present, nor 1986 winner Greg LeMond – who was still recovering from his hunting accident – as well as 1983 and 1984 Tour champ Laurent Fignon being a long way from top form, the 1988 Tour looked as though it was going to be Pedro Delgado's for the taking.

Indeed it was – and yet the Spanish climber made it very hard for himself, the race organisers, the press and the fans when he tested positive for the diuretic probenecid during the race. However, it was not at that point on cycling governing body the UCI's banned list, despite being a product banned by the International Olympic Committee, and so Delgado escaped punishment.

In all other ways, it was an easy win for Delgado, who finished 7 minutes 13 seconds ahead of Dutchman Steven Rooks and almost ten minutes in front of Colombian climber Fabio Parra.

The 1988 Tour also saw the introduction of the 'start village' – an area set-up close to each stage's start-line where local dignitaries, VIPs, sponsors' guests, journalists and the riders themselves can get a coffee, try the local cuisine, shoot the breeze or read the papers – an oasis of relative calm before the off, which is still a major feature of today's Tours, although an increasing number of riders prefer to stay inside their luxurious, air-conditioned team buses before the start, which is a real shame for virtually everyone but them.

LONDON

ROYAUME-UNI

BELGIQUE

ALLEMAGNE

52 km

WASQUEHAL

LIÉVIN

6

147.5 km

5

7

225.5 km

REIMS

219 km

8

160.5 km

NEUFCHÂTEL-EN-BRAY

NANCY

STRASBOURG

9

ÉVREUX

PARIS

158 km

4

22

172.5 km

NEMOURS

BELFORT

149.5 km

10

BESANÇON

213.5 km

3

LE MANS

232 km

11

PONTCHÂTEAU NANTES ANCENIS

ORNICHET-LA BAULE

P

1 km

2

48 km

1

91.5 km

MACHECOUL

LA HAYE-FOUASSIÈRE

FRANCE

SANTENAY

CHALON-
SUR-SAÔNE

21

46 km

MORZINE

223.5 km

20

SUISSE

93.5 km

188 km

CLERMONT-
FERRAND

RUELLE-SUR-
TOUVRE

LIMOGES

18

19

PUY DE DÔME

GRENOBLE

VILLARD-DE-LANS

L'ALPE-
D'HUEZ

227 km

12

13

38 km

BORDEAUX

17

210 km

BLAGNAC

38 km

163 km

PAU TARBES

16

14

ST-GIRONS

LUZ-ARDIDEN

15

GUZET-NEIGE

187.5 km

ESPAGNE

ANDORRE

"I lost that Tour by eight seconds, but if I'd stopped then, I would have fallen apart completely
Runner-up Laurent Fignon on putting his disappointment behind him. The French rid
rode on until eventually retiring in 1993, and died in 2010 having battled canc

Greg LeMond sees Fignon's time and realises he has wo

Start: Luxembourg, on 1 July
Finish: Paris, France, on 23 July

Total distance:
3285.3 km (2040 miles)
Longest stage: 259 km (161 miles)

Highest point:
Col du Galibier: 2645 m (8678 ft)
Mountain stages: 7

Starters: 198
Finishers: 138

Winning time: 87 h 38' 35"
Average speed:
37.487 kph (23.279 mph)

1. Greg LeMond (USA)
2. Laurent Fignon (Fra) at 0' 08"
3. Pedro Delgado (Spa) at 3' 34"

Points: Sean Kelly (Ire)
Mountains:
Gert-Jan Theunisse (Hol)
Young rider: Fabrice Philipot (Fra)

Many would argue that the 1989 edition of the Tour was the greatest ever. Whether you agree with that or not, what can't be denied is that the race provided the closest winning margin ever: just 8 seconds separated Greg LeMond and Laurent Fignon at the finish in Paris.

It was a return to form for both the American and the Frenchman after a number of years in the wilderness since their Tour wins – Fignon in 1983 and 1984, and LeMond in 1986 – and what a return it was.

Spain's Pedro Delgado would have arguably given them a run for their money, too – had he not missed his start time in the prologue, that is. The defending champion was nearly three minutes behind his rivals before the race was barely under way, although

he did rally to finish a third overall in Paris.

Fignon was the better, more aggressive rider in the mountains, but LeMond – as ever au fait with the latest in cycling technology – used his now famous clip-o 'tri bars' to gain an advantage against the clock. Unusually, the final stage was run as an individual time trial, which ended up being the most exciting finale of what had already been a desperately exciting Tour thanks to the yellow jersey yo-yoing back and forth between LeMond and Fignon.

LeMond went into the final stage with a 50-second deficit to Fignon, but turned it over and added 8 seconds to provide an exciting and dramatic end to the most superb three weeks of bike racing.

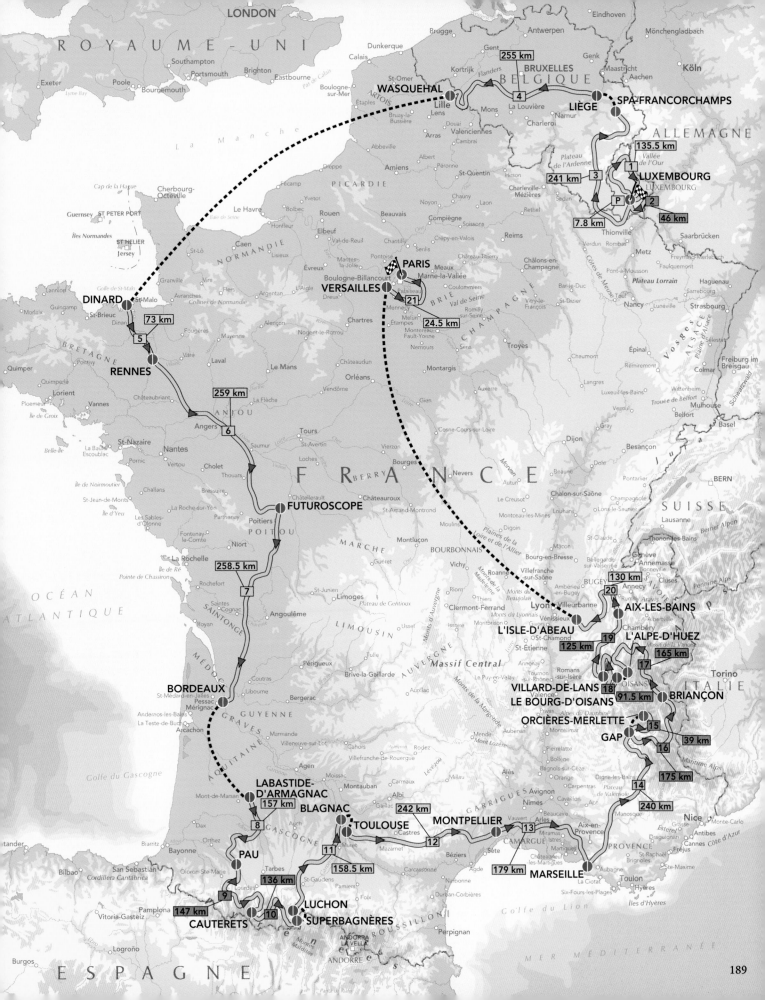

189

Future champion Miguel Indurain (left) attacks with current champ LeMond on Luz-Ardi

Start: Futuroscope, France, on 30 June
Finish: Paris, France, on 22 July

Total distance: 3403.8 km (2115 miles)
Longest stage: 301 km (187 miles)

Highest point: Col du Tourmalet: 2115 m (6939 ft)
Mountain stages: 4

Starters: 198
Finishers: 156

Winning time: 90 h 43' 20"
Average speed: 38.621 kph (23.984 mph)

1. Greg LeMond (USA)
2. Claudio Chiappucci (Ita) at 2' 16"
3. Erik Breukink (Hol) at 2' 29"

Points: Olaf Ludwig (Ger)
Mountains: Thierry Claveyrolat (Fra)
Young rider: Gilles Delion (Fra)

Defending champion Greg LeMond went into the 1990 Tour as the big favourite; an out-of-shape Fignon started, too, but quit as early as stage 5.

Although LeMond did wind up on the top step of the podium in Paris once more, he hadn't made it easy on himself.

In the Futuroscope theme park, short-time-trial specialist Thierry Marie took the second of three career prologue wins but ceded the yellow jersey the next day when the leaders allowed a four-man group to finish more than ten minutes ahead of the main field.

Three of those four – Dutchman Frans Maassen was the odd one out – proceeded to wear the yellow jersey as the race's other riders, and Greg LeMond in particular, slowly but surely ate into their lead.

Canada's Steve Bauer was the first 'breakawayee' to don the yellow tunic, and he held it until stage 10 when the Frenchman Ronan Pensec took charge.

Italy's Claudio Chiappucci was the last man standing – the last of the 'breakaway four' to wear yellow – and he proved the most difficult for LeMond to displace.

The American finally overturned Chiappucci's advantage on the penultimate stage – a time trial around Lac de Vassivière. The stage was won by Holland's Erik Breukink – who eventually finished third overall – but with LeMond doing enough to take the yellow jersey from Chiappucci's shoulders.

It turned out to be the making of Chiappucci nevertheless, who had been relatively anonymous in the peloton prior to his breakaway and subsequent yellow-jersey escapades.

Also making his presence felt – albeit in his trademark 'gentle giant' way – was Pedro Delgado's team-mate and countryman Miguel Indurain. The Spanish powerhouse won stage 16 on Luz-Ardiden. Was this a sign of things to come? Absolutely.

Uzbekistan's Djamolidine Abdoujaparov is just moments from hitting the Champs-Élysées asphalt on the final stage of the 1991 Tour. Despite his injuries, 'Abdou' was helped across the line to ensure he claimed the points title.

Indurain (right) took his chance en route to Val Louron and never relinquished his le

Start: Lyon, France, on 6 July
Finish: Paris, France, on 28 July

Total distance:
3914.4 km (2431 miles)
Longest stage:
286 km (178 miles)

Highest point:
Col du Tourmalet: 2115 m (6939 ft)
Mountain stages: 4

Starters: 198
Finishers: 158

Winning time: 101 h 01' 20"
Average speed:
38.747 kph (24.062 mph)

1. Miguel Indurain (Spa)
2. Gianni Bugno (Ita) at 3' 36"
3. Claudio Chiappucci (Ita) at 5' 56"

Points:
Djamolidine Abdoujaparov (Uzb)
Mountains: Claudio Chiappucci (Ita)
Young rider: Álvaro Mejía (Col)

And so began the reign of Indurain. The softly spoken Spaniard hadn't exactly come from nowhere – 1991 was his seventh Tour – yet he had spent most of his professional career up until that point riding in the service of others, and his Reynolds team leader Pedro Delgado in particular from 1988 onwards. The Reynolds team became Banesto in 1990, and the change in sponsor brought about change in the squad's hierarchy, too, as Delgado and Indurain's roles started to reverse. Indurain had still ridden for Delgado during the 1990 Tour, but it was pretty clear that Indurain was ready to step up from his *super-domestique* role to become Banesto's fully fledged leader.

At the 1991 Tour, he got his chance, striking out for the first time in the race's first long time trial, on stage 8, in which he beat defending champion Greg LeMond to the stage win by 8 seconds. LeMond still had a healthy lead overall at that point, having been part of a successful breakaway on stage but Indurain now knew that LeMond could be beaten.

On the second mountain stage, betwee Jaca, on the Spanish side of the Pyrenees and Val Louron, Indurain struck again, with Italy's Claudio Chiappucci for company – the man who had pushed LeMond so close in 1990. Chiappucci would win the stage, while LeMond would lose well over seven minutes, putting Indurain into yellow for the first time, by a three-minute margin over France's Charly Mottet.

Indurain never let it go after that, winning the race's final time trial and sharing the podium in Paris with Italians Gianni Bugno and Chiappucci.

ROYAUME-UNI

LONDON

BELGIQUE

BRUXELLES

ALLEMAGNE

LUXEMBOURG

ARRAS **259 km** **6**
VALENCIENNES **149.5 km** **5**
LE HAVRE **7**
167 km
REIMS
73 km **8**
ARGENTAN
ALENÇON **161 km** **9**
286 km **4**
RENNES
QUIMPER **207.5 km** **10**
246 km **11**
ST-HERBLAIN
PARIS
MELUN **178 km** **22**

DIJON

FRANCE

210.5 km **3**

LUGNY **57 km** **21**
MÂCON **160 km**
177 km
MORZINE
20
VILLEURBANNE **19**
LYON
114.5 km **1** **P**
5.4 km AIX-LES-BAINS **18**
BRON **2** **255 km**
CHASSIEU
36.5 km
L'ALPE-D'HUEZ

OCÉAN
ATLANTIQUE

LE BOURG-D'OISANS
17
GAP **125 km**

235 km
ALÈS **16** **215 km**
ALBI **15**
CASTRES **172.5 km**
PAU **232 km**
14
JACA **12** **13**
192 km VAL LOURON ST-GAUDENS

ESPAGNE

ITALIE

MER MÉDITERRANÉE

Start: San Sebastián, Spain,
on 4 July
Finish: Paris, France, on 26 July

Total distance:
3975 km (2470 miles)
Longest stage:
268 km (166 miles)

Highest point:
Col de l'Iseran: 2770 m (9088 ft)
Mountain stages: 2

Starters: 198
Finishers: 130

Winning time: 100 h 49' 30"
Average speed:
39.504 kph (24.532 mph)

1. Miguel Indurain (Spa)
2. Claudio Chiappucci (Ita)
   at 4' 35"
3. Gianni Bugno (Ita) at 10' 49"

Points: Laurent Jalabert (Fra)
Mountains: Claudio Chiappucci (Ita)
Young rider: Eddy Bouwmans (Hol)

King of the mountains, Claudio Chiappucci, braves the crowds on the Col des Saisies on stage

The 1992 Tour was the most international yet, visiting six mainland European countries, including France, in recognition of the signing of the Maastricht Treaty and the subsequent formation of the European Union. The race started in San Sebastián, in Spain, and then headed north through France – barely venturing into the Pyrenees – and on up into Belgium, the Netherlands and Germany, back down into Luxembourg, through the Alps with a brief sojourn to Sestriere in Italy before heading directly northwest to the now traditional finish on the Champs-Élysées.

The thirteenth stage to Sestrière was arguably the most spectacular when a polka-dot-jersey-clad Claudio Chiappucci somehow managed to squeeze his way up the Italian mountain through some of the deepest crowds the race had ever seen, almost all of them fervent supporters of the diminutive climber. He won alone at the summit, a minute-and-a-half ahead of fellow Italian Franco Vona, while Indurain, as was his wont, kept his rivals in sight in the mountains and then left them for dead in the time trials.

Indurain's grand-tour dominance was such that he came into the 1992 Tour having already won that year's Giro d'Italia. The Giro-Tour double was a feat that he repeated in 1993.

LONDON

ROYAUME-UNI

BRUSSELS
167 km
ROUBAIX
WASQUEHAL
196 km
5

206.5 km
8
VALKENBURG
7
196.5 km
KOBLENZ
ALLEMAGNE

65 km
9
LUXEMBOURG
217 km
10

NOGENT-SUR-OISE
STRASBOURG

NANTERRE
PARIS
LA DÉFENSE
21
141 km
249.5 km
11

222 km
20
MULHOUSE

64 km
19
BLOIS
TOURS

FRANCE
DOLE

18
212 km

267.5 km
12

189 km
17
MONTLUÇON
ST-GERVAIS-
LES-BAINS

212 km
198 km
LA BOURBOULE
16
15
ST-
ÉTIENNE
13
254.5 km

BORDEAUX
63.5 km
4
14
LE BOURG-
D'OISANS
SESTRIERE
L'ALPE-
D'HUEZ
186.5 km
LIBOURNE

3
210 km

SAN SEBASTIÁN
255 km
PAU
P
8 km
2
1
194.5 km

ESPAGNE

ITALIE
SUISSE
BELGIQUE

197

1993
80th Edition

Marking his territory, a young Lance Armstrong shows a sign of things to come in Verd[...]

Start: Le Puy du Fou, France,
on 3 July
Finish: Paris, France, on 25 July

Total distance:
3714.3 km (2306 miles)
Longest stage:
286.5 km (178 miles)

Highest point:
Cime de la Bonette:
2802 m (9193 ft)
Mountain stages: 5

Starters: 180
Finishers: 136

Winning time: 95 h 57' 09"
Average speed:
38.709 kph (24.038 mph)

1. Miguel Indurain (Spa)
2. Tony Rominger (Swi) at 4' 59"
3. Zenon Jaskula (Pol) at 5' 48"

Points:
Djamolidine Abdoujaparov (Uzb)
Mountains: Tony Rominger (Swi)
Young rider:
Antonio Martin (Spa)

The Puy du Fou theme park hosted the start of the 1993 Tour de France, where Miguel Indurain stormed the 6.8-km prologue time trial to take the race's first yellow jersey and begin his campaign for a third consecutive Tour title.

It seemed almost inevitable that 'Big Mig' would win again and, having purposely let his lead go to sprinters Wilfried Nelissen and Mario Cipollini during the first week to ease the pressure on his team-mates, Indurain took the lead back after the Lac de Madine time trial on stage 9, and this time held it all the way to Paris.

Was his dominance at the Tour simply boring though? Some would say so, while others would marvel at his power and composure on the bike, particularly in those time trials where he was truly unbeatable. At least he was most of the time: with a buffer of four-and-a-half minutes to Colombian climber Álvaro

Mejía and 5 minutes 41 seconds to Swiss star Tony Rominger, Indurain could perhaps afford to take his foot off the accelerator a little, suffering a rare defeat in the race's final time trial, to Rominger.

Mejía dropped off the podium having lost too much time against the clock, and it ended in Paris with Indurain winning his third title by a second shy of five minutes from Rominger, while in third place was Poland's Zenon Jaskula, who became the first rider from an Eastern European country to finish in the top three.

A young American named Lance Armstrong also began his Tour story in 1993, winning stage 8 in Verdun by outsprinting Mexican Raúl Alcalá and France's Ronan Pensec. Later in the season, the 21-year-old Texan would win the road race world championships in Oslo, Norway, and really put himself on the map.

LONDON

ROYAUME-UNI

La Manche

BELGIQUE

BRUXELLES

ALLEMAGNE

PÉRONNE

AMIENS

158 km
6

196.5 km
20

225.5 km
5

ÉVREUX

PARIS

MONTLHÉRY

VIRY-CHÂTILLON

BRÉTIGNY-SUR-ORGE

48 km
19

DINARD

189.5 km
3

AVRANCHES
4

81 km

VANNES

227.5 km
2

215 km
1

LE PUY
DU FOU
6.8 km

LES SABLES-D'OLONNE

LUÇON

FRANCE

184.5 km

199 km
7

VERDUN

CHALONS-
SUR-MARNE

LAC DE
MADINE
9

59 km

OCÉAN
ATLANTIQUE

BORDEAUX

199.5 km
18

ORTHEZ

PAU

TARBES

190 km

ST-LARY-
SOULAN

17

230 km
16

ANDORRA

231.5 km

15

PERPIGNAN

223 km

MONTPELLIER
13

14

181.5 km

MARSEILLE

203 km
10

SERRE-
CHEVALIER

VILLARD-
DE-LANS

179 km
11

ISOLA
2000

286.5 km
12

Nice

SUISSE

ITALIE

ESPAGNE

MER MÉDITERRANÉE

Golfe du Lion

199

Race leader Johan Museeuw and Britain's Chris Boardman line up at the start of stage 4 in Dover in 1994. It was the second time that the Tour had come to Britain, having first visited in 1974. It would return in 2007, starting in London, and will come back a fourth time for the 2014 *Grand Départ*, in Yorkshire.

1994
81st Edition

Start: Lille, France, on 2 July
Finish: Paris, France, on 24 July

Total distance:
3978.7 km (2470 miles)
Longest stage:
270.5 km (168 miles)

Highest point:
Val Thorens: 2275 m (7464 ft)
Mountain stages: 7

Starters: 189
Finishers: 117

Winning time: 103 h 38' 38"
Average speed:
38.383 kph (23.836 mph)

1. Miguel Indurain (Spa)
2. Piotr Ugrumov (Lat) at 5' 39"
3. Marco Pantani (Ita) at 7' 19"

Points: Djamolidine
Abdoujaparov (Uzb)
Mountains: Richard Virenque (Fra)
Young rider: Marco Pantani (Ita)

Featuring what are arguably the race's two most legendary climbs – the twenty-one hairpin bends that make up Alpe d'Huez and 'The Giant of Provence', Mont Ventoux – this was a classic Tour route save for one thing: the trip across the Channel to Britain.

Then-race director Jean-Marie Leblanc, a fully-paid-up Anglophile, was instrumental in getting his Tour to the UK for only the second time. That first foray – to Plymouth in 1974 – was, however, best forgotten, and instead Dover, Brighton – where the riders made short work of the climb of Ditchling Beacon – and then, the next day, Portsmouth played host to two successful days of racing before the 1994 Tour was ferried back to Cherbourg and more familiar surroundings.

There had already been a somewhat British feel to proceedings right from the off when Chris Boardman powered his way into the race's first yellow jersey in the prologue in Lille, only to lose it the day before the race hopped on the Eurotunnel – which had opened exactly two months earlier – for the transfer under the sea.

It was curious, then, that after Boardman had become the first British rider to don the famous *maillot jaune* since Tom Simpson in 1962, another British rider, Sean Yates, should take the yellow jersey upon the race's return to French soil, in Rennes.

However, when defending champion Miguel Indurain grabbed hold of the reins by winning the 64-km (40-mile) individual time trial between Périgueux and Bergerac three days later, it was business as usual, and the Spaniard never let go, despite spirited attempts from Luc Leblanc, Piotr Ugrumov and Marco Pantani to wrest it from his shoulders, notably on the climbs to Hautacam and Val Thorens – mountains which both featured in the Tour for the first time in 1994.

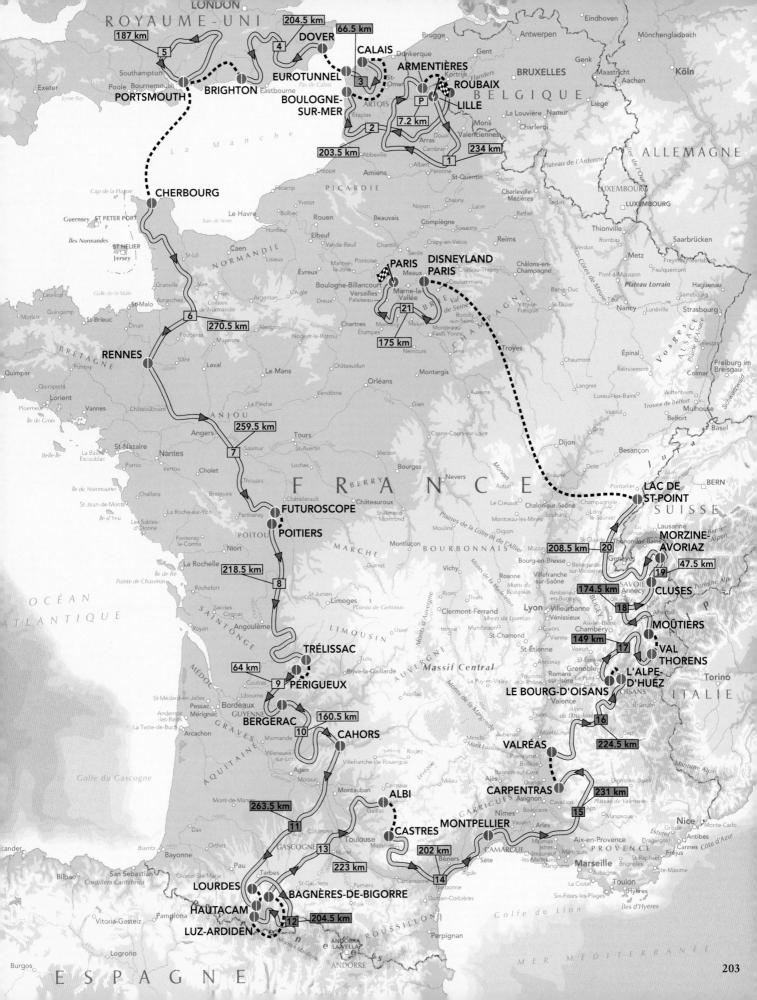

LONDON

ROYAUME-UNI

187 km
5
Southampton
Poole Bournemouth
PORTSMOUTH   BRIGHTON   Eastbourne

204.5 km
4
66.5 km
DOVER
EUROTUNNEL
CALAIS
BOULOGNE-SUR-MER
3
ARMENTIÈRES
ROUBAIX
P
LILLE
7.2 km

203.5 km
2
234 km
1

CHERBOURG

6
270.5 km

RENNES

259.5 km
7

FUTUROSCOPE
POITIERS

218.5 km
8

TRÉLISSAC

64 km
9   PÉRIGUEUX

BERGERAC
160.5 km
10
CAHORS

263.5 km
11
13
223 km
14

ALBI
CASTRES
202 km
MONTPELLIER

LOURDES
BAGNÈRES-DE-BIGORRE
HAUTACAM
12   204.5 km
LUZ-ARDIDEN

ESPAGNE

ANDORRE

PARIS   DISNEYLAND PARIS
21
175 km

LAC DE ST-POINT

208.5 km
20
174.5 km
18
149 km
17

MORZINE-AVORIAZ
47.5 km
19
CLUSES
MOÛTIERS
VAL THORENS
L'ALPE-D'HUEZ
LE BOURG-D'OISANS
16
224.5 km

VALRÉAS

CARPENTRAS
231 km
15

SUISSE

ITALIE

203

Camaraderie for Casartelli – the peloton allows Motorola to cross the finish line first in [

Start: St-Brieuc, France, on 1 July
Finish: Paris, France, on 23 July

Total distance:
3547.3 km (2204 miles)
Longest stage:
261 km (162 miles)

Highest point:
Col du Tourmalet:
2115 m (6939 ft)
Mountain stages: 5

Starters: 189
Finishers: 115

Winning time: 92 h 44' 59"
Average speed:
39.193 kph (24.339 mph)

1. Miguel Indurain (Spa)
2. Alex Zülle (Swi) at 4' 35"
3. Bjarne Riis (Den) at 6' 47"

Points: Laurent Jalabert (Fra)
Mountains: Richard Virenque (Fra)
Young rider: Marco Pantani (Ita)

The 1995 Tour started with an evening prologue time trial around St-Brieuc, during which Britain's Chris Boardman – the stage favourite following his win at the 1994 prologue – crashed on a wet descent, ending his race before it had barely begun.

Stage 4 between Alençon and Le Havre took the peloton over the spectacular Pont de Normandie to celebrate the opening that year of the bridge that spans the Seine estuary.

On stage 8, Spain's Miguel Indurain kicked things up a gear, winning the time trial and taking the yellow jersey, which he then defended all the way to Paris. It was the last of Indurain's five Tour wins, and now that Lance Armstrong has had his seven wins between 1999 and 2005 taken away from him, Indurain remains the only rider to have won five consecutive Tours.

What should have been a celebration of the first rider to win five in succession in 1995 was marred, however, by the death of Italian rider Fabio Casartelli. The 1992 Olympic road race champion crashed on the descent of the Col de Portet d'Aspet on stage 15 between St-Girons and Cauterets. It's known as a very fast, dangerous descent – Raymond Poulidor had crashed heavily there in 1973, too, ending his campaign that yea[

Casartelli died as a result of the head injuries he sustained. The next day, stage 16 was neutralised, and the Italian's Motorola team-mates, includin[Canada's Steve Bauer and the USA's Lance Armstrong and Frankie Andreu, were allowed to cross the line first, side-by-side, with the peloton holding back and finishing a few metres behind.

On stage 18, Armstrong then took an emotional solo stage win, pointing at the sky in memory of Casartelli as he crossed the line in Limoges.

ROYAUME-UNI

LONDON

Southampton · Portsmouth · Brighton · Eastbourne

Exeter · Poole · Bournemouth

Lyme Bay

Cap de la Hague
Cherbourg-Octeville

Guernsey ST PETER PORT
Îles Normandes
ST HELIER
Jersey

PERROS-GUIREC **233.5 km**

NION

Morlaix · Guingamp

ST-BRIEUC **1**
P
7.3 km

2
235.5 km

Quimper · Quimperlé

Lorient · Vannes

Belle-Île

La Baule-Escoublac

St-Nazaire

OCÉAN ATLANTIQUE

Île de Noirmoutier

St-Jean-de-Monts

Île d'Yeu

Les Sables-d'Olonne

La Rochelle
Île de Ré
Pointe de Chassiron

Rochefort

Royan

BORDEAUX
St-Médard-en-Jalles
Pessac

Arcachon
Andernos-les-Bains
La Teste-de-Buch

246 km **17**

Golfe du Gascogne

Dax

Biarritz
Bayonne

San Sebastián

Bilbao
Cordillera Cantábrica

Vitoria-Gasteiz

Logroño

Burgos

ESPAGNE

DUNKIRK
Calais

Boulogne-sur-Mer
Étaples
Bruay-la-Bussière

261 km **5**

FÉCAMP
Dieppe

LE HAVRE
Honfleur
Caen
Lisieux

4
162 km

ALENÇON
MAYENNE **3**
67 km
VITRÉ
Fougères
Rennes
Laval
Le Mans

DINAN

St-Malo
Golfe de St-Malo

Granville
Avranches
Vire
Argentan
Collines de Normandie
L'Aigle
Dreux
Chartres
Châteaudun
Vendôme
Tours
St-Avertin
Loches
Châteauroux

Châteaubriant

Angers
Cholet
Thouars
Bressuire
Châtellerault
Poitiers

Nantes

Pornic
Challans

Fontenay-le-Comte
Niort

Parthenay

Saintes
Cognac
Angoulême

Coutras
Libourne
Bergerac

Mont-de-Marsan

Villeneuve-sur-Lot
Agen

Auch
Colomiers
Toulouse
Muret

PAU
TARBES
(Stage 16 neutralised with results annulled)

149 km

ST-GIRONS
St-Gaudens

16

CAUTERETS
15
206 km

ANDORRA LA VELLA
ANDORRA

GUZET-NEIGE **14** **164 km**
Foix

ROUSSILLON

BELGIQUE
Brugge · Gent · Antwerpen · Mönchengladbach · Eindhoven · Genk · Maastricht · Aachen · Köln

BRUXELLES **6** **202 km**
Kortrijk
Flanders
St-Omer
Lille
Louvière
Mons
Namur
Valenciennes
Douai
Arras
Abbeville
Amiens
Péronne
St-Quentin
Hirson
Charleville-Mézières

HUY LIÈGE
SERAING
CHARLEROI
8
54 km **7**
203 km

Plateau de l'Ardenne

ALLEMAGNE

LUXEMBOURG
LUXEMBOURG

Vallée de l'Our

Sedan
Verdun
Metz
Saarbrücken
Thionville
Rombas
Plateau Lorrain
Nancy
Lunéville
Hagenau
Saverne
Strasbourg

Reims
Châlons-en-Champagne
Épernay
Bar-le-Duc
St-Dizier
Vitry-le-François
Épinal
Remiremont
Colmar
Freiburg im Breisgau
Mulhouse
Belfort
Basel

Beauvais
Compiègne
Soissons
Laon
Noyon
Crépy-en-Valois
Senlis
Chantilly
Pontoise

PARIS
Marne-la-Vallée
Boulogne-Billancourt
STE-GENEVIÈVE-DES-BOIS **20** **155 km**
Versailles
Melun
Montereau-Fault-Yonne
Romilly-sur-Seine
Troyes
Chaumont
Langres
Vesoul
Gray
Besançon

Nogent-le-Rotrou
Orléans
Montargis
Sens
Auxerre

BERRY
Bourges
Nevers
Moulins
Vichy
Roanne

Cosne-Cours-sur-Loire
Plaines de la Loire et de l'Allier
Digoin
Autun
Le Creusot
Chalon-sur-Saône
Beaune
Dijon
Dole
Lons-le-Saunier
Champagnole
St-Claude

Châteauroux
St-Amand-Montrond
Montluçon
Bourg-en-Bresse
Mâcon

MARCHE
Guéret
LIMOGES **18** **166.5 km**
LAC DE VASSIVIÈRE **19** **46.5 km**
Plateau de Gentioux
Ussel
Tulle
Brive-la-Gaillarde
Aurillac

LIMOUSIN
Monts d'Auvergne
Clermont-Ferrand
Monts du Lyonnais
Montbrison

Villefranche-sur-Saône
Ambérieu-en-Bugey
Annecy
LE GRAND-BORNAND **160 km**
Thonon-les-Bains
Lac Léman
Lausanne
BERN
Berner Alpen

SUISSE

Genève
Annemasse
9
Aix-les-Bains
Chambéry
162.5 km
199 km
10 AIME
LA PLAGNE
L'ALPE-D'HUEZ
LE BOURG-D'OISANS
Massif de la Vanoise
Torino

ITALIE

Lyon
Villeurbanne
Vénissieux
ST-ÉTIENNE
St-Chamond
11
Givors
Annonay
Tournon-sur-Rhône
Valence
Romans-sur-Isère
Voiron
Grenoble
OISANS
Vizille

12
222.5 km
Le Puy-en-Velay
Monts de la Margeride
MENDE
Mont Lozère
Alès
Bagnols-sur-Cèze
Orange
Carpentras
Avignon
Valence
Montélimar
Pierrelatte
Bollène

Massif Central

AUVERGNE
Issoire

ST-ORENS-DE-GAMEVILLE
Castres
REVEL
13 **245 km**
Mazamet
Béziers
Narbonne
Perpignan

Rodez
Villefranche-de-Rouergue
Millau
Lévezou
Albi
Carmaux
Montauban
Moissac
Marmande
CARRIGUES
Nîmes
Montpellier
Sète
Agde

CAMARGUE
Arles
Miramas
Istres
Aix-en-Provence
PROVENCE
Salon-de-Provence
Draguignan
Grasse
Cannes
Antibes
Nice
Monte-Carlo
Côte d'Azur

Marseille
La Ciotat
Six-Fours-les-Plages
Toulon
Hyères
Îles d'Hyères
St-Raphaël
Fréjus
St-Maxime

Golfe du Lion

MER MÉDITERRANÉE

FRANCE

Bjarne Riis impressed on his way to his 1996 Tour win – the first and only by a Dane – but his admission to doping in 2007 meant that the Tour organisers at first chose to scrub his name from the list, and then reinstated him, albeit with an asterisk – the implication being that perhaps a number of his rivals weren't entirely clean, either, and so picking a replacement winner could have been tricky.

The key stage proved to be the snow-hit stage 9 between Val-d'Isère and Sestriere in Italy, which was instead started at Le Monêtier-les-Bains and run over the remaining 46 km (28.5 miles) of the scheduled stage, striking the Col de l'Iseran and the Col du Galibier from the route.

It proved that stages don't have to be long to make all the difference: Riis attacked on the climb to the Montgenèvre ski resort and won alone at Sestriere, taking almost 30 seconds out of his main rivals, including the defending champion Miguel Indurain on a quest to score a record-breaking sixth Tour win. Riis's stage win was enough to secure the yellow jersey, which he defended all the way to Paris.

When Festina's Richard Virenque and Laurent Dufaux, and Switzerland's Tony Rominger had been expected to be in the mix for victory, not to mention Indurain, the top two places on the podium came as a relative surprise. True, Riis had finished third in 1995, but his 22-year-old Telekom team-mate, Jan Ullrich, was the real revelation.

Riis was heralded as the man who broke Indurain's run of Tour wins, and the way he dominated the race suggested that there was a lot more to come. Ullrich's win in the penultimate stage, however, beating Indurain by almost a minute, suggested a bright future for Riis's young German team-mate.

Bjarne Riis claimed two stage victories as well as overall crown, becoming the first Danish champi...

Start: 's-Hertogenbosch, Netherlands, on 29 June
Finish: Paris, France, on 21 July

Total distance: 3764.9 km (2340 miles)
Longest stage: 262 km (163 miles)

Highest point: Sestriere: 2033 m (6670 ft)
Mountain stages: 5

Starters: 198
Finishers: 129

Winning time: 95 h 57' 16"
Average speed: 39.227 kph (24.356 mph)

1. Bjarne Riis (Den)
2. Jan Ullrich (Ger) at 1' 41"
3. Richard Virenque (Fra) at 4' 37"

Points: Erik Zabel (Ger)
Mountains: Richard Virenque (Fra)
Young rider: Jan Ullrich (Ger)

ROYAUME-UNI

Gloucester
Swansea
Oxford
Luton
Watford
Colchester
LONDON
Southampton
Portsmouth
Brighton
Eastbourne
Poole
Bournemouth
Exeter

La Manche

Cherbourg-
Octeville
Guernsey ST PETER PORT
ST HELIER
Jersey
Îles Normandes

BELGIQUE
Rotterdam
Dordrecht
Nijmegen
'S-HERTOGENBOSCH
1
209 km
P
9.4 km
Eindhoven
Antwerpen
2
247.5 km
BRUXELLES
Gent
Flanders
Genk
Maastricht
Aachen
Köln
Mönchengladbach
ALLEMAGNE

WASQUEHAL
St-Omer
Lille
Bruay-la-
Bussière
195 km
3
Lens
Douai
Valenciennes
Cambrai
Mons
La Louvière
Namur
Liège
Charleroi
LUXEMBOURG
LUXEMBOURG

Dunkerque
Calais
Boulogne-sur-Mer
Étaples
ARTOIS

Abbeville
Amiens
Albert
Péronne
St-Quentin
Hirson
Plateau de l'Ardenne
Sedan
Charleville
232 km
4
Rethel
Reims
Verdun
Côtes de Meuse
Pont-à-Mousson
Metz
Thionville
Rombas
Freyming-Merlebach
Faulquemont
Saarbrücken
Sarreguemines
Haguenau

NOGENT-SUR-OISE
Chantilly
Crépy-en-Valois
SOISSONS
Laon
Châlons-en-Champagne
Vitry-le-François
St-Dizier
Toul
Nancy
Lunéville
Épinal
VOSGES
Strasbourg
Freiburg im Breisgau

PARIS
21
147.5 km
PALAISEAU
BRIE
Val de Seine
Melun
Montereau-Fault-Yonne
Troyes
Chaumont
Langres
LAC DE MADINE
5
242 km
Remiremont
Luxeuil-les-Bains
Colmar
Mulhouse
Trouée de Belfort
Belfort
Basel

NORMANDIE
Le Havre
Honfleur
Bolbec
Yvetot
Rouen
Beauvais
Compiègne
Noyon
Chauny

BRETAGNE
Quimper
Lorient
Vannes
Nantes

OCÉAN ATLANTIQUE

BORDEAUX
226.5 km
19

HENDAYE
154.5 km
18
PAMPLONA
262 km
17
ARGELÈS-GAZOST
LOURDES-HAUTACAM

AGEN
199 km
16
VILLENEUVE-SUR-LOT
63.5 km
20
ST-ÉMILION
15
176 km

SUPERBESSE
186.5 km
14
BRIVE-LA-GAILLARDE
TULLE
BESSE
13
177 km
LE PUY-EN-VELAY
12
143.5 km
VALENCE
11
202 km
GAP
10
208.5 km
46 km
SESTRIERE
9
TURIN
ITALIE

LE MONÊTIER-LES-BAINS
VAL-D'ISÈRE
LES ARCS
8
30.5 km
BOURG-ST-MAURICE
CHAMBÉRY
7
200 km
AIX-LES-BAINS
6
207 km
BESANÇON
ARC-ET-SENANS
SUISSE
BERN

207

1997
84th Edition

Start: Rouen, France, on 5 July
Finish: Paris, France, on 27 July

Total distance:
3942.3 km (2450 miles)
Longest stage:
262 km (163 miles)

Highest point:
Andorra Arcalis: 2240 m (7349 ft)
Mountain stages: 5

Starters: 198
Finishers: 139

Winning time: 100 h 30' 35"
Average speed:
39.237 kph (24.366 mph)

1. Jan Ullrich (Ger)
2. Richard Virenque (Fra) at 9' 09"
3. Marco Pantani (Ita) at 14' 03"

Points: Erik Zabel (Ger)
Mountains: Richard Virenque (Fra)
Young rider: Jan Ullrich (Ger)

Bjarne Riis arrived at the 1997 Tour de France in Rouen with the best intentions of defending his title. The man who had finished runner-up to him in 1996 – Germany's Jan Ullrich – remained faithfully on the Dane's Telekom squad, and was expected to help his team leader in the mountains.

Britain's Chris Boardman won the prologue time trial in Rouen to take the race's first yellow jersey, just as he had in 1994, beating Ullrich by just 2 seconds, while Riis finished down in thirteenth place, a further 13 seconds behind. Although at that early point in the race it meant little, prologues nevertheless have a tendency to gauge which of the Tour favourites have arrived at the race with the best form and the most hunger to perform.

In this case, it did prove to be Ullrich, and once it became painfully clear that the young German was the stronger man in the mountains, Riis turned his attentions to helping his team-mate win the race against the might of the Festina team, which numbered Richard Virenque, Laurent Dufaux and Christophe Moreau among its ranks.

Riis settled for seventh place overall, happy to have won his Tour in 1996 and now, aged 33, happy to help his team-mate do the same. Ullrich, Germany's first Tour winner at the tender age of 23, sent his home nation cycling-crazy, hoping for a spell of dominance to compare with Miguel Indurain's.

The final stage began at Disneyland Paris just as it had done in 1994, and finished on the Champs-Élysées where Ullrich could boast a 9-minute 9-second victory over second-placed Virenque. Marco Pantani was third, having lit up the race in the mountains and taken two stage wins, including stage 13 to Alpe d'Huez. However, the best was yet to come for the Italian climber.

Bjarne Riis proved a worthy lieutenant to the baby-faced Jan Ullrich, assisting his team-mate to Germany's first Tour victory

LONDON

ROYAUME-UNI

Southampton · Portsmouth · Brighton · Eastbourne
Exeter · Poole · Bournemouth

Cap de la Hague · Cherbourg-Octeville
Guernsey · ST PETER PORT · Îles Normandes · ST HELIER · Jersey

ST-VALERY-EN-CAUX

FORGES-LES-EAUX

192 km 1

7.3 km P

ROUEN

2 **262 km**

VIRE

224 km 3

PLUMELEC

223 km

4

LE PUY DU FOU

CHANTONNAY

5 **261.5 km**

LA CHÂTRE

LE BLANC

6 **215.5 km**

MARENNES

7 **194 km**

BORDEAUX

SAUTERNES

161.5 km

8

PAU

182 km

9 **252.5 km** 10

LOUDENVIELLE **LUCHON**

LOUDENVIELLE

ANDORRA ARCALIS

192 km 11

PERPIGNAN

DISNEYLAND PARIS

PARIS

21 **149.5 km** 20

63 km

COLMAR

175.5 km

172 km 18

19

MONTBÉLIARD

DIJON

17

218.5 km

FRIBOURG

SUISSE

16 **181 km**

MORZINE

15 **208.5 km**

COURCHEVEL

148 km 14

L'ALPE-D'HUEZ

55.5 km 12 13

ST-ÉTIENNE

203.5 km

LE BOURG-D'OISANS

FRANCE

ITALIE

BELGIQUE
BRUXELLES
ALLEMAGNE
LUXEMBOURG

ESPAGNE

OCÉAN ATLANTIQUE

Golfe de Gascogne

MER MÉDITERRANÉE

Golfe du Lion

"It was a difficult decision to make, but one that we think was essential for
Tour de France and for cycling, and something that we hope will also put an
to the unhealthy climate that has hung over this race since the start in Dubli

Tour boss Jean-Marie Leblanc talks to the press about his decision to throw the Festina squ
off the race, in the hope that the sport could move forward towards a healthier fut

You might be forgiven for remembering the 1998 Tour de France for all the wrong reasons. What should have been a stunning *Grand Départ* in Dublin, Ireland, was massively overshadowed by a doping controversy that arguably kick-started a widespread awareness and subsequent condemnation of drugs in cycling – a battle that is still ongoing.

When Festina team *soigneur* – or 'team helper' – Willy Voet was stopped on the France/Belgium border by customs officials who unearthed a wealth of doping riches, including EPO, in the boot of the Belgian's car just three days before the start of the Tour, the race – and professional cycling in general – was plunged into turmoil. Who was doping? What were they taking? How did they get hold of the doping products?

The Tour struggled on, but following the sixth stage between La Châtre and Brive-la-Gaillarde (the race having returned to French shores from Ireland on stage 3), the Festina riders were thrown off the race by Jean-Marie Leblanc.

Tour director Leblanc later admitted that he was at his wits' end in the wake of the scandal; being at the helm of a French institution in very real danger of going under was not a job to be sniffed at. Amid arguments, strikes, further confessions and more arrests, the stricken 1998 Tour nevertheless continued.

Like in 1997, Denmark's Bjarne Riis tried to help his younger team-mate and defending champion Jan Ullrich in the battle that had developed between the German and Italy's Marco Pantani, but the Italian was just too strong.

The key stage was a cold and wet stage 15 – a true epic that crossed the Croix de Fer, the Col du Télégraphe

and the Col du Galibier before a summi finish at Les Deux Alpes. Along the way a yellow-clad Ullrich cracked in a big way, and had to be shepherded to the finish by German team-mate Udo Bölts and a strong-looking Riis, while Pantan veritably soared, climbing with his hand on the drops of the handlebars and taki the yellow jersey from Ullrich's slumpe shoulders by sealing victory that day.

His overall win in Paris, by nearly three-and-a-half minutes from Ullrich, was, tragically, to be the pinnacle of Pantani's career. 'The Pirate', as he was called, by virtue of his hooped earrings and the bandana he often wore on his head, was found dead in a Rimini hotel room on Valentine's Day 2004 – death by cocaine overdose the official verdict.

Mercurial climber Pantani v
regarded as the saviour of the T

Start: Dublin, Ireland, on 11 July
Finish: Paris, France, on 2 August

Total distance:
3877.1 km (2409 miles)
Longest stage:
252 km (156 miles)

Highest point:
Col du Galibier: 2645 m (8678 ft)
Mountain stages: 5

Starters: 189
Finishers: 96

Winning time: 92 h 49' 46"
Average speed:
39.983 kph (24.829 mph)

1. Marco Pantani (Ita)
2. Jan Ullrich (Ger) at 3' 21"
3. Bobby Julich (USA) at 4' 08"

Points: Erik Zabel (Ger)
Mountains:
Christophe Rinero (Fra)
Young rider: Jan Ullrich (Ger)

LONDON
ROYAUME-UNI
and 2

DUBLIN
5.6 km P
ENNISCORTHY
180.5 km
205.5 km
2

BELGIQUE
ALLEMAGNE
LUXEMBOURG
LUXEMBOURG

ROSCOFF
169 km
3
PLOUAY
252 km
4
LORIENT

PARIS
147.5 km
21
MELUN

LA CHAUX-DE-FONDS
242 km
NEUCHÂTEL
BERN
SUISSE
AUTUN
19
LE CREUSOT
20
MONTCEAU-LES-MINES
218.5 km
18
52 km

CHOLET
228.5 km
5
CHÂTEAUROUX
LA CHÂTRE

FRANCE

204.5 km
6

MEYRIGNAC-L'ÉGLISE
58 km
7
BRIVE-LA-GAILLARDE
CORRÈZE

(Stage 17 annulled)
17
149 km
ALBERTVILLE
AIX-LES-BAINS
16
204 km
GRENOBLE
15
189 km
LES DEUX-ALPES
14
VIZILLE
186.5 km
VALRÉAS
CARPENTRAS

190.5 km
8

MONTAUBAN
210 km
9
PAU

FRONTIGNAN-LA PEYRADE
196 km
13
222 km
12
CAP D'AGDE

10
196.5 km
LUCHON
11
170 km
TARASCON-SUR-ARIÈGE
PLATEAU DE BEILLE
ANDORRE
LA VELLA

ESPAGNE

OCÉAN
ATLANTIQUE

ITALIE

211

Start: Le Puy du Fou, France, on 3 July
Finish: Paris, France, on 25 July

Total distance:
3686.8 km (2291 miles)
Longest stage:
236.5 km (147 miles)

Highest point:
Col du Galibier: 2645 m (8678 ft)
Mountain stages: 4

Starters: 180
Finishers: 141

Winning time: 91 h 32' 16"*
Average speed:
40.276 kph (25.011 mph)*

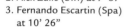

1. Lance Armstrong (USA)*
2. Alex Zülle (Swi) at 7' 37"
3. Fernando Escartin (Spa)
   at 10' 26"

Points: Erik Zabel (Ger)
Mountains:
Richard Virenque (Fra)
Young rider: Benoît Salmon (Fra)

* Lance Armstrong was officially stripped of his seven Tour titles in 2012, with no rider listed as the winner from 1999 to 2005

For the second time in its history, the race began at France's 'mediaeval theme park' the Puy du Fou, 50 km (30 miles) southeast of Nantes. This was a race that had come to be dubbed 'the Tour of Redemption' – the antidote to the horrors of the previous year's Festina Affair.

Winner Lance Armstrong was welcomed with open arms by fans and the media – an American, and therefore enough of an outsider, perhaps, not to have anything to do with the established and wizened old European pros for whom doping was part of the sport. In addition, he came with an amazing story, having fought back from cancer – virtually back from the dead. What wasn't to like? The timing was perfect; only now do we know that it was too good to be true.

From Miguel Indurain's last Tour win in 1995, via Riis, Ullrich, Pantani and now Armstrong, the Tour enjoyed five different winners in five editions, the excitement and unpredictability of which certainly did the race no harm in the wake of 'Festina'.

Little did anyone expect that 1999 in fact signalled the start of an unprecedented run of seven straight victories for Armstrong: seven consecutive wins that would shock the cycling world with their dominance, and then shock the cycling world again– and the world in general, such was the scale of the fraud – when they were taken away from him in 2012.

All of Armstrong's Tour de France wins – from this first one in 1999 all the way through to his last in 2005 – have been struck from the record books by cycling's governing body, the UCI, thanks to a US Anti-Doping Agency (USADA) investigation that exposed

Armstrong as one of the ring-leaders in a meticulously organised doping system of the Texan's teams.

Lance Armstrong claims the first of his seven tainted Tour de France titles

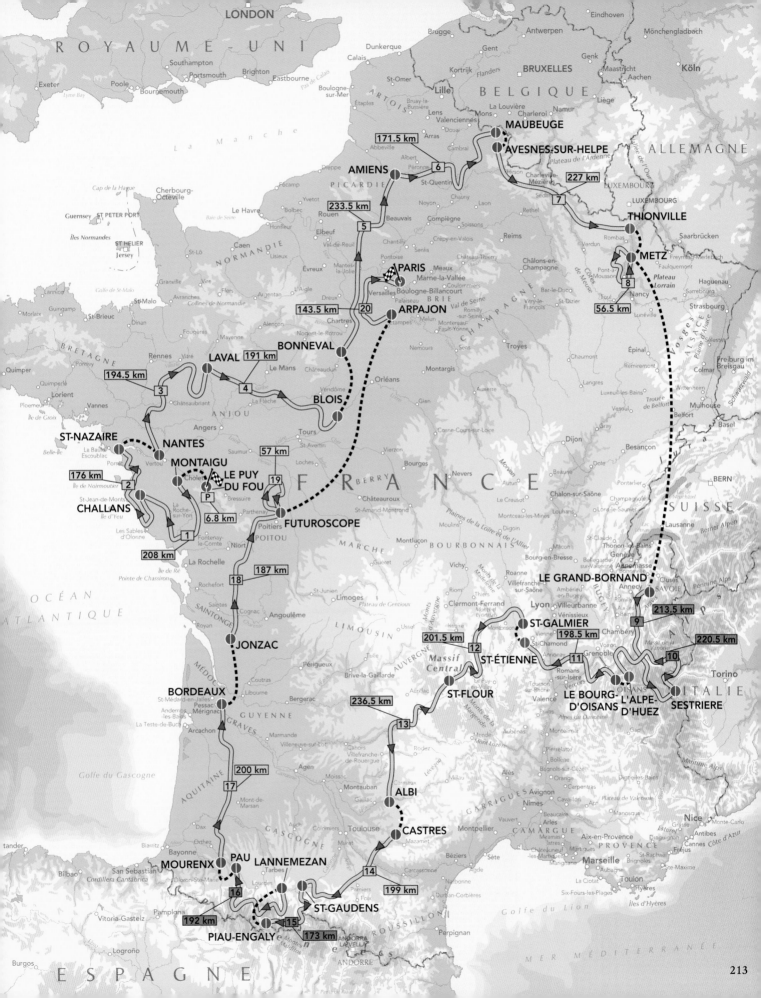

ROYAUME-UNI

LONDON
Southampton
Exeter
Poole Brighton Eastbourne
Bournemouth Portsmouth
Lyme Bay
Cap de la Hague Cherbourg-
Octeville Le Havre
Guernsey ST PETER PORT
Îles Normandes
ST HELIER
Jersey
La Manche

BELGIQUE
BRUXELLES
Brugge Antwerpen Eindhoven Mönchengladbach
Gent Genk Maastricht Köln
Kortrijk Flanders Aachen
Lille
St-Omer Mons La Louvière Charleroi Namur Liège
Calais Bruay-la- Valenciennes
Pas de Calais Buissière Lens Douai Cambrai Hirson Charleville- ALLEMAGNE
Boulogne- Abbeville Albert Péronne Mézières Sedan LUXEMBOURG
sur-Mer Arras St-Quentin
171.5 km 6 **227 km**
AMIENS MAUBEUGE Plateau de l'Ardenne
PICARDIE AVESNES-SUR-HELPE LUXEMBOURG
Dieppe Rouen Beauvais Noyon Laon 7 Rombas Saarbrücken
Fécamp Yvetot Chauny THIONVILLE
233.5 km Compiègne Soissons Reims Verdun Metz-Merlebach
Bolbec Elbeuf 5 Chantilly Crépy-en-Valois Châlons-en- Pont-à- METZ Plateau
Honfleur Val-de-Reuil Senlis Château-Thierry Champagne Mousson 8 Lorrain
NORMANDIE Évreux Pontoise Marne-la-Vallée Bar-le-Duc Vitry-le- Nancy **56.5 km**
Caen Lisieux Mantes- PARIS Meaux St-Dizier François Lunéville
St-Lô la-Jolie Boulogne-Billancourt Melun Romilly-
Avranches Argentan L'Aigle Dreux Versailles Palaiseau sur-Seine Troyes Épinal
Flers Chartres 20 Étampes ARPAJON Sens Chaumont
Vire Alençon Nogent-le-Rotrou **143.5 km** Montereau- Langres
Collines de Normandie Le Mans Fault-Yonne
St-Malo Mayenne Châteaudun Auxerre Vesoul

BRETAGNE LAVAL **191 km** Vendôme Orléans Montargis
Rennes Vitré 4 BONNEVAL Dijon
Pontivy **194.5 km** La Flèche BLOIS Gien Cosne-Cours-sur-Loire Beaune
3 Châteaubriant ANJOU Tours Chalon-sur-Saône Pontarlier SUISSE
St-Avertin FRANCE BERRY Nevers Autun
NANTES Angers Saumur Loches Bourges Montceau-les-Mines Lons-le-Saunier
ST-NAZAIRE **176 km** MONTAIGU Vierzon Châteauroux Le Creusot Mâcon Bourg-en-Bresse
Vertou LE PUY **57 km** St-Amand-Montrond Plaines de la Loire et de l'Allier St-Claude Thonon-les-Bains
2 DU FOU 19 PLAINES MARCHE Moulins Digoin BOURBONNAIS Genève Genève
CHALLANS P Poitiers Roanne Bellegarde- LE GRAND-BORNAND
1 **6.8 km** FUTUROSCOPE POITOU Vichy Villefranche- sur-Valserine Annecy SAVOIE
208 km La Rochelle **187 km** Guéret sur-Saône Lyon Aix-les-Bains
18 Niort LIMOUSIN Clermont-Ferrand Villeurbanne 9 **213.5 km**
Rochefort Montluçon Ussel Monts Vénissieux ST-GALMIER Chambéry **220.5 km**
Île de Ré JONZAC Limoges d'Auvergne **201.5 km** **198.5 km** 10
OCÉAN Saintes Brive-la-Gaillarde Aurillac 12 11 LE BOURG- SESTRIERE
ATLANTIQUE Cognac Tulle Massif ST-ÉTIENNE D'OISANS ITALIE
Angoulême Central St-Flour Annonay L'ALPE- Torino
Périgueux **236.5 km** ST-FLOUR Valence D'HUEZ
BORDEAUX Libourne 13 Gap
St-Médard-en-Jalles Bergerac Rodez Montélimar
GUYENNE Villefranche- ALBI Nîmes
MÉDOC Marmande de-Rouergue Carmaux Avignon
GRAVES Villeneuve-sur-Lot Montauban Arles PROVENCE
200 km Agen Moissac GASCOGNE Toulouse CAMARGUE Aix-en-Provence
17 Mont-de- CASTRES Béziers Cannes
Marsan Sète Marseille Antibes
MOURENX PAU LANNEMEZAN Narbonne Toulon
192 km Tarbes ROUSSILLON Golfe du Lion
16 **199 km** MER MÉDITERRANÉE
PIAU-ENGALY 15 ST-GAUDENS 14
ANDORRE
ESPAGNE **173 km**

213

2000
87th Edition

From a start at a mediaeval theme park in 1999 to a *Grand Départ* from the polar opposite – as theme parks go – in technology-fuelled theme park Futuroscope in 2000, the Tour has never been afraid to mix tradition with modernity.

The 2000 Tour also introduced fans to a young British rider called David Millar who won the 16.5-km (10-mile) opening-stage time trial, continuing where Chris Boardman had left off in 1998, while also becoming only the fourth Briton in the Tour's history to wear the yellow jersey. Lance Armstrong finished second in Futuroscope, just 2 seconds behind Millar, although the American had bigger plans for later in the race.

Spain's Javier Otxoa broke away early on in the 205-km (127-mile) tenth stage from Dax to Hautacam, a stage on which Armstrong also demonstrated the same dominance that had won him his first Tour in 1999. While Otxoa clung on to win the stage by 42 seconds from Armstrong, the Texan used the Hautacam's flanks to drop his rivals and take the yellow jersey.

For the first time since 1987, the race returned to Mont Ventoux in 2000. As ever, it was a dramatic stage that finished atop 'The Bald Mountain', and it was the famously bald Italian rider Marco Pantani who triumphed there on stage 12. However, while most would have expected the diminutive climber and 1998 Tour winner to display his considerable skills in the mountains, the fact that Armstrong was the only rider who could stay with him, and then let the Italian win the stage – a relatively normal practice as Armstrong still had the yellow jersey and had further distanced his other rivals – angered Pantani. Armstrong was in turn incensed that Pantani was ungrateful for his 'gift', and a war of words broke out between them in the press.

Once again, the Ventoux had proved its ability to tower over all those who try to conquer it, both physically and metaphorically, arousing fiery passion in those taking on its slopes.

Start: Futuroscope, France, on 1 July
Finish: Paris, France, on 23 July

Total distance:
3667.5 km (2279 miles)
Longest stage:
254.5 km (158 miles)

Highest point:
Col du Galibier: 2645 m (8678 ft)
Mountain stages: 5

Starters: 177
Finishers: 127

Winning time: 92 h 33' 08"*
Average speed:
39.556 kph (24.579 mph)*

1. Lance Armstrong (USA)*
2. Jan Ullrich (Ger) at 6' 02"
3. Joseba Beloki (Spa) at 10' 04"

Points: Erik Zabel (Ger)
Mountains: Santiago Botero (Col)
Young rider:
Francisco Mancebo (Spa)

* Lance Armstrong was officially stripped of his seven Tour titles in 2012, with no rider listed as the winner from 1999 to 2005

Lance Armstrong and Marco Pantani storm Mont Ventoux

LONDON

ROYAUME-UNI

BELGIQUE

ALLEMAGNE

PARIS

21 138 km

TROYES 254.5 km FREIBURG IM BREISGAU 59 km

VITRÉ 202 km 5 198.5 km 6 20 MULHOUSE 19

BELFORT 252 km 18

ST-NAZAIRE VANNES 70 km NANTES 4 3 161.5 km TOURS FRANCE SUISSE

FUTUROSCOPE 1 16.5 km LOUDUN 7 205.5 km LAUSANNE 17

2 194 km ÉVIAN 155 km

LIMOGES MORZINE

203.5 km 8 196 km 16

COURCHEVEL 15 173.5 km ITALIE

BRIANÇON

249 km

VILLENEUVE-SUR-LOT 14

AGEN 181 km CARPENTRAS MONT VENTOUX 149 km

9 AVIGNON 12 185.5 km

DAX 13

205 km BAGNÈRES-DE-BIGORRE REVEL DRAGUIGNAN

10 11 218.5 km

LOURDES-HAUTACAM

ESPAGNE

MER MÉDITERRANÉE

David Millar crashes during the opening time trial in Dunk

Start: Dunkirk, France, on 7 July
Finish: Paris, France, on 29 July

Total distance:
3453.2 km (2146 miles)
Longest stage:
232.5 km (144 miles)

Highest point:
Col du Tourmalet:
2115 m (6939 ft)
Mountain stages: 5

Starters: 189
Finishers: 144

Winning time: 86 h 17' 28"*
Average speed:
40.016 kph (24.850 mph)*

1. Lance Armstrong (USA)*
2. Jan Ullrich (Ger) at 6' 44"
3. Joseba Beloki (Spa) at 9' 05"

Points: Erik Zabel (Ger)
Mountains: Laurent Jalabert (Fra)
Young rider: Óscar Sevilla (Spa)

* Lance Armstrong was officially stripped of
his seven Tour titles in 2012, with no rider
listed as the winner from 1999 to 2005

After winning the Tour's opening time trial and taking the yellow jersey in 2000, Scotland's David Millar was the favourite to repeat the feat in Dunkirk at the start of the 2001 Tour. However, while giving it everything, the Cofidis rider crashed on the final corner of the 8.2-km (5.1-mile) course, and could only remount and limp home way off the winning time of France's Christophe Moreau, who gave the home crowd something to cheer about – despite the fact that Moreau had only returned from a doping ban in 1999 for his role in the Festina Affair.

In 2004, Millar, too, would admit to having doped, and would be banned until just before the start of the 2006 Tour when he returned to the sport with the Spanish Saunier Duval squad as a staunchly anti-doping figure serving on the World Anti-Doping Agency's Athlete Committee.

Now that Armstrong's third Tour win in 2001 – like his other six wins between 1999 and 2005 – has been wiped from the slate, it becomes painfully clear just how dark a time the 1990s and 2000s were for professional cycling, and things were set to get even worse before they were to supposedly get better.

ROYAUME-UNI

LONDON

Southampton
Brighton
Eastbourne
Poole
Bournemouth

Exeter
Lyme Bay

Cap de la Hague
Cherbourg-Octeville

Îles Normandes
ST PETER PORT
Guernsey
ST HELIER
Jersey

BELGIQUE

Eindhoven
Mönchengladbach

ANTWERP
198.5 km

Brugge
Gent
DUNKIRK
8.2 km
CALAIS
BOULOGNE-SUR-MER
ST-OMER
218.5 km

Genk
Maastricht
Köln
Aachen

ALLEMAGNE

Liège
SERAING
HUY

LUXEMBOURG
215 km
LUXEMBOURG

Thionville
Saarbrücken

VERDUN
67 km
Metz

BAR-LE-DUC
COMMERCY
STRASBOURG

PARIS
ÉVRY
CORBEIL-ESSONNES
160.5 km
ORLÉANS
149.5 km

COLMAR
162.5 km
211.5 km

Mulhouse
Belfort
Basel

222.5 km
Besançon
PONTARLIER

SUISSE
BERN

FRANCE

ST-AMAND-MONTROND
61 km
MONTLUÇON
194 km

185 km
Lyon

AIX-LES-BAINS

BRIVE-LA-GAILLARDE
SARRAN

209 km
GRENOBLE
L'ALPE-D'HUEZ
32 km
CHAMROUSSE

ITALIE
Torino

229.5 km
CASTELSARRASIN
LAVAUR

232.5 km
PAU
TARBES
141.5 km
LUZ-ARDIDEN
ST-LARY-SOULAN
14
13
FOIX
AX-LES-THERMES
194 km
166.5 km
PERPIGNAN

OCÉAN ATLANTIQUE

Bordeaux

ESPAGNE

ANDORRE

MER MÉDITERRANÉE

Marseille
Nice

217

King of the mountains Laurent Jalabert (right) battles with Richard Virenque at Les Deux-Alp

Start: Luxembourg, on 6 July
Finish: Paris, France, on 28 July

Total distance:
3277.5 km (2035 miles)
Longest stage:
226.5 km (141 miles)

Highest point:
Col du Galibier: 2645 m (8678 ft)
Mountain stages: 5

Starters: 189
Finishers: 153

Winning time: 82 h 05' 12"*
Average speed:
39.88 kph (24.765 mph)*

1. Lance Armstrong (USA)*
2. Joseba Beloki (Spa) at 7' 17"
3. Raimondas Rumsas (Lit)
   at 8' 17"

Points: Robbie McEwen (Aus)
Mountains: Laurent Jalabert (Fra)
Young rider: Ivan Basso (Ita)

* Lance Armstrong was officially stripped of his seven Tour titles in 2012, with no rider listed as the winner from 1999 to 2005

Before the 2000 Tour, Mont Ventoux hadn't featured on the race route since 1987, but it was back on the menu again already in 2002.

Luxembourg hosted the Tour's *Grand Départ*, which included the prologue time trial, the whole of the first stage and the start of stage 2.

Defending champion Lance Armstrong took the race's first yellow jersey by virtue of winning the prologue by just under 2 seconds from French fans' favourite Laurent Jalabert, who, following his nasty accident at Armentières at the 1994 Tour, had transformed himself from a formidable sprinter into a climber – albeit a mildly fraudulent one in that he would tactically steal the points towards the 'king of the mountains' jersey whenever he could, building up enough of a lead in the competition to prevent the 'real' climbers having any chance of making up the deficit later.

Using what was nevertheless a pretty smart tactic in terms of publicity earned

'Jaja' the polka-dot jersey in both 2001 and 2002 – and the French public, still waiting for their next Tour winner after Bernard Hinault in 1985, loved him for i

There was more for French fans to enjoy on stage 14 when seven-time polka dot jersey winner Richard Virenque won the Ventoux stage by two minutes. So keen for something to cheer about were they that they could seemingly overlook Virenque's role in the 1998 Festina Affair and his nine-month ban from the sport (his 'KoM' titles stood regardless), and blithely continue their support of housewives' favourite 'Reechard' nonetheless.

In Paris, it was Armstrong's fourth straight Tour win at the time, but today the name of the winner remains blank in the official records, just like it does for each of the other six Tours that the American 'won'.

ROYAUME-UNI

LONDON

ALLEMAGNE

BELGIQUE

LUXEMBOURG

192.5 km

1

7 km

P

2   181 km

LUXEMBOURG

174.5 km

3

METZ

SAARBRÜCKEN

REIMS

SOISSONS

195 km

5

FORGES-LES-EAUX

ROUEN

176 km

7

6

199.5 km

CHÂTEAU-THIERRY

ÉPERNAY

4

PARIS

20

MELUN

144 km

67.5 km

BAGNOLES-
DE-L'ORNE

AVRANCHES

ST-MARTIN-
DE-LANDELLES   ALENÇON

217.5 km

8

52 km

PLOUAY

9

LANESTER

LORIENT

FRANCE

SUISSE

BERN

MÂCON

50 km   19

RÉGNIÉ-DURETTE

BOURG-EN-BRESSE

18

CLUSES

17

176.5 km

AIME

142 km

LA PLAGNE

16   179.5 km

15

LES
DEUX-ALPES

226.5 km

MONT VENTOUX

VAISON-LA-ROMAINE

221 km   14

BAZAS

147 km

10

LODÈVE

171 km

BÉZIERS

PAU

LANNEMEZAN

LAVELANET

11

12

13

158 km

LA MONGIE

199.5 km

PLATEAU DE BEILLE

ANDORRE

ESPAGNE

ITALIE

Lance Armstrong, in yellow, takes down Spain's Iban Mayo on the climb to Luz-Ardiden in the 2003 Tour, after catching his handlebars on a spectator's bag, while Jan Ullrich takes evasive action.

2003
90th Edition

High fives all round as Armstrong claims his fifth

Start: Paris, France, on 5 July
Finish: Paris, France, on 27 July

Total distance:
3426.6 km (2128 miles)
Longest stage:
230.5 km (143 miles)

Highest point:
Col du Galibier: 2645 m (8678 ft)
Mountain stages: 7

Starters: 198
Finishers: 147

Winning time: 83 h 41' 12"*
Average speed:
40.956 kph (25.434 mph)*

1. Lance Armstrong (USA)*
2. Jan Ullrich (Ger) at 1' 01"
3. Alexandre Vinokourov (Kaz)
   at 4' 14"

Points: Baden Cooke (Aus)
Mountains: Richard Virenque (Fra)
Young rider: Denis Menchov (Rus)

* Lance Armstrong was officially stripped of
his seven Tour titles in 2012, with no rider
listed as the winner from 1999 to 2005

The 2003 Tour celebrated 100 years since the first edition of the race in 1903, and as a result started and finished in Paris, passing through Lyon, Marseille, Toulouse, Bordeaux and Nantes, just as it had during that first edition.

Appropriately, there was no shortage of excitement during the race, either, as Jan Ullrich pushed Lance Armstrong all the way to Paris, only conceding defeat in the final time trial, where the German crashed in the pouring rain. It was the closest Armstrong had come yet to losing the Tour since 1999. Were it not for Joseba Beloki's crash while descending the Col de la Rochette into Gap on stage 9, the American might have been pushed even harder.

Going into the stage, Beloki trailed Armstrong by just 40 seconds. After hitting a slippery section of tarmac, melted by the hot summer sun, the

Spaniard crashed spectacularly, and painfully. The resultant broken wrist, thigh and elbow ended his race, but mo remarkable of all was how Armstrong avoided the stricken Beloki, having beer forced off the road and into a field, whi he rode down before leaping across the ditch at the bottom, remounting his bi and continuing on the road further do the mountain. Win number five was in the bag, and no one and nothing – not even an impromptu spot of off-road riding – was going to stand in his way. rivals had crashed left, right and centre and Armstrong himself had even crashe brought down when a spectator's bag got caught on his handlebars. Armstron picked himself up and won that stage t Luz-Ardiden, whereas his rivals' crashes had put them out of contention. The Texan could seemingly do no wrong. Or so we were led to believe.

222

ROYAUME-UNI

LONDON

ALLEMAGNE

BELGIQUE

BRUXELLES

LUXEMBOURG

CHARLEVILLE-MÉZIÈRES · SEDAN

204.5 km · 2

167.5 km · 3

MEAUX

ST-DENIS · 6.5 km

152 km · 20

VILLE-D'AVRAY

PARIS · P

MONTGERON · 1

LA FERTÉ-SOUS-JOUARRE

ST-DIZIER

JOINVILLE · 4

69 km

168 km

TROYES

195.6 km · 5

FRANCE

NEVERS

SUISSE

BERN

230 km · 6

230.5 km · 7

MORZINE

SALLANCHES

LYON

219 km · 8

49 km · 19

NANTES

PORNIC

ST-MAIXENT-L'ECOLE

OCÉAN ATLANTIQUE

L'ALPE-D'HUEZ

LE BOURG-D'OISANS

ITALIE

GAP · 9

184.5 km

219.5 km · 10

203.5 km · 18

BORDEAUX

181 km · 17

47 km

GAILLAC · 12 · CAP DÉCOUVERTE

DAX

TOULOUSE

153.5 km

MARSEILLE

BAYONNE

PAU

BAGNÈRES-DE-BIGORRE

NARBONNE

197.5 km · 16

15

159.5 km

ST-GIRONS

11

197.5 km · 13

LUZ-ARDIDEN

14

LOUDENVIELLE

191.5 km

AX 3 DOMAINES

ANDORRE

ESPAGNE

MER MÉDITERRANÉE

223

Start: Liège, Belgium, on 3 July
Finish: Paris, France, on 25 July

Total distance:
3391.1 km (2106 miles)
Longest stage:
237 km (147 miles)

Highest point:
Col de la Madeleine:
2000 m (6562 ft)
Mountain stages: 5

Starters: 188
Finishers: 147

Winning time: 83 h 36' 02"*
Average speed:
40.553 kph (25.183 mph)*

1. Lance Armstrong (USA)*
2. Andreas Klöden (Ger) at 6' 19"
3. Ivan Basso (Ita) at 6' 40"

Points: Robbie McEwen (Aus)
Mountains: Richard Virenque (Fra)
Young rider: Vladimir Karpets (Rus)

* Lance Armstrong was officially stripped of
his seven Tour titles in 2012, with no rider
listed as the winner from 1999 to 2005

Lance Armstrong powers to victory at Alpe d'Hu

While the 2003 Tour had provided Lance Armstrong with a few obstacles to hop over – not least a ditch on the Col de la Rochette after a sortie across an open field, as well as a back-in-form Jan Ullrich – it was business as usual in 2004 as the Texan romped to a sixth successive victory, surpassing such greats as Miguel Indurain, Eddy Merckx, Bernard Hinault and Jacques Anquetil, all with 'only' five wins apiece.

Of course, now that Armstrong's Tours have been erased from the history books, those other famous names stand proud at the top of the tree once more – Indurain arguably slightly prouder than most as the only rider to have won his five Tours in consecutive years (1991–1995).

In 2004, though, Armstrong was, quite simply, rampant in the mountains,

and only Italy's Ivan Basso – riding for Bjarne Riis's CSC outfit – could stay anywhere near him on the climbs. The American won at Plateau de Beille, Villard-de-Lans, Le Grand-Bornand and at Alpe d'Huez – the latter run as a mountain time trial. That mountain TT summed up Armstrong's Tour perfectly: he was the best in the mountains, but also the best against the clock – the latter a discipline in which Basso was less proficient.

Ullrich finished out of the top three for the first time in his career – although only just, in fourth – while his T-Mobile team-mate and compatriot Andreas Klöden stepped into the breach to finish a surprise second, with Basso third.

LONDON

ROYAUME-UNI

BELGIQUE

WATERLOO
LIÈGE

210 km

BRUXELLES

WASQUEHAL

CHARLEROI

NAMUR

ALLEMAGNE

6.1 km

197 km

202.5 km

ARRAS

CAMBRAI

AMIENS

64.5 km

200.5 km

LUXEMBOURG

PICARDIE

NORMANDIE

PARIS

163 km

204.5 km

ST-BRIEUC

LAMBALLE

km

8

QUIMPER

CHARTRES

BONNEVAL

MONTEREAU-
FAULT-YONNE

196 km

CHÂTEAUBRIANT

6

ANGERS

BESANÇON

55 km

19

LONS-LE-SAUNIER

SUISSE

166.5 km

18

ANNEMASSE

GUÉRET

160.5 km

9

ST-LÉONARD-DE-NOBLAT

LIMOGES

10

237 km

LE GRAND-
BORNAND

204.5 km

17

15.5 km

16

VILLARD-DE-LANS

L'ALPE-D'HUEZ

LE BOURG-D'OISANS

ITALIE

ST-FLOUR

15

180.5 km

FIGEAC

11

164 km

VALRÉAS

CASTELSARRASIN

NÎMES

192.5 km

197.5 km

12

14

LANNEMEZAN

CARCASSONNE

LA MONGIE

13

PLATEAU DE BEILLE

205.5 km

ANDORRE

ESPAGNE

MER MÉDITERRANÉE

225

2005
92nd Edition

*"To the people who don't believe in cycling, the cynics and the sceptics: I'm sorry for yo
I'm sorry you can't dream big, and I'm sorry you don't believe in miracles. But this is o
hell of a race. This is a great sporting event and you should stand around and belie
You should believe in these athletes, and you should believe in these people*

Lance Armstrong signs off from winning what he thought would be his last Tour de Fran

Start: Fromentine, France, on 2 July
Finish: Paris, France, on 24 July

Total distance: 3608 km (2242 miles)
Longest stage: 239.5 km (149 miles)

Highest point: Col du Galibier: 2645 m (8678 ft)
Mountain stages: 5

Starters: 189
Finishers: 155

Winning time: 86 h 15' 02"*
Average speed: 41.654 kph (25.883 mph)*

1. Lance Armstrong (USA)*
2. Ivan Basso (Ita) at 4' 40"
3. Jan Ullrich (Ger) at 6' 21"

Points: Thor Hushovd (Nor)
Mountains: Michael Rasmussen (Den)
Young rider: Yaroslav Popovych (Ukr)

* Lance Armstrong was officially stripped of his seven Tour titles in 2012, with no rider listed as the winner from 1999 to 2005

The USA's Dave Zabriskie provided the second surprise of the 2005 Tour when he blasted to victory in the prologue time trial, beating his compatriot and former team-mate Lance Armstrong by 2 seconds.

The first surprise had come just a few minutes before the final result was confirmed, when Armstrong had caught and passed the man thought likely to be one of his biggest rivals at that year's race, Jan Ullrich, who had started ahead of him in the time trial between Fromentine on the mainland and the island of Noirmoutier, reached by the Noirmoutier bridge.

Zabriskie would lose the jersey after a crash during stage 4's team time trial, won by Armstrong's Discovery Channel squad, which gave Armstrong the yellow jersey for the first time. He didn't quite wear it all the way to Paris – crowd favourite and Zabriskie's CSC team-mate Jens Voigt wore it on stage 10 before it went back to Armstrong for the remainder of the race. Armstrong then sealed the victory with a win in the final time trial.

The race also saw the emergence of Denmark's Michael Rasmussen, whose attacking style on the climbs netted him stage win and the 'king of the mountain title. He went into the final time trial in third place overall, but multiple, almost comedic, crashes lost him his podium spot to Ullrich, who had made somethin of a recovery after his disastrous start on the bridge to Noirmoutier.

Ullrich would later admit to having "made a mistake" and worked with infamous doping doctor Eufemiano Fuentes, and had his third place at the 2005 Tour wiped from the record books Along with Armstrong's later docking o his Tour victories, and second-placed Ivan Basso's later two-year suspension for intent to dope – again at the hands of Fuentes – the original 2005 Tour podiu today makes for depressing viewing.

Lance Armstrong powers past Jan Ullrich in the prolo

ROYAUME-UNI

LONDON
Southampton · Portsmouth · Brighton · Eastbourne
Exeter · Poole · Bournemouth
Lyme Bay

Cap de la Hague
Cherbourg-Octeville

Guernsey · ST PETER PORT
Îles Normandes
ST HELIER · Jersey

La Manche

BELGIQUE
BRUXELLES
Antwerpen · Gent · Brugge
Kortrijk · Flanders · Genk · Maastricht · Aachen
Lille · Mons · La Louvière · Namur · Liège · Köln
Calais · Dunkerque · Douai · Valenciennes · Charleroi
Boulogne-sur-Mer · Lens · Cambrai
Dieppe · Abbeville · Albert · Péronne · St-Quentin · Hirson · Charleville-Mézières · Sedan
Amiens · Rethel

ALLEMAGNE
Mönchengladbach
Eindhoven

LUXEMBOURG
LUXEMBOURG
Thionville · Saarbrücken
Verdun · Metz · Freyming-Merlebach
Rombas · Faulquemont · Pont-à-Mousson · Sarrebourg

PFORZHEIM
KARLSRUHE
228.5 km · 7
NANCY
Toul · Haguenau
LUNÉVILLE
Strasbourg · 8
231.5 km
GÉRARDMER
Épinal · Remiremont · Colmar
9 · 171 km
MULHOUSE
Basel · Zürich

PICARDIE
Fécamp · Yvetot · Rouen · Beauvais · Compiègne · Soissons · Laon
Le Havre · Bolbec · Elbeuf · Chantilly · Crépy-en-Valois · Château-Thierry · Reims · Châlons-en-Champagne
Baie de Seine · Honfleur · Val-de-Reuil · Mantes-la-Jolie · Senlis · Coulommiers · Epernay · Vitry-le-François · Chaumont

NORMANDIE
Caen · Lisieux · Évreux · Dreux · PARIS · Meaux · Marne-la-Vallée
St-Lô · Argentan · L'Aigle · Chartres · Boulogne-Billancourt · Versailles · BRIE · Bar-le-Duc
Vire · Flers · Alençon · Nogent-le-Rotrou · Étampes · Nemours · Fontainebleau · Romilly-sur-Seine · Langres
Granville · Avranches · Collines de Normandie

144.5 km · 21
CORBEIL-ESSONNES
MONTARGIS
TROYES · 6 · 199 km
67.5 km · Orléans
BLOIS · 212.5 km · 183 km · 5
TOURS · 4 · CHAMBORD · Gien · Auxerre · Dijon
Vendôme · Cosne-Cours-sur-Loire

St-Malo · Dinan · Fougères · Mayenne · Laval · Châteaudun
Lannion · St-Brieuc · Vitré · Le Mans
Paimpol · Guingamp · Pontivy · Rennes · La Flèche · Châteaubriant
BRETAGNE · ANJOU · St-Avertin · Loches · Bourges · Nevers · Le Creusot
Quimperlé · Vannes · Nantes · Vertou · Saumur · Vierzon · Château-Chinon · Autun
Lorient · Île de Groix · Châteaubriant · Cholet · Thouars · BERRY · Châteauroux · St-Amand-Montrond · Moulins

FRANCE

19 km · 1
NOIRMOUTIER-EN-L'ÎLE · Pornic
Île de Noirmoutier
FROMENTINE · St-Jean-de-Monts · La Roche-sur-Yon
Île d'Yeu · LES ESSARTS
CHALLANS · LA CHÂTAIGNERAIE
Les Sables-d'Olonne · 2 · Bressuire · Châtellerault · Poitiers
181.5 km · Fontenay-le-Comte · POITOU
La Rochelle · Niort · MARCHE
Île de Ré · Rochefort · BOURBONNAIS
Pointe de Chassiron

153.5 km
Clermont-Ferrand · 19
55.5 km · Villefranche-sur-Saône
Riom · Thiers · 20 · Villeurbanne
Monts du Beaujolais · Lyon
Vénissieux · Givors

192.5 km
Chambéry · 10
COURCHEVEL
Massif de la Vanoise · Torino
11 · 173 km
GRENOBLE · BRIANÇON
ITALIE

SUISSE
BERN
Lausanne · Berner Alpen
Genève · Annemasse · Bonneville · Cluses · Pennine Alps
Thonon-les-Bains · Annecy · Rumilly

OCÉAN ATLANTIQUE

ESPAGNE

SAINTONGE · LIMOUSIN · AUVERGNE
Saintes · Cognac · Angoulême · Périgueux · St-Flour · ISSOIRE
Royan · Libourne · Brive-la-Gaillarde · Tulle · Aurillac · Massif Central
MÉDOC · Bordeaux · Bergerac · ST-ÉTIENNE
St-Médard-en-Jalles · Pessac · GUYENNE · LE PUY-EN-VELAY
Andernos-les-Bains · Mérignac · GRAVES · Villeneuve-sur-Lot · Cahors · MENDE
Arcachon · La Teste-de-Buch · Marmande · Villefranche-de-Rouergue · Rodez · 189 km
Montauban · Carmaux · 18
Golfe de Gascogne · AQUITAINE · Moissac · Milhau · Lévézou
Mont-de-Marsan · Agen · ALBI
Dax · GASCOGNE · Colomiers · Toulouse · Castres
239.5 km · Auch · 17 · Muret · REVEL
Bayonne · Orthez · Mazamet
MOURENX · PAU · Tarbes · Ariège
Biarritz · Oloron-Ste-Marie · LÉZAT-SUR-LÈZE · Carcassonne
San Sebastián · Lourdes · St-Gaudens · Pamiers
Bilbao · Cordillera Cantábrica · 16 · 15 · Foix
Vitoria-Gasteiz · Pamplona · ANDORRE · 205.5 km
180.5 km · ANDORRA LA VELLA
Logroño · ST-LARY-SOULAN · AX 3 DOMAINES · ROUSSILLON · Perpignan

Vichy · Roanne
189 km
173.5 km
13 · Avignon
ALÈS · Nîmes
DIGNE-LES-BAINS · 187 km · 12
MIRAMAS · Aix-en-Provence
MONTPELLIER · AGDE · Sète · Béziers · Marseille
14 · 220.5 km · Narbonne · Durban-Corbières
CAMARGUE · PROVENCE
St-Raphaël · Fréjus · Cannes · Côte d'Azur
Nice · Monte-Carlo · Antibes
Toulon · Hyères · Six-Fours-les-Plages · Îles d'Hyères
Golfe du Lion · MER MÉDITERRANÉE

*"I think a lot of people thought I was crazy, but my way of thinking was that the o
chance I had of winning the Tour was to go from the beginning [of the stage
I didn't really know if it would work or not, but I had nothing to los*

Floyd Landis tells the press about his epic breakaway on stage

Floyd Landis and his Phonak team control the peloton from Béziers to Montéli

Start: Strasbourg, France, on 1 July
Finish: Paris, France, on 23 July

Total distance:
3657.1 km (2271 miles)
Longest stage:
230 km (143 miles)

Highest point:
Col du Galibier: 2645 m (8678 ft)
Mountain stages: 5

Starters: 176
Finishers: 139

Winning time: 89 h 40' 27"
Average speed:
40.781 kph (25.325 mph)

1. Óscar Pereiro (Spa)
2. Andreas Klöden (Ger) at 0' 32"
3. Carlos Sastre (Spa) at 2' 16"

Points: Robbie McEwen (Aus)
Mountains:
Michael Rasmussen (Den)
Young rider:
Damiano Cunego (Ita)

With Lance Armstrong having retired following the 2005 Tour, the 2006 edition was wide open.

In the build-up, perennial runners-up during the Armstrong years – Ivan Basso and Jan Ullrich – were the big favourites, but which of them was most capable of clinching the win in the American's absence?

It turned out that neither of them even made it to the start line in Strasbourg; the so-called Operación Puerto investigation in Spain into dodgy sports doctor Eufemiano Fuentes's clients unearthed a number of famous cycling names, including both Ullrich and Basso, which resulted in their respective teams pulling them out of the race. Both eventually admitted to having been in touch with Fuentes – Basso with intent to blood-dope, which earned him a two-year ban regardless of whether he actually did or not, while Ullrich's admission in 2012 to having been in contact with Fuentes was a little less specific, as he talked only of his regret, which saw the German's 2005 and 2006 results annulled.

In the race favourites' absence, American Floyd Landis – another forme team-mate of Armstrong, now riding for the Swiss Phonak outfit – came to the fore. Landis initially took the yellow jersey on stage 11, but then intentionall let it pass to the shoulders of Spanish rider Óscar Pereiro to alleviate the burden of his team having to ride to defend the jersey so early on in the race.

The stand-out performance in the 2006 Tour was Floyd Landis's epic solo breakaway. Having cracked and lost 8 minutes on the stage to La Toussuire on stage 16, it looked as though Landis was out of the running. However, the following day he simply rode away from the peloton, crossing the line alone in Morzine to put himself back within 30 seconds of Pereiro overall. Then, the superior time triallist, Landis easily reclaimed the yellow jersey in the final time trial.

Four days after the finish, it was announced that Landis had tested positive for an abnormal testosterone/epitestosterone ratio and he was strippe of the title.

An unusually perfect British summer's day saw the riders on their way from London en route to Canterbury on stage 1 of the 2007 Tour. Aussie sprinter Robbie McEwen would win the stage, while Switzerland's Fabian Cancellara held on to the race lead.

2007
94th Edition

Swift Swiss Fabian Cancellara charges down the M

Start: London, UK, on 7 July
Finish: Paris, France, on 29 July

Total distance:
3569.4 km (2217 miles)
Longest stage:
236.5 km (147 miles)

Highest point:
Col de l'Iseran: 2770 m (9088 ft)
Mountain stages: 6

Starters: 189
Finishers: 141

Winning time: 91 h 00' 26"
Average speed:
39.226 kph (24.359 mph)

1. Alberto Contador (Spa)
2. Cadel Evans (Aus) at 0' 23"
3. Levi Leipheimer (USA)
   at 0' 31"

Points: Tom Boonen (Bel)
Mountains:
Juan Mauricio Soler (Col)
Young rider:
Alberto Contador (Spa)

The 2007 Tour de France was the ultimate London to Paris bike ride as the British capital hosted the famous French race's *Grand Départ*. Against all odds, a glorious, faultless blue summer sky greeted the riders on Saturday 7 July in central London while huge crowds lined the route of the prologue course, which started on Whitehall and finished on The Mall, via Buckingham Palace, Constitution Hill and Hyde Park.

Despite the best efforts of home riders Bradley Wiggins and David Millar – who finished fourth and thirteenth, respectively – they were no match for the time-trialling man of the moment, Switzerland's Fabian Cancellara, who blasted through the London streets to take the race's first yellow jersey.

It was the third time that the Tour had come to the UK. The first time, in Plymouth in 1974, was best forgotten, but the two stages in 1994 in Kent, Sussex and Hampshire were extremely well received, and the Tour organisers had been keen to return ever since.

The second and final day of the race on British shores took the riders from London to Canterbury before the Tour entourage was ferried back to France where it picked up from Dunkirk for stage 2.

Geographically, once the race returned to the mainland, it was business as usual but the sporting side of things was about to take a turn for the worse, although it got temporarily very exciting before the wheels fell off.

Denmark's Michael Rasmussen had been a revelation at the 2006 Tour, attacking constantly in the mountains, which gave him the polka-dot jersey, as well as a stage win.

Along with a wiry, young Spanish rider called Alberto Contador, Rasmussen set the 2007 Tour alight in the Alps and the Pyrenees, and the two looked set to batt it out all the way to Paris – until Rasmussen was thrown off the race whil in the yellow jersey, after it was revealed that he'd lied on his 'whereabouts' form for dope testers to be able to find him in the run-up to the race, and so his Rabobank team reluctantly sent him packing.

In Paris, 24-year-old Contador won his first Tour, just 23 seconds ahead of runner-up Cadel Evans of Australia, and only 31 seconds ahead of US rider Levi Leipheimer.

ROYAUME-UNI

LONDON
P
7.9 km
CANTERBURY
1
203 km

La Manche

BELGIQUE
168.5 km
2
GHENT
Brugge
DUNKIRK
Kortrijk
WAREGEM
Lille

ALLEMAGNE

3
236.5 km

PICARDIE

COMPIÈGNE
VILLERS-
COTTERÊTS
193 km
4

PARIS
146 km
20
MARCOUSSIS

FRANCE

JOIGNY
182.5 km
5
CHABLIS
SEMUR-EN-AUXOIS
AUTUN
199.5 km
6

SUISSE

BOURG-EN-BRESSE
197.5 km
7
LE GRAND-
BORNAND
8
165 km
TIGNES
VAL-D'ISÈRE
159.5 km
9

55.5 km
19
COGNAC
ANGOULÊME

OCÉAN
ATLANTIQUE

211 km
18
CAHORS

BRIANÇON

ITALIE

TALLARD
54 km
178.5 km
ALBI
13
229 km
10

CASTELSARRASIN
188.5 km
CASTRES
12
MONTPELLIER
MAZAMET
11
182.5 km
MARSEILLE

ORTHEZ
PAU
17
218.5 km
16
196 km
15
FOIX
14
197 km

GOURETTE-
COL D'AUBISQUE
LOUDENVIELLE
PLATEAU-
DE-BEILLE

ESPAGNE

MER MÉDITERRANÉE

233

Brest, in Brittany, waved off the start of the ninety-fifth Tour de France – a race with no defending champion due to Alberto Contador having left Discovery Channel to join the Kazakh Astana team for the 2008 season. Astana posted two positive dope tests by way of Alexandre Vinokourov and Andrey Kashechkin during the 2007 Tour. The Tour organisers didn't invite the team as a result; the last thing the race needed was any more doping scandals.

Spain's Carlos Sastre stepped up to the plate, but Lance Armstrong would later call Sastre's 2008 Tour win "a bit of a joke", although that attack was tempered when Sastre's CSC team manager Bjarne Riis, whose own Tour win in 1996 was achieved through the use of EPO, found Tour organiser Christian Prudhomme on the finish line on the Champs-Élysées to present Sastre to him with the words, "Here's your clean Tour winner," suggesting an element of redemption on Riis's part and a suggestion that in a sea of suspicion and uncertainty, Sastre, at least, could be counted on as a paragon of virtue.

Armstrong later apologised to the Spaniard, but the American's barb had referred to the relative lack of competition that Sastre faced in the Astana team's absence, and in fact one of the biggest challenges for the CSC-Saxo Bank squad was trying to manage the ambitions of both Sastre and the Schleck brothers, Andy and Frank.

When Sastre finally took the yellow jersey – by winning on top of Alpe d'Huez – it was from his own team-mate, the yellow-clad Frank Schleck, who wasn't allowed to react to the attack and just had to mark their team's rivals.

The dinner table at the team's hotel

that night must have been a little quiet t say the least, but Sastre proved they had backed the right man by limiting his losses to Cadel Evans in the final time trial, and the final result was a 58-secon win over the Australian in Paris.

Carlos Sastre attacks on Alpe d'Huez to seal overall victo

Start: Brest, France, on 5 July
Finish: Paris, France, on 27 July

Total distance:
3559.5 km (2211 miles)
Longest stage:
232 km (144 miles)

Highest point:
Cime de la Bonette:
2802 m (9193 ft)
Mountain stages: 5

Starters: 180
Finishers: 145

Winning time: 87 h 52' 52"
Average speed:
40.504 kph (25.153 mph)

1. Carlos Sastre (Spa)
2. Cadel Evans (Aus) at 0' 58"
3. Bernhard Kohl (Aut) at 1' 13"

Points: Óscar Freire (Spa)
Mountains: Bernhard Kohl (Aut)
Young rider: Andy Schleck (Lux)

LONDON

ROYAUME-UNI

BELGIQUE

ALLEMAGNE

LUXEMBOURG

SUISSE

FRANCE

ITALIE

ESPAGNE

OCÉAN
ATLANTIQUE

La Manche

164.5 km
ST-BRIEUC
ST-MALO
2
1
97.5 km
PLUMELEC
AURAY
3
208 km

143 km
PARIS
21
ÉTAMPES

232 km
CHOLET
5
NANTES
4
29.5 km
CHÂTEAUROUX
AIGURANDE
6
195.5 km

ST-AMAND-MONTROND
20
53 km
CÉRILLY
MONTLUÇON
19
ROANNE
165.5 km

196.5 km
L'ALPE-D'HUEZ
17
210.5 km

SUPERBESSE
BRIOUDE
ST-ÉTIENNE
18
LE BOURG-D'OISANS
183 km
CUNEO
15
EMBRUN
JAUSIERS
16
PRATO NEVOSO
DIGNE-LES-BAINS
157 km

AURILLAC
7
FIGEAC
159 km

172.5 km
8
TOULOUSE
224 km
LANNEMEZAN
9
PAU
10
156 km
HAUTACAM
BAGNÈRES-DE-BIGORRE
167.5 km
11
FOIX
LAVELANET
12
168.5 km
NARBONNE
13
182 km
NÎMES
14
194.5 km

235

Lance Armstrong makes his Tour comeback in Mona[co]

Start: Monaco, on 4 July
Finish: Paris, France, on 26 July

Total distance:
3459.5 km (2148 miles)
Longest stage:
224 km (139 miles)

Highest point:
Col du Grand-St-Bernard:
2473 m (8113 ft)
Mountain stages: 7

Starters: 180
Finishers: 156

Winning time: 85 h 48' 35"
Average speed:
40.316 kph (25.036 mph)

1. Alberto Contador (Spa)
2. Andy Schleck (Lux) at 4' 11"
3. Lance Armstrong (USA)
   at 5' 24"

Points: Thor Hushovd (Nor)
Mountains: Franco Pellizotti (Ita)
Young rider: Andy Schleck (Lux)

Astana were back for the 2009 Tour, and this time they'd swelled their ranks with a certain Lance Armstrong, who had decided to make a comeback to the sport. It created a big buzz around that year's Tour, which was exaggerated by the fact that the race was starting in the principality of Monaco.

It was pretty clear, however, that new team-mates Contador and Armstrong weren't exactly the best of friends, and they spent most of the race doing their own thing, apart from in the team time trial on stage 4, after which Armstrong missed out on wresting the yellow jersey from Fabian Cancellara's shoulders by just two-tenths of a second. After 2005, Armstrong would in fact never wear the yellow jersey again.

The 2008 Tour winner Carlos Sastre was nowhere to be seen – the Spanish climber eventually finished seventeenth overall – while British time trial specialist Bradley Wiggins had started his 2009 season in better shape than ever, having lost weight and decided to concentrate solely on the road after winning two gold medals on the track during the Beijing Olympics.

Nevertheless, Wiggins surprised everyone – not least himself – by keeping in contact with the likes of the Schleck brothers, Contador and Armstrong in the big mountains, earning himself fourth place overall in Paris. Since Armstrong finished a place ahead of Wiggins, in third, but has since had his Tour results scrubbed out, one could argue that Wiggins completed the 2009 podium – albeit not officially. Besides, he would go on to top the podium just a few years later.

Britain's Mark Cavendish was beginning to put sprinting back on the map at the Tour, too, having won four stages at the 2008 edition, while in 2009 he won a quite astonishing six stages.

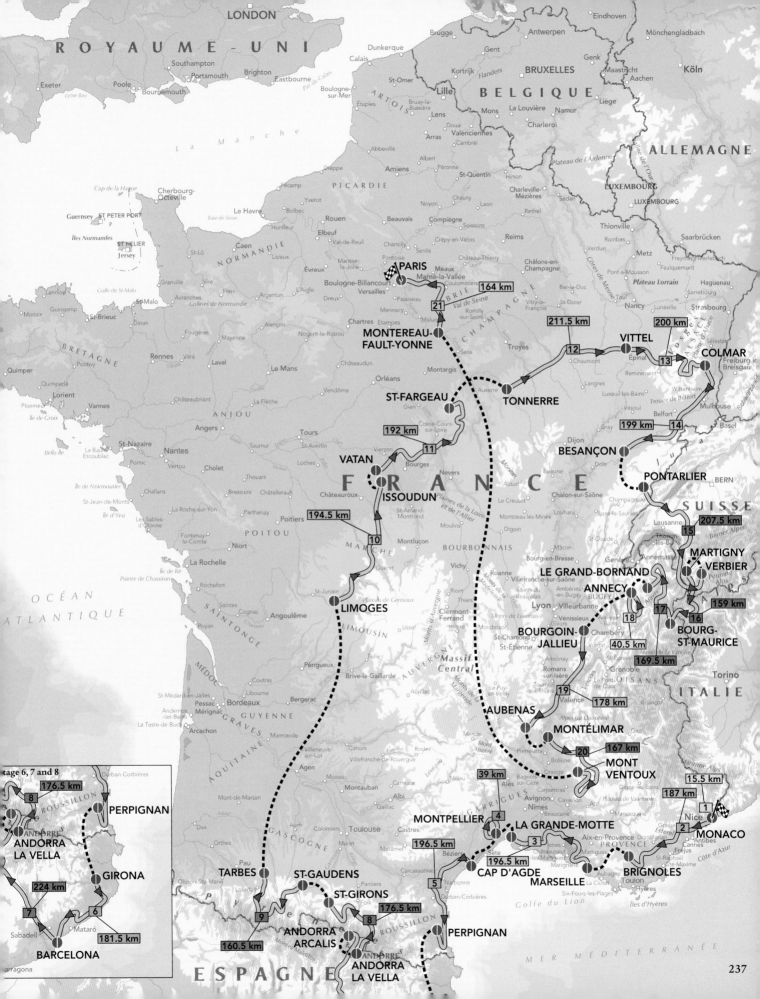

LONDON

ROYAUME-UNI

BELGIQUE

BRUXELLES

ALLEMAGNE

LUXEMBOURG

PARIS

164 km
21

MONTEREAU-
FAULT-YONNE

211.5 km
12

VITTEL

200 km
13

COLMAR

ST-FARGEAU

TONNERRE

199 km
14

192 km
11

VATAN

BESANÇON

PONTARLIER

SUISSE

194.5 km
10

ISSOUDUN

F R A N C E

207.5 km
15

MARTIGNY
VERBIER

159 km
16

LE GRAND-BORNAND

ANNECY

BOURG-
ST-MAURICE

LIMOGES

BOURGOIN-
JALLIEU

40.5 km
18

17

169.5 km

OCÉAN ATLANTIQUE

ITALIE

19

178 km

AUBENAS

MONTÉLIMAR

167 km
20

MONT
VENTOUX

15.5 km
1

187 km

39 km

Nice

Stage 6, 7 and 8

176.5 km
8

PERPIGNAN

MONTPELLIER

4

LA GRANDE-MOTTE

2

MONACO

ANDORRA
LA VELLA

GIRONA

3

196.5 km

BRIGNOLES

224 km

MARSEILLE

7

181.5 km
6

196.5 km

CAP D'AGDE

5

BARCELONA

TARBES

ST-GAUDENS

ST-GIRONS

176.5 km
8

9

PERPIGNAN

160.5 km

ANDORRA
ARCALIS

ANDORRE
LA VELLA

ESPAGNE

MER MÉDITERRANÉE

237

2010
97th Edition

Start: Rotterdam, Netherlands, on 3 July
Finish: Paris, France, on 25 July

Total distance:
3641.9 km (2263 miles)
Longest stage:
228 km (141 miles)

Highest point:
Col du Tourmalet:
2115 m (6939 ft)
Mountain stages: 6

Starters: 198
Finishers: 169

Winning time: 91 h 59' 27"
Average speed:
39.585 kph (24.582 mph)

1. Andy Schleck (Lux)
2. Denis Menchov (Rus) at 1' 22"
3. Samuel Sánchez (Spa) at 3' 01"

Points: Alessandro Petacchi (Ita)
Mountains:
Anthony Charteau (Fra)
Young rider: Andy Schleck (Lux)

Alberto Contador – Tour winner in both 2007 and 2009 – dominated proceedings at the 2010 Tour, both on the road and in the aftermath.

Things had got under way innocently enough in the famous port of Rotterdam in the Netherlands, where Saxo Bank's Fabian Cancellara got the better of HTC's German TT specialist Tony Martin to the tune of 10 seconds.

On stage 15, however, came 'Chaingate'. While climbing the Port de Balès in the Pyrenees, Andy Schleck managed to unship his chain – which seemed like the perfect opportunity, Contador must have thought, to attack the stricken Luxembourger. Schleck was, quite rightly, furious – but no one could ever have quite foreseen that Schleck would ever end up as the winner of the 2010 Tour when he physically finished second to Contador in Paris by 39 seconds (ironically the same amount of time that he lost to Contador as a result of his mechanical problem).

Schleck was awarded the title at a special ceremony in February 2012 after Contador had been disqualified from taking a third title due to testing positive for the drug clenbuterol during the race.

Lance Armstrong, riding his last Tour for his new RadioShack team, was the victim of a number of crashes, which put him out of immediate contention, and he limped home in his last Tour in a lowly twenty-third place.

Besides RadioShack, there was another new kid on the block: British team Sky – a top-notch outfit boasting some of the world's best riders – which came at just the right moment as Mark Cavendish and Bradley Wiggins, on the back of the 2008 Olympics success in track cycling, had helped to pull in interest on the road, too.

Wiggins had broken his contract with Jonathan Vaughters' Garmin squad to join his 'home' team for 2010 and, by 2012, Cavendish had been persuaded to sign up at Sky, too.

Alberto Contador's celebrations were short lived, with the Spaniard subsequently stripped of his title after a positive drugs te

ROYAUME-UNI

LONDON

ALLEMAGNE

BELGIQUE

ROTTERDAM
223.5 km
1
P
8.9 km

BRUSSELS
2 201 km
WANZE
3
SPA
213 km

ARENBERG-PORTE DU HAINAUT
CAMBRAI
153.5 km
4

REIMS
ÉPERNAY
5
187.5 km

PARIS
102.5 km
20
LONGJUMEAU

MONTARGIS
227.5 km
6

FRANCE

165.5 km
STATION DES ROUSSES
GUEUGNON
TOURNUS
7
MORZINE-AVORIAZ
189 km
8
9
204.5 km
SAVOIE

CHAMBÉRY
ST-JEAN-DE-MAURIENNE

BOURG-DE-PÉAGE
210.5 km
12
BOURG-LÈS-VALENCE
10
179 km
ITALIE

PAUILLAC
52 km
19

BORDEAUX

MENDE
RODEZ
GAP
184.5 km
SISTERON
11

198 km
18

SALIES-DE-BÉARN
PAU 199.5 km
187.5 km
PAMIERS
184.5 km
REVEL
196 km
13
14
15
16
17
174 km
COL DU TOURMALET
LUCHON
AX 3 DOMAINES

239

"I'm still alive. Wouter Weylandt wasn't that luck[...]
Dutch rider Johnny Hoogerland remains philosophical after being knocked from his bike b[...]
press car and suffering deep lacerations having landed on a barbed-wire fence on stage[...]
remembering Belgian rider Weylandt who had died in a crash at the Giro d'Italia two months earl[...]

The race sets off over the tidal Passage du G[...]

Start: Passage du Gois, France, on 2 July
Finish: Paris, France, on 24 July

Total distance:
3430 km (2130 miles)
Longest stage:
226.5 km (141 miles)

Highest point:
Col Agnel: 2744 m (9003 ft)
Mountain stages: 6

Starters: 198
Finishers: 167

Winning time: 86 h 12' 22"
Average speed:
39.788 kph (24.708 mph)

1. Cadel Evans (Aus)
2. Andy Schleck (Lux) at 1' 34"
3. Frank Schleck (Lux) at 2' 30"

Points: Mark Cavendish (GBr)
Mountains: Samuel Sánchez (Spa)
Young rider: Pierre Rolland (Fra)

The 2011 Tour started with a procession across the Passage du Gois – a road submerged by the tide twice a day, which links the island of Noirmoutier with the French mainland. It had infamously been used in the 1999 Tour, too, when a number of riders fell foul of its slippery surface and crashed out. This time, the organisers saw sense, and stage 1 was only waved officially on its way once everyone had ridden across the unusual stretch of road in one piece.

There was an even greater focus than usual on the Alps in the 2011 edition of the race, which celebrated the 100th-year anniversary of the mountain range first being included in the race.

Tour director Christian Prudhomme described in *Cycle Sport* magazine how one stage of his 2011 race, in particular, really brought home the bacon.

"I'd gone ahead of the race on the Col d'Izoard (stage 18), and was at the Fausto Coppi and Louison Bobet monument laying some flowers, along with Eddy Merckx, Bernard Hinault and Bernard Thévenet. Then the race radio, in the car just a few metres away, crackled into life: 'Attack by Andy Schleck!' And suddenly

I was a little boy again, listening to the radio, in love with cycling, yet this time [...] was in this amazingly privileged positio[...] surrounded by the biggest names in cycling history – Hinault, Thévenet, Merckx, Coppi, Bobet – with Schleck going on the attack more than 60 km (37 miles) from the finish."

Schleck won the stage, but it was Cade[...] Evans who stood proudly atop the final podium on the Champs-Élysées in Paris [...] as the race's first Australian winner. Almost as proud, however, were Schleck and older brother Frank, who finished second and third overall, becoming the first siblings to finish together on the podium.

Sprint star Mark Cavendish, meanwhi[...] overhauled Spain's José Joaquín Rojas t[...] become the first British rider to win the green points jersey, which was only the second Tour de France 'competition jersey' to be won by a Briton after Rober[...] Millar's 'king of the mountains' title – with its accompanying polka-dot jersey – in 1984.

Bradley Wiggins's yellow jersey was sti[...] a year away...

LONDON

ROYAUME-UNI

BELGIQUE

ALLEMAGNE

LUXEMBOURG

SUISSE

FRANCE

ESPAGNE

ITALIE

OCÉAN ATLANTIQUE

MER MÉDITERRANÉE

Golfe du Gascogne

Golfe du Lion

La Manche

164.5 km 5 CAP FRÉHEL

CARHAIX

DINAN

MÛR-DE-BRETAGNE

172.5 km 4 LORIENT

REDON

198 km 3

23 km 2 LES ESSARTS

PASSAGE DU GOIS 1 MONT DES ALOUETTES

OLONNE-SUR-MER

191.5 km

226.5 km 6 LISIEUX

PARIS

95 km 21 CRÉTEIL

LE MANS

218 km 7

CHÂTEAUROUX

AIGURANDE

189 km 8

ISSOIRE

SUPERBESSE SANCY

208 km 9

AURILLAC

ST-FLOUR

158 km 10

CARMAUX

BLAYE-LES-MINES

LAVAUR 11 167.5 km

211 km

CUGNAUX

152.5 km 13 PAU

LOURDES 12 ST-GAUDENS

LUZ-ARDIDEN 14 168.5 km

PLATEAU DE BEILLE

LIMOUX

15 192.5 km

MONTPELLIER

ST-PAUL-TROIS-CHÂTEAUX

16 162.5 km

GAP

GALIBIER/SERRE-CHEVALIER 17

179 km

18 200.5 km

PINEROLO

MODANE 19

L'ALPE-D'HUEZ 109.5 km

GRENOBLE

42.5 km 20

241

Overall winner Bradley Wiggins leads out world champion and Sky team-mate Mark Cavendish on the Champs-Élysées. This was Cavendish's third stage win of the 2012 Tour and his twenty-third career Tour stage victory, while Wiggins became the first Briton to win the Tour.

"We're just going to draw the raffle numbers now
Bradley Wiggins takes to the microphone on
Champs-Élysées in Paris to give his victory speech to the wo

Start: Liège, Belgium, on 30 June
Finish: Paris, France, on 22 July

Total distance:
3496.9 km (2172 miles)
Longest stage:
226 km (140 miles)

Highest point:
Col du Tourmalet:
2115 m (6939 ft)
Mountain stages: 5

Starters: 198
Finishers: 153

Winning time: 87 h 34' 47"
Average speed:
39.80 kph (24.734 mph)

1. Bradley Wiggins (GBr)
2. Chris Froome (GBr) at 3' 21"
3. Vincenzo Nibali (Ita) at 6' 19"

Points: Peter Sagan (Svk)
Mountains: Thomas Voeckler (Fra)
Young rider:
Tejay van Garderen (USA)

Bradley Wiggins arrived at the 2012 as ready as he would, or could, ever be, having dedicated himself to a brutal training regime in the first half of the year, while targeting just a handful of stage races to hone his form.

The Briton finished third overall at the Tour of the Algarve in February, then won Paris-Nice, the Tour of Romandy and the Critérium du Dauphiné in June. By 30 June – the start of the Tour – he'd hit peak fitness.

Just as it had in 2004, Liège, Belgium, hosted the start of the race, and in the prologue time trial history repeated itself as Fabian Cancellara did exactly what he had done in Liége in 2004, blasting to the win and the race's first yellow jersey. Wiggins finished second, just 7 seconds off the pace, but went on to win both of the race's other, longer time trials, on stages 9 and 19.

Second in turn to Wiggins at both of those time trials was his British Team Sky team-mate Chris Froome, who proved to be a key lieutenant in the mountains, and whose consistently strong riding netted him second overall in Paris. They were ably aided and abetted by Michael Rogers and Richie Porte, both of whom took a bit of stick for being Aussie riders helping a Pom to win the Tour. Fellow Aussie Cadel Evans – the defending champion on rival team BMC – never enjoyed the same level of team support as Wiggins at Sky, who some – controversially – opined looked like Lance Armstrong's US Postal squad in the early 2000s, such was their dominance in the race.

2012 saw Bradley Wiggins become the f
British rider to win the Tour de Fra

LONDON

ROYAUME-UNI

BELGIQUE

BOULOGNE-SUR-MER
197 km
3
TOURNAI
207.5 km
2
VISÉ
P
6.4 km
SERAING
LIÈGE
ORCHIES
ALLEMAGNE
ABBEVILLE
214.5 km
4
LUXEMBOURG
198 km
1
ST-QUENTIN
ROUEN
5
196.5 km
ÉPERNAY
207.5 km
6
METZ
PARIS
RAMBOUILLET
20
TOMBLAINE
7
199 km
CHARTRES
120 km
LA PLANCHE DES BELLES FILLES
19
53.5 km
BONNEVAL
BELFORT
PORRENTRUY
FRANCE
BESANÇON
8
157.5 km
ARC-ET-SENANS
9
41.5 km
SUISSE
MÂCON
BELLEGARDE-SUR-VALSERINE
10
BRIVE-LA-GAILLARDE
194.5 km
ALBERTVILLE
ANNONAY/DAVÉZIEUX
12
ST-JEAN-DE-MAURIENNE
11
LA TOUSSUIRE/LES SYBELLES
226 km
148 km
ITALIE
18
222.5 km
ST-PAUL-TROIS-CHÂTEAUX
217 km
BLAGNAC
13
158.5 km
15
SAMATAN
143.5 km
PAU
17
CAP D'AGDE
FOIX
LIMOUX
191 km
16
14
197 km
PEYRAGUDES
LUCHON
ESPAGNE

245

Start: Porto-Vecchio, France,
on 29 June
Finish: Paris, France, on 21 July

Total distance:
3403.5 km (2115 miles)
Longest stage:
242 km (150 miles)

Highest point: Col de Pailhères:
2001 m (6565 ft)
Mountain stages: 7

Starters: 198
Finishers: 169

Winning time: 83 h 56' 40"
Average speed:
40.55 kph (25.20 mph)

1. Chris Froome (GBr)
2. Nairo Alexander Quintana
   Rojas (Col) at 4' 20"
3. Joaquim Rodriguez Oliver
   (Spa) at 5' 04"

Points: Peter Sagan (Svk)
Mountains: Nairo Alexander
Quintana Rojas (Col)
Young rider: Nairo Alexander
Quintana Rojas (Col)

Britain's Chris Froome went one better than his runner's-up spot behind Sky team-mate Bradley Wiggins in 2012 to become the winner of the 100th edition of the Tour de France.

Just like fellow Briton Wiggins's results the year before, Froome's build-up races indicated exactly what was to come. Already in February, Froome had won the Tour of Oman, then Critérium International in Corsica in March, and the Tour de Romandie in late April. Victory at June's Critérium du Dauphiné — the same Alpine stage race Wiggins had won ahead of the Tour in 2012 — showed that Froome really was ready to go.

The spectacular Grand Départ in Corsica saw German sprinter Marcel Kittel win the opening stage and wear the race's first yellow jersey, which passed to Jan Bakelants the next day after the Belgian, with the peloton bearing down on him, held on for a thrilling solo stage victory.

Along with Sky, Australian outfit Orica-GreenEdge enjoyed an excellent race, with a win by Simon Gerrans on stage three and then victory for the squad in stage four's team time trial in Nice, back on the French mainland, which also gave Gerrans yellow. He then passed it on to team-mate Daryl Impey at the conclusi of stage six; Impey became the first Sou African to wear cycling's ultimate prize.

It was from Impey that Froome first took the jersey, annihilating his rivals on stage eight and its summit finish at Ax 3 Domaines in the Pyrenees, and defending the lead for the rest of the ra

Sky's own Aussie, Richie Porte, repeat his excellent work of 2012, but with Wiggins not there to defend his title, and Froome elevated to team leader, it was Porte who became Froome's right-hand man, demonstrating that he, too, has all the makings of a future grand-tour champion.

An excellent ride by Nairo Quintana looked as though it was going to reward him with the white jersey as best young rider, but a late surge by the Colombian climber also netted him the 'king of the mountains' title and, most importantly of all, the second step on the podium in Paris.

Quintana had shown that he has the ability to one day go a step higher, while a below-par Alberto Contador — winner in 2007 and 2009 — finished in Paris kee to forget his fourth place overall, after Spanish compatriot Joaquim Rodriguez had rounded out the top three.

Chris Froome, in yellow, is shepherded home at the front of the peloton by his Sky team-ma

2014

101st Edition

Start: Leeds, UK, on 5 July
Finish: Paris, France, on 27 July

Total distance:
3656 km (2272 miles)
Longest stage:
237 km (147 miles)

Highest point: Col d'Izoard:
2360 m (7742 ft)
Mountain stages: 6

You could be forgiven for thinking, after all the excitement of the 100th edition of the Tour de France in 2013 — its Grand Départ in Corsica, climbs of both Alpe d'Huez and Mont Ventoux, and a stunning dusk finish on the Champs-Elysées in Paris — that the Tour might be happy to stay out of the limelight and revert to a more traditional, almost less impressive route for 2014.

But you'd be wrong. A Grand Départ in Yorkshire — the furthest north the race has ever started — takes the Tour to the heartland of British cycling, and provides yet another exciting and original start to the race. There's also a return to London, which hosted the start of the 2007 Tour, for the finish of stage three, before a return to France that takes in the cobbles of northern France, the tough climbs of the Alps and the Pyrenees and a grand finale in Paris.

Having featured in the 100th edition, neither the Ventoux nor Alpe d'Huez appear in 2014; the Tour's two most iconic climbs have been given a year off. But there are plenty of celebrated mountains on the menu to whet the appetite nevertheless, and the Col d'Izoard, Pla d'Adet, the Col du Tourmalet and Hautacam all feature.

Assuming good health and an injury-free build-up, defending champion Chris Froome is likely to start as the favourite, while Sky team-mate — and 2012 champion — Bradley Wiggins, who missed the 2013 edition, should be an extremely able co-captain. Earlier in the 2014 season, Nairo Quintana — runner-up in 2013 — wasn't certain to start in Yorkshire, potentially targeting victory at the Tour of Italy and the Tour of Spain instead. But regardless of whether the Colombian lines up to challenge Team Sky's Tour dominance, Froome et al will face stiff competition from the likes of Spain's Alberto Contador and Luxembourg's Schleck brothers, who are both hoping for a return to form — Fran from a year ban for a positive test for the diuretic drug xipamide and Andy from the long-term effects of a pelvis fracture sustained in 2012. If all the potential contenders do make it to the start line in Leeds on July 5th, the 2014 Tour has all the makings of a classic race.

2014 sees the Tour return to its most well u climb, the Col du Tourmalet. Thomas Voec shows the pain required to be first over summit when it was last climbed in 20

Middlesbrough

191 km 1 HARROGATE
YORK
198 km 2 LEEDS
Huddersfield
SHEFFIELD
Manchester
Liverpool

ROYAUME-UNI
Birmingham
Norwich
CAMBRIDGE
159 km 3
Milton Keynes
Gloucester Luton
Oxford
LONDON

Swansea
Cardiff Bristol
Exeter
Plymouth

PAYS-BAS
AMSTERDAM
'S-GRAVENHAGE
Rotterdam

156 km 5
YPRES
ARENBERG,
PORTE DU HAINAUT
BELGIQUE
BRUXELLES
ALLEMAGNE

LE TOUQUET
PARIS-PLAGE
164 km 4
LILLE
ARRAS

6 194 km
PICARDIE

233 km 7
REIMS
ÉPERNAY
TOMBLAINE
NANCY 8
161 km
GÉRARDMER
161 km 10 9 166 km
LA PLANCHE DES
BELLES FILLES
MULHOUSE

PARIS
EVRY
136 km 21
186 km 11
BESANÇON
SUISSE

FRANCE

BOURG-EN-BRESSE
183 km
OYONNAX
12
ST-ÉTIENNE 13 200 km
GRENOBLE CHAMROUSSE
14
177 km RISOUL
TALLARD
222 km
15
NÎMES

PÉRIGUEUX 20
54 km BERGERAC
208 km 19

MAUBOURGUET,
VAL D'ADOUR
145 km 18
PAU
HAUTACAM
SAINT-
GAUDENS
CARCASSONNE
237 km
16
BAGNÈRES-
DE-LUCHON
SAINT-LARY-SOULAN, 17
PLA D'ADET
125 km
ANDORRE

ESPAGNE

Stages 1 to 3

Stage: 1
Start: Leeds
Finish: Harrogate

Classification: Flat
Distance: 191 km (118 miles)

Stage: 2
Start: York
Finish: Sheffield

Classification: Hilly
Distance: 198 km (123 miles)

Stage: 3
Start: Cambridge
Finish: London

Classification: Flat
Distance: 159 km (98 miles)

The 2014 Tour's opening stage, between Leeds and Harrogate, virtually invites home hero Mark Cavendish to win the race's first yellow jersey, finishing as it does in the town where his mother lives; whoever wins this flat first stage will take it. But when he had that opportunity in 2013, on a similar opening stage in Corsica, Cavendish was thwarted by German fast-man Marcel Kittel, who went on to win another three stages, to Cavendish's eventual two.

Whoever wears the *maillot jaune* on the second stage from York to Sheffield will be hard-pressed to defend it on a much lumpier affair that threatens to shake up the general classification once more. The principal difficulty along the way is the climb of Holme Moss, in the Pennines, which will be familiar to many thanks to multiple appearances on the route of the Tour of Britain over the years. The sprinters' teams will have their work cut out to try to keep things in check, and the other teams will all be hoping to get a man into whichever breakaway eventually sticks.

The race then leaves Yorkshire behind with a road transfer south to Cambridge for the start of the third and final stage on British shores. The day's route heads down through Essex and into central London, where a spectacular sprint finish on The Mall is on the cards. Many of those among what will be huge crowds hoping for a Cavendish win will remember the 2007 Tour having started here when a prologue time trial was won by Swiss powerhouse Fabian Cancellara, who rolled out from The Mall again the next day in yellow en route to Canterbury, where Australian sprinter Robbie McEwen took the stage victory.

But in 2014, the London stage finish signals the end of the race's time in the UK, and a hop across the Channel to the coastal resort of Le Touquet for the start of stage four puts the 'France' back into 'Tour de France'.

After two days in the wilds of the Yorkshire Dales and the Peak District, stage 3 sets off from the beautiful university city of Cambridge.

Glasgow · Edinburgh

Newcastle upon Tyne

Carlisle

Middlesbrough

Belfast

Blackpool · Preston · **HARROGATE** · **YORK**
191 km · 1
198 km · 2 · **LEEDS** · Kingston upon Hull
Manchester · Bolton · Huddersfield
Liverpool · St Helens · Stockport · **SHEFFIELD**

R O Y A U M E - U N I

Stoke-on-Trent · Nottingham · Norwich
Derby
Telford · Wolverhampton · Leicester · Peterborough
Birmingham · Northampton
CAMBRIDGE · Ipswich
159 km · 3 · Colchester
Milton Keynes
Gloucester · Oxford · Luton
Watford
Cardiff · Bristol · **LONDON**

Swansea

Southampton · Brighton · Eastbourne
Bournemouth · Portsmouth · Dunkerque · Brugge
Poole · Calais · YPRES · Gent · Antwerpen
Exeter · Lyme Bay · Boulogne-sur-Mer · Kortrijk · 156 km · 5 · Flanders · BRUXELLES
Plymouth · La Manche · St-Omer · LILLE · Maastricht · Aachen
LE TOUQUET · 4 · Bruay-la-Bussière · ARENBERG, · Liège
PARIS-PLAGE · 164 km · Lens · PORTE DU HAINAUT · Charleroi
ARRAS · Douai · Valenciennes · BELGIQUE
Abbeville · Cambrai · Plateau de l'Ardenne
Cap de la Hague · Dieppe · Amiens · St-Quentin · LUXEMBOURG
Cherbourg-Octeville · PICARDIE · Péronne · Hirson · LUXEMBOURG
Guernsey · ST PETER PORT · Fécamp · 6 · Chauny · Laon · Sedan · Thionville
Îles Normandes · Yvetot · 194 km · Noyon · Charleville-Mézières · Metz
Baie de Seine · Bolbec · Rouen · Compiègne · Soissons · Rethel
ST HELIER · Val-de-Reuil · Beauvais · REIMS · 233 km
Jersey · St-Lô · Elbeuf · Chantilly · Crépy-en-Valois · Verdun · 7
Caen · Lisieux · Honfleur · Senlis · Château-Thierry · Châlons-en-Champagne
Granville · NORMANDIE · Évreux · Mantes-la-Jolie · Pontoise · ÉPERNAY · Bar-le-Duc
Avranches · Vire · Argentan · L'Aigle · PARIS · Meaux · Coulommiers · Vitry-le-François · St-Dizier
Collines de Normandie · Dreux · Boulogne-Billancourt · Marne-la- · BRIE · NANCY
St-Brieuc · Dinan · Versailles · Palaiseau · Vallée · Val de Seine · TOMBLAINE
136 km · 21 · Mennecy
BRETAGNE · Alençon · Chartres · ÉVRY · Montereau- · Chaumont
Lannion · Mayenne · Étampes · Fault-Yonne · Langres
Morlaix · Le Mans · Nemours · CHAMPAGNE
Brest · Guingamp · Laval · Nogent-le-Rotrou · Sens · Troyes
Douarnenez · Pontivy · La Flèche · Châteaudun · Auxerre
Quimper · Rennes · ANJOU · Montargis · Vesoul
Quimperlé · Vitré · Orléans · Gien · Dijon · Gray
Lorient · Vannes · Châteaubriant · Vendôme · Cosne-Cours-sur-Loire · BESANÇON
Ploemeur · Angers · Tours · St-Avertin · 186 km · Dole · 11
Île de Groix · Saumur · Loches · Vierzon · Nevers · Beaune
St-Nazaire · Nantes · La Baule-Escoublac · Cholet · F R A N C E · Bourges · BERRY · Chalon-sur-Saône
Pornic · Vertou · Thouars · Châteauroux
Belle-Île · Challans · Bressuire
Île de Noirmoutier · La Roche-sur-Yon · Parthenay · St-Jean-de-Monts

251

Stages 4 to 10

Stage: 4
Start: Le Touquet Paris-Plage
Finish: Lille

Classification: Hilly
Distance: 164 km (101 miles)

Stage: 5
Start: Ypres
Finish: Arenberg, Porte du Hainaut

Classification: Flat
Distance: 156 km (96 miles)

Stage: 6
Start: Arras
Finish: Reims

Classification: Flat
Distance: 194 km (120 miles)

Stage: 7
Start: Épernay
Finish: Nancy

Classification: Flat
Distance: 233 km (144 miles)

Stage: 8
Start: Tomblaine
Finish: Gérardmer

Classification: Hilly
Distance: 161 km (100 miles)

Stage: 9
Start: Gérardmer
Finish: Mulhouse

Classification: Hilly
Distance: 166 km (103 miles)

Stage: 10
Start: Mulhouse
Finish: La Planche des Belles Filles

Classification: Mountains
Distance: 161 km (100 miles)

Once back on French soil, it's not long before the race heads off piste again — this time into Belgium. The Ypres start to stage five commemorates 100 years since the start of the First World War, when the Flemish town was of key strategic importance. What's likely to be an emotional start to the day's stage will give way to a time of difficulty of a different kind as the peloton take on the cobblestones that only just about pave many of the roads of northern France, and will be familiar to both riders and fans from the route of the Paris-Roubaix one-day race. The last time the Tour came through this part of the world, and across these cobbles, was in 2010, when crashes galore brought down a number of big names, and put paid to overall contender Frank Schleck's ambitions when he had to retire from stage three with a broken collarbone. They'll all be trying to avoid such a fate this time in the hopes of heading into the Vosges mountains on stage eight in the best condition possib

The mountain range in north-east France is not a patch on the upcoming Alps or Pyrenees, but the *ballons* — meaning ball, or balloon, thanks to the climbs' rounded, rather than peaked, summits — come thick and fast around here for three stages, culminating with the tough finish at La Planche des Belle Filles on stage 10. It was here on the seventh stage of the 2012 Tour that Chr Froome showed 2011 champion Cadel Evans a clean pair of heels to take the stage win, while Bradley Wiggins took third, and with it the yellow jersey, whic he then held on to all the way to Paris. The climb should again show who the real favourites are for the 2014 title.

Jens Voigt checks on his injured team-mate Frank Schleck after a crash during stage 3 of the 2010 Tour de Fra

Stages 11 to 15

Stage: 11
Start: Besançon
Finish: Oyonnax

Classification: Flat
Distance: 186 km (115 miles)

Stage: 12
Start: Bourg-en-Bresse
Finish: St-Étienne

Classification: Hilly
Distance: 183 km (113 miles)

Stage: 13
Start: St-Étienne
Finish: Chamrousse

Classification: Mountains
Distance: 200 km (124 miles)

Stage: 14
Start: Grenoble
Finish: Risoul

Classification: Mountains
Distance: 177 km (109 miles)

Stage: 15
Start: Tallard
Finish: Nîmes

Classification: Flat
Distance: 222 km (137 miles)

Following a rest day in Besançon, the riders head south out of the city on stage 11, destination Oyonnax — nestled in a valley in the shadow of the Jura mountains, just north of the Alps. A tough first week can be ticked off the list, and the sprinters get their chance to come to the fore once more. Expect a bunch gallop in Oyonnax, and possibly again on the next day's lumpier stage from Bourg-en-Bresse to Saint-Etienne, although no doubt a group of chancers will hope to make a break stick before the start of the Alps proper.

Stage 13 heralds the first day in the high mountains, although it's really only on the final climb up to the finish at the ski station of Chamrousse that the riders will be fully tested. If La Planche des Belles Filles on stage 10 was a dress rehearsal to indicate how the top riders were feeling, Chamrousse will be the real deal, and anyone failing to find their climbing legs can probably kiss a podium place in Paris good-bye. The 18-km (11-mile) climb has been used only once before in the Tour, and that was for an individual time-trial stage in 2001. That 32-km (19-mile) stage from Grenoble was won by Lance Armstrong, who beat Germany's Jan Ullrich by exactly a minute. The result was later nullified after Armstrong's admission in 2013 that he had cheated to win all seven of 'his' Tours.

Stage 14 the following day promises to be nothing short of spectacular as th[e] riders take on two legendary climbs in t[he] form of the Col du Lauteret and the Co[l] d'Izoard, while the day ends with anoth[er] summit finish at another ski resort — th[is] time the resort of Risoul, which appear[s] on the Tour route for the first time.

Climbers and sprinters alike will be pleased to see the flat, but long, run between Tallard and Nîmes for stage 15. The race's second and final rest day follows it.

Winner of three consecutive Tours in the 50s, Fran[çois]
Louison Bobet moves clear of Ferdi Kübler on [the]
Col d'Izoard, en route to his second victory in 19[xx]

Stages 16 to 21

Stage: 16
Start: Carcassonne
Finish: Bagnères-de-Luchon

Classification: Mountains
Distance: 237 km (147 miles)

Stage: 17
Start: Saint-Gaudens
Finish: Saint-Lary-Soulan,
Pla d'adet

Classification: Mountains
Distance: 125 km (77 miles)

Stage: 18
Start: Pau
Finish: Hautacam

Classification: Mountains
Distance: 145 km (90 miles)

Stage: 19
Start: Maubourguet, Val d'Adour
Finish: Bergerac

Classification: Flat
Distance: 208 km (129 miles)

Stage: 20
Start: Bergerac
Finish: Périgueux

Classification: Individual time trial
Distance: 54 km (34 miles)

Stage: 21
Start: Évry
Finish: Paris

Classification: Flat
Distance: 136 km (84 miles)

For those still left in the race, waking up in Carcassonne for the start of the third and final week will be tough on both body and mind — especially as the toughest stages are yet to come.

Stage 16 is a relatively gentle introduction to the Pyrenees, taking the riders over the Col de Portet d'Aspet and the Port de Balès before a long descent to the finish in the spa town of Bagnères-de-Luchon. But stage 17 and 18 are hard to split in terms of toughness; both could easily lay claim to the title of the 2014 Tour's 'queen stage'.

The 17th stage between Saint-Gaudens and the town of Saint-Lary-Soulon, towered over by the climb of Pla d'Adet, features four Pyrenean climbs of such similar heights and gradients — and toughness — that the stage profile resembles more a Stegosaurus's back than the usual 'shark's teeth' cliché.

But whoever empties the tank to win at Pla d'Adet will need to recharge their batteries quickly. Stage 18 features the veritably monstrous Col du Tourmalet — a mountain beaten only by Mont Ventoux and Alpe d'Huez in order of the Tour's most iconic climbs, and 2014 will be its 79th appearance in the race, making it the race's most-used mountain, having first featured in 1910.

Before Paris, there's one more chance for the sprinters' teams to bag a win on the 19th stage between Maubourguet Pays du Val d'Adour and Bergerac, and then comes the race's one and only time trial: a 54-km (34-mile) individual race against the clock that will decide the race if things are still close between the leaders. The race winner will be all but crowned that night in Périgueux in the Dordogne. The riders will then take a flight to Evry, just south of Paris, to start the final processional stage towards the Champs-Elysées. Only once they arrive on the capital's famous cobblestones will the blue touch paper be lit; this is the unofficial sprinters' world championships.

The peloton on the Champs Élysées, with the Arc de Triomphe in the background, during the final stage of the 2010 Tc

The Tour's most memorable places

This stadium-less sport has nevertheless made arenas out of towns, roads and climbs – some the sites of exceptional riding, some places made infamous due to misfortune , some simply areas of natural beauty that, as a backdrop for some exciting racing, never fail to disappoint. All, though, for better or worse, have helped shape Tour de France history – a race that simply is defined by the places it visits.

259

Mont Ventoux,
France

'The police motorbike rider came up to Aimar to tell him that he'd followed him down off the Ventoux – and had clocked him at 140 kph'

'The Giant of Provence' has delivered heartache to so many riders and fans since its first inclusion in the Tour de France in 1951: always tough, always decisive and always, it appears, controversial.

Chiefly, it must take at least partial blame for a rider having died on its flanks: British rider Tom Simpson's death at the 1967 Tour was attributed to him having ingested amphetamines before the start of that thirteenth stage in Marseille, exacerbated, however, by the extreme heat of the day and the effort of climbing the brutal Ventoux on the exposed southern slopes from the town of Bédoin.

It was also the scene of a ding-dong battle between Marco Pantani and Lance Armstrong at the 2000 Tour. Armstrong, already in yellow, allowed Pantani to win the stage – which offended the Italian climber, in turn angering Armstrong to the extent that the American promised that there would be "no more gifts" ever again.

The toughness of the 1912 m (6273 ft) climb is well documented, and a constant stream of amateur riders flock to Provence to take on the challenge.

It would be folly, however, to talk about the Ventoux only in terms of the difficulty of the climb: the fast, difficult descent from the observatory on its summit down to the town of Malaucène on the Ventoux's north side has also often played a key role at the Tour. Only when the Ventoux was first climbed, in 1951, did it go up from Malaucène. Every other time, it has been climbed from Bédoin.

The mountain featured on the Tour route for the fifteenth time in 2013.

Stage 15 finished on its summit, so there was no descent this time, but, on the fifteenth stage of the 1994 Tour, Italian rider Eros Poli swept through Bédoin a a sole breakaway rider, and was faced with dragging his six-foot-four frame up the Ventoux's terrible slopes. For such a big man, it was no mean feat, and by the time he'd struggled to the top, the 25-minute advantage he'd held over the chasers at the bottom had been cut to less than five.

A breakneck 21-km descent down to Malaucène, plus a further all-out 20-km effort to the finish in Carpentras, saw Poli come home as the day's winner with a three-and-a-half minute advantage over the second-placed rider, fellow Italian Alberto Elli. It was a phenomenal achievement, and a rare instance of a rider getting the better of the Ventoux.

In 1967, defending Tour champion Lucien Aimar (left) also used the descent to similarly devastating effect. The Frenchman had in fact been with the tragic Simpson's group on the climb when the Briton collapsed, and just a few minutes further on, Aimar fell victim to a puncture.

It left him two-and-a-half minutes off the pace of the front group at the top of the climb, and so began a manic, high-speed chase to get back on terms. Aimar did it, too, and was there in Carpentras to duke it out for the stage victory, won by Holland's Jan Janssen. Aimar was fifth.

Later, one of the police motorbike riders came up to Aimar to tell him that he'd followed him down off the Ventoux – and had clocked him at 140 kph.

St tienne Firminy Bourg Rives Voiron Moirans Gde Chartreuse Allevard Massif de la Var... St Jean de Maurienne St Michel Col Mt Mod...

Beaurepaire Mt Pilat 1434 Argental le Chau Chambon Tullins ISÈRE 2087 St Jean de Maurienne Aig. d'Arves Mt Thabor 3177 Bar...

Annonay St Vallier St Marcellin Grenoble Domène Gdes Rousses 3470 3514 Col du Lautaret 2058

Haise Dieu Craponne s.A. Monistrol s.L. Yssingeaux Tournon Romans s.Isère Vizille le Bourg d'Oisans la Grave 3986 Meije Col du Mt G... 485...

HAUTE-LOIRE Tence St Péray Bourg de Péage Valence Vif la Mure 4103 les Écrins Brian...

St Paulien le Puy 1438 Mezenc le Cheylard la Voulte s.R. Chabeuil Grand Veymont 2346 Corps 2793 Massif du Pelvoux Pic de Rochebru... l'Argentière

Grandrieu 1754 le Monastier Lamastre St Péray Livron Die 1180 St Bonnet DAUPHINÉ Co...

RAL S O Privas ARDÈCHE Crest DRÔME Col de la Croix Haute Col Bayard 1246 HAUTES-ALPES Embrun Guille...

Margeride Langogne Thueyts Vals les Bains 1519 Loriol 1592 Aspres s.Buech Veynes Gap Durance Parpaillon 3048 Gd Bérard

Mende Villefort les Vans Largentière Aubenas Montélimar Dieulefit Serres Tallard Seyne Barcelonnet 3053 Mt Pel...

1702 Mt Lozère 1554 Chassezac Vallon Viviers DONZÈRE DAM le Teil Valréas Rémuzat la Motte du Caire Trois Évêchés 2927 Allos

Florac Bessèges Ardèche Bourg St Andéol Pierrelatte Nyons Ouvèze Laragne Sisteron Gd Coyer 2709

la Grand Combe St Ambroix Cèze MONDRAGON DAM Aygues Vaison les Baronnies Mt Ventoux 1912 Mne de Lure Chau Arnoux BASSES-ALPES Digne

1567 St Jean du Gard Alès Bagnols s.C. Orange Sarrians Carpentras VAUCLUSE Pernes Forcalquier Bléone les Mées

St Hippolyte du Fort Anduze GARD Uzès Villeneuve les A. Avignon l'Isle s. la Sorgue Apt Moustiers Ste Marie Castella...

Ganges Quissac Vidourle Remoulins Aramon Cavaillon Coulon Manosque Riez Verdon Comps

Nîmes Gard Tarascon M. de Lubéron Durance Aups Plans de Canjuers

Sommières Beaucaire Ste Rémy Orgon Pertuis PROVENCE Draguignan

Lunel Vauvert Arles Salon de P. Lambesc Meyrargues Barjols VAR les Arcs

Montpellier St Gilles la Crau BOUCHES-DU-RHÔNE Miramas Arc Aix en P. Ste Victoire St Maximin Brignoles Vidauban

Paulhan Aiguesmortes Istres E. de Berre Rognac Trets Gardanne Ste Baume Carnoules Cogolin

Frontignan le Grau du Roi E de Vaccarès Port de Fos Martigues Roquevaire Marseille 1154 Sollies Pont MAURES Cava...

Sète Étang de Thau Stes Maries St Louis C.Couronne Aubagne le Beausset Toulon Hyères Bormes

Agde Cap d'Agde Petit Rhône 50 m. C.Croisette L.H. la Ciotat Bandol la Seyne les Salins I. du La...

GOLFE DU LION C.Sicié P.Ile de Giens I. de Port Cros

100 m. 200 m. I. Porquerolles L.H. Iles d'Hyères

1000 m.

MER MÉDITER...

Dublin, Ireland

'Doping was rife in professional cycling, and the red-blood-cell booster EPO – which dangerously thickened the blood in the arteries – was the drug of choice in the late 1990s'

Unfortunately for poor old Dublin, memories of the 1998 Tour de France's *Grand Départ* there are more than a little spoiled by the seismic event that was the Festina Affair. When, three days before the start of the race, Belgian *soigneur* Willy Voet was apprehended by customs officers on the border between Belgium and France with a car-boot-load of illicit substances destined for the Festina squad in Ireland, it sent shock waves through the cycling world.

True, Voet wasn't caught in Dublin, but it's where the aftershocks were felt most keenly, and to say it put a dampener on proceedings is the understatement of the century.

This was an event that really kick-started the still-ongoing war against doping in cycling. It had had various false starts before: in the wake of Tom Simpson's death as a result of drugs on Mont Ventoux at the 1967 Tour, and following the publication of *A Rough Ride* by former pro Paul Kimmage – himself an Irishman, as it happened – which blew the lid off doping in the sport, although

it was a book taken nowhere near as seriously as it should have been when it appeared in 1990.

Voet being caught, and the falling of the Festina house of cards that followed highlighted something too few had either dared, or had concrete proof of, to speak out about: doping was rife in professional cycling, and the red-blood-cell booster EPO – which dangerously thickened the blood – was the drug of choice in the late 1990s.

In a more positive link to Tour folklore, Dublin is also the birthplace of 1987 champion Stephen Roche. After a successful amateur career in France, Roche turned pro for the Peugeot team 1981, and promptly beat Bernard Hinault to win the now-defunct Tour of Corsica.

In 1987, he won the Tour of Italy, then the Tour de France and then won the world road race championships in Austria to complete 'the triple'.

He now runs a hotel in Antibes, near Nice, in France. His son, Nicolas, is also a pro rider who rides for Bjarne Riis's Saxo-Tinkoff team.

263

Normandy,
France

'I was in agony in the last 20 kilometres... It was horrible – I didn't know where I was'

The French region of Normandy – or, rather, two regions: Upper and Lower Normandy – featured for the first time in the third edition of the Tour de France, in 1905, when Caen was both the finish of stage 10 and the start of the eleventh and final stage.

As well as retaining that quintessential Frenchness – it's all picnic tables and boxes of wine when the Tour comes through, which is most years – Normandy has increasingly grown in popularity with British cycling fans, who make the trip across in their thousands, arriving at Cherbourg, Le Havre and Dieppe on the ferry, often with their bikes, to populate the roadside with their French cousins, and even share the wine when the *Entente Cordiale* allows.

In 2013, the Tour visits Mont-St-Michel – one of Lower Normandy's most visited tourist attractions – for the stage 11 individual time trial. Prior to that, the island town's first and last appearance on the route was in 1990, when it hosted the finish of stage 4 from Nantes – a bunch gallop won by young Belgian sprinter Johan Museeuw.

A year later, at the 1991 Tour, Normandy was on the route again. France's Thierry Marie (left), a time-trial specialist of some repute, had done what he did best to win the race-opening prologue in Lyon. The next day, however, the leader's jersey was lost to defending champion Greg LeMond after the morning's road stage before moving to the young shoulders of Rolf Sørensen that afternoon following the team time trial.

When a crash forced Sørensen out of the race three days later, and LeMond gallantly refused to profit from the Dane's misfortune, the 259-km sixth stage between Arras and Le Havre set off without a yellow jersey, and Marie decided that it was the ideal opportunity to try to seize it back for himself.

The Castorama chancer was a Normandy lad, too, so a few hours in front of his roadside fans and the TV cameras were going to do no harm at all, and he slipped off the front of the bunch 25 kilometres into the stage.

Fast forward six hours and, having at one point held a massive 22-minute lead, Marie still held a slim advantage over the chasing peloton.

"I was in agony in the last 20 kilometres," said Marie. "It was horrible – I didn't know where I was."

Nothing for it, then, but to belt out Normandy 'anthem', *Ma Normandie*, grit his teeth, and hope to hold on for as long as possible.

His singing, picked up by the cameras boosted him from regional to national hero, while the 234 km he spent alone ahead of the field before winning in Le Havre made it the second-longest successful breakaway in the race's post-war history, after compatriot Alber Bourlon's 253 km between Carcassonne and Luchon in the 1947 Tour.

Marie had clung on to win by just shy of two minutes, but it was also a case of mission accomplished when it came to the yellow jersey: the daring raid had given the Frenchman back the race lead, too, if only for two more days.

LA MANCHE

Berck Plage

le Crotoy

Cayeux s. Mer

Valérys S.

le Tréport

Gama

Dieppe

Blangy sur Bresle

St Valéry en Caux

Bethune

Fécamp

Cany Barville

Neufchâtel

Aumale

Etretat

SEINE - INFÉRIEURE

St Pierre Eglise

L.Hpte de Barfleur

Barfleur

Cherbourg

Baie de la Seine

Montivilliers

Bolbec

Yvetot

Clères

Forges les Eaux

le Havre

C. de la Hève

Lillebonne

Caudebec en Caux

Gournay

ville

Valognes

quebec

Cotentin

Grandcamp les Bains

Trouville

Honfleur

Seine

Rouen

Douve

Deauville

Pont Audomer

Fleury sur Andelle

du Puits

Isigny

Carentan

Aure

Bayeux

Cabourg

Pont l'Eveque

Cormeilles

Elbeuf

Louviers

les Andelys

Lessay

Lison

Caen

Troarn

Mézidon

Lisieux

Beaumont le Roger

Evreux

Vernon

Périers

St Lô

Balleroy

Villers Bocage

Orne

Bernay

EURE

Coutances

MANCHE

Mt Pincon

CALVADOS

Livarot

Conches

Mantes

gnéville

Gavray

Vire

359

Thury Harcourt

Dives

Vimoutiers

Bréteuil

St André de l'Eure

nville

Villedieu

Condé sur Noireau

Falaise

N

A

Iton

Verneuil

Dreux

S

o

Vire

Flers

Argentan

Laigle

Houd

Ms Michel

See

Avranches

Mortain

Briouze

309

Mt d'Amain

Touvouvre

Chateauneuf en Thimerais

Man

Dol

Pontorson

St Hilaire du Harcouët

Domfront

Couterne

ORNE

Sées

Mortagne

Ramb

Trans

Pré en Pail

Sarthe

Alençon

La Loupe

Eure

Anneau

Antrain

Ambrières

les Avaloirs

417

Bellême

Chartr

mbourg

Quesnon

Fougères

Ernée

Mayenne

Fresnay s.S.

Mamers

Nogent le Rotrou

EURE ET LOI

St Aubin du Cormier

M

Bais

les Coëvrons

357

Beaumont s.S.

la Ferté Bernard

Illiers

Vov

ET - VILAINE

MAYENNE

Sillé le Guillaume

Bonnétable

Brou

Bonneval

Châteaubourg

Vilaine

Laval

Evron

Sarthe

Huisne

Vibraye

Cloyes

Châteaudun

Rennes

Vitré

Ste Suzanne

Connerré

R

Argentré du Plessis

Vaiges

Loué

Le Mans

SARTHES

St Calais

Mondoubleau

O

Orlé

ichen

la Guerche de B.

Meslay s.M.

la Suze s.S.

Ecommoy

le Grand Lucé

Savigny s. B.

Loir

Morée

Meung s. L.

Janzé

Semnon

ain de B.

Craon

Oudon

Château Gontier

Sablé s. S.

Château du Loir

Vendôme

Beaugency

Mer

Derval

Pouancé

Segré

la Flèche

la Chartre s. le Loir

Neuillé Pt Pierre

Châteaurenault

LOIR-ET-CHER

Blois

Bracieux

éméné Penfao

Nozay

Candé

le Lion d'Anges

Sarthe

Loir

Durtal

le Lude

Château la Vallière

INDRE

Beuvra

Erdre

MAINE

Angers

Trélazé

U

Loir

Nort

La Plagne,
France

'The oxygen mask required after his effort showed that it was the climb that had the last laugh'

"Just who is that rider coming up behind?" Phil Liggett asks the TV audience watching at home. "Because that looks like Roche. That looks like Stephen Roche... It's Stephen Roche!"

The genuine surprise in the cycling commentator's voice is impossible to mask. Stephen Roche, who would go on to win that 1987 Tour de France, saved his race there on the final climb up to the finish of stage 21.

Roche's main rival that year, Pedro Delgado (above) – who was already in yellow, and leading the Irishman by 25 seconds going into the stage – had attacked at the bottom of the climb and, with Roche (above left) unable to respond, it looked as though the Spanish rider was going to sew the Tour victory up.

Roche dug deep, however, and by the top he'd managed to reduce the deficit to just 4 seconds. By stealing back a few seconds from Delgado on a climb-filled day the next day, and then beating him by just over a minute in the time trial on the penultimate day, it was Roche who won the race overall in Paris, by just 40 seconds.

Despite Roche's fightback, you can't exactly say that the Irishman 'owns'

La Plagne. In fact, the oxygen mask required after his effort showed that it was the climb that had the last laugh.

Laurent Fignon, though – he's a rider you can say conquered the mountain. He's done it twice, too – which is 50 percent of the time that the Tour has visited the climb. Although everyone remembers Roche – and, more specifical Liggett's commentary – La Plagne has only been used by the Tour four times.

The first time the climb was used – in 1984 – Fignon already had the race sewn up, but it didn't stop him taking the sta victory and more than a minute out of h closest rivals.

In 1987, too, it was Fignon who took the stage win, outsprinting Spain's Anselmo Fuerte, although it was somewhat overshadowed by Roche's heroics. Admittedly, by that point in the race Fignon was well off the pace, more than 15 minutes down on Delgado. The Frenchman's '83 and '84 overall Tour wins must have seemed like another era by then, although it turns out they weren't, really: Fignon battled back to fitness to contend for the title in 1989, but was pipped by Greg LeMond for that year's win by 8 seconds.

Givry • Chalon s. Saône • St Germain du Bois • JURA • Champagnole • Orbe • Yverdon • Thun

LOIRE • Buxy • Lons le Saunier • Clairvaux • Mt Risoux 1384 • L. de Joux • Moudon • Romont • Bulle • Spiez • Grind

Seille • Louhans • Cuiseaux • St Laurent • le Brassus • Morges • Lausanne • Thuner S • Zweisimmen • Alpe

Cuisery • St Amour • Col de la Faucille 1323 • Morez • Vevey • Saanen • Lötschbe Tunnel

Tournus • Pont de Vaux • Montrevel • Ain • Nantua • Gex 1723 • Nyon • L. Léman • Aigle • Wildhorn • Leuk • Brig

Cluny • Crêt de la Neige • Genève • Thonon les Bains • Evian • B • Wildhorn • Sierre

Mâcon • Pont de Veyle • Bourg • Oyonnax • Annemasse • Bonneville • Dent du Midi 3260 • Martigny • Pennine

Mt St Rigaud • Veyle • AIN • Bellegarde • St Julien en G. • la Roche s.F. • Cluses 3097 • Orsières • Alpi • Zerm • Matterhorn

Beaujeu • Belleville • Dombes • Bellegarde • Ht.e SAVOIE • Arve • Buet 4481 • Chamonix • VALLE • Alagn

Villefranche S. • Villars • Pont d'Ain • Ambérieu • GENISSIAT DAM • St Rambert • Annecy • Sallanches • Mt Blanc 4810m 15.781 ft • Col du Gd St Bernard 2472 • Châtillon

HÔNE • Trevoux • Miribel • Meximieux • Rumilly • L. d'Annecy • St Gervais • Pré St Didier • D'AOSTA

l'Arbresle • Rhône • Crémieu • Culoz • Ugines • Beaufort s.D. • Petit S Bernard 2157 • Dora Baltea

Lyon • Villeurbanne • Belley • L. du Bourget • Faverges • Albertville • Bourg St Maurice • Gd de Sassière 3756 • Gran Paradiso 4061 • Ivrea

zelles s.l. • Givors • Bourgoin • la Tour du Pin • Yenne • Aix les B. • Chambéry • St Pierre d'Alb. • Moutiers • TIGNES DAM • Alpi • 3619 • Levanna • Pont Canavese

Vienne • Pont de Beauvoisin • les Echelles • Montmélian • SAVOIE • Gd de Casse 3861 • Lanslebourg • Ceres • Orco

Rive de Gier • la Côte St André • Voiron • G. de Chartreuse • Allevard • Massif de la Vanoise 2084 • 3841

tienne • Mt Pilat 1434 • Beaurepaire • Rives • Moirans • St Jean de Maurienne • St Michel • Col du Mt Cenis • Chivass

Domène • 2087 • ISÈRE • G. des Rousses 3470 • Aig.s d'Arves 3514 • Mt Thabor 3177 • Modane • Susa • Dora Riparia • Moncalieri

monay • St Vallier • Tullins • Grenoble • Vizille • la Graye • Arc • Bardonecchia • PIEM

Tournon • Romans s.Isère • St Marcellin • Vif • le Bourg d'Oisans • 3986 Meije • Col du Lautaret 2058 • Chisone • Col du Mt Genèvre

Dout • 4103 les Ecrins • 1854 • Briançon • Alpes • Pinerola

Bourg de Péage • Grand Veymont 2346 • la Mure • Massif du Pelvoux • Pic de Rochebrune 3324 • Torre Pelice po • Barge

Lamastre • St Péray • Valence • Chabeuil • Corps • l'Argentière • Dauphiné • Cottiennes

la Voulte s.R. • Livron • Drac • Devoluy 2793 • M.Viso 3841 • Saluzzo

Privas • Crest • Die • 1180 • St Bonnet • NÉ • Guillestre • Dronero

HE les Bains • Loriol • Col de la Croix Haute • du • Durance • Embrun • Gd Bérard 3048 • Parpaillon • Maira

DRÔME • 1592 • Col Bayard 1246 • HAUTES-ALPES • Ubaye • Cuneo

Montélimar • Veynes • Gap • Tallard • Barcelonnette • M.t Pelat 3053 • St Etienne de T. • Demonte

le Tiel • Dieulefit • Aspres s.Buech • Serres • Seyne • Trois Evêchés 2927 • Villan Mor

Viviers • NZÈRE DAM • Valréas • Rémuzat • la Motte du Caire • Allos • Gd Cover 2709 • C. di Tenda 1870 • Sav

Bourg St Andéol • Pierrelatte • Nyons • Ouvèze • Laragne • Sisteron • BASSES-ALPES • Mt Mounier 2818 • Alpes Maritimes • Foss

èche • Pont St Esprit • MONDRAGON DAM • Vaison • Buis les Baronnies • BASSES-ALPES • Gd Coyer • St Martin Vésubie • Tend

Aygues • Mt Ventoux 1912 • Mgne de Lure • Digne • Provence • Var • Puget Theniers • ALPES

gnols s.G. • Orange • Sarrams • Ch.an Arnoux • Bléone • Annot • MARITIMES • Bréi

Villeneuve les A. • Carpentras • Pernes • Forcalquier • les Mées • Asse • Levens • Sos

oulins • Avignon • l'Isle s. • Ant • Moustiers Ste Marie • 1778 • VAUCLUSE

London,
United Kingdom

'Warm temperatures, perfect blue skies and huge, enthusiastic crowds... Many of the riders talked afterwards of their shock and surprise at what a fantastic reception they received'

So astonishing was the London weather that accompanied the 2007 Tour's *Grand Départ* in the UK capital, it was as though the tourist board had done some kind of a deal with someone important. Warm temperatures, perfect blue skies and huge, enthusiastic crowds met the magnificent men and their riding machines; many of the riders talked afterwards of their shock and surprise at what a fantastic reception they received, while the Tour organisation promised that they'd be back.

Contrast that 2007 experience with the first time the race had visited British shores in 1974, which was, in fact, the first time that the race had headed out of mainland Europe. Then, in Plymouth, the Tour raced up and down the newly built Plympton bypass, and no one – neither the press nor the public – paid it much attention. There was only one happy rider on that occasion, and that was stage winner Henk Poppe.

The Tour came to British shores again in 1994, which was a much happier occasion. London still wasn't on the route, but thousands of spectators enjoyed a stage between Dover and Brighton, and then a stage on the second day based around Portsmouth.

However, just seven years after last hosting the start of the Tour, London w feature again in 2014 when Yorkshire – and, more specifically, Leeds – hosts the *Grand Départ*. That opening stage will finish in Harrogate, while a second stage from York to Sheffield – will stay in Yorkshire before London hosts the finis of the third stage, starting in Cambridge

Armed with even more knowledge and experience than ever before in the wake of sprinter Mark Cavendish's twenty-five stage wins since 2008, as well as Bradley Wiggins's and Chris Foome's overall victories in 2012 and 2013, the public reaction and turnout in Yorkshire is certain to be nothing short of spectacular. The London Olympics, meanwhile, proved what hunger there is for road cycling in the capital – as if the 2007 Tour start there hadn't been proof enough already.

Foulness I.

Swindon
London
Romford
Southend

BERKS
Henley
Slough
W. Ham
Tilbury
Thames
Sheerness
Margate

Chippenham
Reading
MIDD
Greenwich

Devizes
Windsor
Kingston on
Rochester
Chatham
Canterby

WILTS
Newbury
Woking
Croydon
Maidstone
North
Downs

Basingstoke
SURREY
KENT

ANGLETERRE
Reigate
Dover

Wylye
Amesbury
Haslemere
Tunbridge
Wells
The Weald
Hythe
Folkes

Salisbury
Winchester
WEST
Horsham
Shaftesbury
HAMPSHIRE
SUSSEX
EAST
Rye
New Romney

orne
Southampton
South Downs
Lewes
Hastings
Dungeness
C. Gris

Blandford
New
Fareham
Chichester
Brighton
LH.

Poole
Bournemouth
Forest
Gosport
Solent
Portsmouth
Worthing
Newhaven
Eastbourne
Pas de
Boulo

Cowes
Ryde
Beachy
Hd.

The
Needles
Newport
Isle of Wight
25 m.
le P

Swanage
St Catherines
Ventnor

St Albans
Hd.
Pt. LH.

50 m.

LA MANCHE

le To
Paris

Berck l

le C

Cayeux s. M

50 m.
le Tréport

Dieppe

St Valéry en Caux
25 m.

Béthune

la Hague
Fécamp
Cany
Barville
Neufchâtel

LH.
St Pierre
Eglise
LH pte de Barfleur
Etretat
SEINE - INFÉRIEUF

Octeville
Barfleur
Montivilliers
Bolbec
Yvetot
Clères

Cherbourg
Baie de la Seine
C. de la Hève

Valognes
le Havre
Lillebonne
Caudebec en Caux

Bricquebec
Cotentin
Grandcamp les Bains
Trouville
Honfleur
Rouen

Carteret
Douve
Isigny
Deauville
Seine

Ecréhou
Aure
Bayeux
Pont
Audomer
Elbeuf

la Haye du Puits
Carentan
Cabourg
Pont
l'Eveque
Louviers

St Helier
Lessay
Lison
Caen
Cormeilles
Risle

Périers
Balleroy
Troarn
Lisieux
EURE

St Lô
Villers Bocage
Mézidon

Coutances
MANCHE
Mt Pincon
CALVADOS
Bernay
Beaumont
le Roger
Evreu

Regnéville
Gavray
359
Thury Harcourt
Livarot
Conches

Chausey
Vire
Condé
sur Noireau
Falaise
Dives
Vimoutiers
St André
de l'Eure

Granville
Villedieu
See
Iton
Verneuil

St Malo
Flers
Argentan
Laigle
269

Malo
Cancale
M. S. Michel
Avranches
Mortain
Brioüze
309

Cherbourg
la Haye

Puy de Dôme, France

'The two rivals matched each other pedal-stroke for pedal-stroke before Poulidor pulled away, although it was Anquetil who got the last laugh, winning his fifth and final Tour that year'

The Puy de Dôme, an extinct volcano in the Massif Central, has seen its fair share of 'Tour moments' – mainly thanks to its narrow road leading to the summit at 1415 m (4642 ft).

The climb reaches a maximum gradient of 13 percent on its upper slopes, and it was there that Raymond Poulidor put 42 seconds into rival Jacques Anquetil at the 1964 Tour. The famous photograph of their shoulder-to-shoulder tussle lower down the climb is perhaps one of the best-known Tour images; the two rivals matched each other pedal-stroke for pedal-stroke before Poulidor (above) pulled away, although it was Anquetil who got the last laugh, winning his fifth and final Tour that year.

In 1975, the next man to win five Tours – Eddy Merckx – was possibly robbed of a sixth victory thanks to the Puy de Dôme. The narrow roads meant that the feverish crowd was virtually on top of the riders, and the Belgian was dealt a punch in the kidneys by a spectator. Merckx was already in pursuit

of Bernard Thévenet at that point – was the spectator a supporter? – and it was the Frenchman who went on to release the stranglehold Merckx had held on the Tour by beating the Belgian by 2 minutes 47 seconds in Paris.

The climb was first used by the Tour in 1952, and has been used twelve times since then, and for the last time in 1988. The sheer size of the Tour today means that the organisation has struggled to take the race there since – there's very little room at the car park at the top – but there are a number of people who would like to see them find a way.

The Puy de Dôme remains a lesser-known climb compared to Alpe d'Huez, the Tourmalet or Mont Ventoux, and that's because it's a private road, which isn't permanently open for riders to challenge themselves. However, the battles played out on the climb's slopes, and photographs like the one of Anquetil and Poulidor, have cemented its place in Tour history.

me Palleteau · le Souterraine · Creuse · Bonnat · BOUSSAC · MONTLUÇON · Varennes s.A. · la Clayette · Marcigny · M

magnac · MARCHE · Gueret · Gouzon · Commentry · St Pourçain s.Sioule · Lapalisse · Mts de la Madeleine · Charlieu · 1012 St Rig · Mts Beau

Laval · s.G. · Benevent l'Ab.C. · Chéneailles · Evaux · St Eloy les Mines · St Germain des Fosses · Pouilly s.C. · du Beaujolai · Thizy · Ville

701 · St Sulpice Laurière · CREUSE · Anzances · Gannat · Vichy · Cusset · St Just en Chev · RHON

NNE · Tourion · Aubusson · Bellegarde en M. · Sioule · Châtelguyon · St Remy s.Durolle · Bois Noirs · Amplepuis · RHO

Ambazac · Bourganeuf · Pontaumur · Riom · Pont du Chau · Thiers · Mts du Lyonnais · Tarare · LA

Limoges · St Léonard de Noblat · Felletin · la Courtine · Giat · Puy de Dôme 1463 · Clermont Ferrand · Lezoux · Courpière · Boën · Feurs · LYONNAI · L

Eymoutiers · Vienne · Plateau · Rochefort Montagne · Billom · Dore · Mts du Forez · LOIRE · Chazelle

ierre uffière · St Germain les Belles · de Eygurande · PUY-DE-DÔME · Cunlhat · Ambert · St Rambert · Montbrison · Gi · St

rieux · Millevaches · Ussel · la Bourboule · Pont Dore · Issoire · Mts du Livradois · Chamond

Vigeois · Uzerche · CORRÈZE · Treignac · Meymac · 1886 · Puy de Sancy · la Chaise Dieu · le Chambon · St Etie

Egletons · Bort les Orgues · Mont Dore · Lempdes · Craponne · Firminy · Bourg Argentat · M

illac · Tulle · Neuvic · Rhue · Condat en F · Signal du Luguet · Brioude · St Paulien · Monistrol s.L. · Annon

fort · Donzenac · Corrèze · Riom ès Montagne · MASSIF · Massiac · HAUTE-LOIRE · Yssingeaux · du Vivarais

Brive · Argentat · Mauriac · CANTAL · Murat · Neussargues · Langeac · le Puy · Tence · Mts

Terrasson · Pleaux · Puy Mary 1787 · Plomb du Cantal 1858 · St Flour · Allier · 1438 · Megal · Mezenc

Meyssac · St Cernin · cantal · Sangues · Velay · le Monastier 1754 · le Cheylard · Lama

Martel · Beaulieu s.D. · Aurillac · Vic s.Cère · Chaudesaigues · St Chely l'Apcher · Grandrieu · Loire · CENTRAL · SO · Priva

Sarlat · Souillac · Bretenoux · Cère · Arpajon · Truyère · Mur de Barrez · Mts de la Margeride · Aumont · Langogne · Thueyts · ARDÈCHE · Vals les

Dordogne · St Céré · Lacapelle Marival · Maurs · Laguiole · Nasbinals · 1554 · Mts d'Aubrac · 1471 · 1519 · Mt Tanargue · Auben

omme · Gramat · Gourdon · Labastide Murat · Figeac · Entraygues · LOZÈRE · Marvejols · Largentière · les Vans · le

nche · Célé · Capdenac · Lot · Espalion · Mende · Villefort · Chassezac · Nallon · Bou

que · St Géry · Cajarc · Aubin · Marcillac · St Geniez · Chanac · 1702 · MtLozère · Vivi · DONZÈRE

zech · Cahors · Lot · Villeneuve d'A · Rodez · Ste Enimie · Séverac le Chau · Florac · Bessèges · Cèze

LOT · Villefranche de Rouergue · Aveyron · AVEYRON · Laissac · Gorges du Tarn · St Ambroix · St Es

telnau · Lalbenque · Rieupeyroux · la Salvetat · Viaur · Salles Curan · Meyrueis · la Grand Combe · Alès

mtratier · Caylus · Mts de l'Aigoual · St Jean du Gard · Anduze · GARD · Uzès

rte · Caussade · Cassagnes Bégonhès · Millau · Peyreleau · Mt 1567 Aigoual · Bagnols

araise · T-GARONNE · St Antonin · Viaur · Cordes · Carmaux · Requista · Nant · le Vigan · St Hippolyte du Fort · Remoulin

Montauban · Nègrepelisse · St Affrique · Cornus · Ganges · Vidourle · Gard · Ara

ch · Tarn · Gaillac · Ambialet · Tarn · le Caylar · Ouissac · Nîmes · Beauc

de · Villemur s.le T. · Albi · St Sernin s.Rance · Sorgues · Camarès · Hérault · Sommières · Lunel

Grisolles · Lisles T. · TARN · Realmont · Dourbie · Lodève · U · Vauvert · St Gil

St Sulpice · Rabastens · Graulhet · Dadou · Montredon Labessonnié · Lacaune · Clermont · Gignac · Montpellier · Aiguesmortes · Cam

ac · Girou · Lavaur · Lautrec · Mts de Lacaune · Bédarieux · HÉRAULT · Paulhan · le Grau du Roi

Toulouse · Agout · la Salvetat · Olargues · Pézenas

dain · Caraman · Puylaurens · Castres · Labruguière · Thoré · St Pons · Frontignan

GARONNE · Baziège · Revel · Mazamet · L.H.

Col du Tourmalet, France

'It dominates the Pyrenees, but it dominates the riders, too, when they encounter it'

The Col du Tourmalet is a climb inextricably linked with the Tour de France. It's the most-used climb in the race, having made seventy-eight appearances on the route since its debut in 1910. It's almost hard not to go over it: geographically, it dominates the Pyrenees, but it dominates the riders, too, when they encounter it, whether that be from the western side from the town of Luz-St-Sauveur or the eastern side from Ste-Marie-de-Campan, via the ski town of La Mongie.

Octave Lapize, the French winner of the 1910 edition, was first to trudge over the Tourmalet's summit, but it had clearly taken its toll: he was the one who, after cresting the next climb on the day's agenda – the Col d'Aubisque – accused the race organisers of trying to kill the riders with the inhumanity of taking the Tour into the Pyrenees for the first time.

The Tourmalet became part of Tour history after then race organiser Henri Desgrange's assistant, Alphonse Steines, was tasked with checking out the viability of using the Pyrenees on the race route. January perhaps wasn't the best time to take a look at the mountains, but Steines ignored the dangerous snowstorms he encountered to tell Desgrange that the climbs should definitely be included on the route.

Even without the snow in the summer months, the Tourmalet and its surrounding neighbours still provided more than a stiff challenge due to their gradients and, even more importantly, the fact that the roads were still unmade in those days.

At the 1913 Tour, Eugène Christophe broke his forks on his way down the eastern side of the Tourmalet. There was nothing for him to do but run down the rest of the descent with his bike where he made repairs at a blacksmith's in Ste-Marie-de-Campan. Despite his efforts, he was subsequently penalised for having used outside assistance – the blacksmith's assistant had operated the bellows for Christophe to make the repairs to his forks himself.

Both routes up to the summit at 2115 m (6939 ft) are tough, which means that the descents off the top in both directions are equally tough – whether you're running down with a broken bike, *à la* Christophe, or, more conventionally, are on your bike: cycling commentator Paul Sherwen said he once saw fellow British rider Sean Yates's cycling computer after a descent off the Tourmalet, and it read that his maximum speed had been 112 kph.

DORDOGNE

Castelnau de M.   Bourg   Coutras   Isle   Montignac   Terrasson
Lacanau   St André de Cubzac   Mussidan   le Bugue   St Cyprien   Sarlat
Ste Hélène   Monpont   Dordog
St Medard en J.   Libourne   Castillon et Capitourlan   Bergerac   Domme
Bordeaux   Ambarès et Lagrave   Branne   Ste Foy la G.de   Lalinde   Gourd
Pessac   GIRON   Créon   Dordogne   Beaumont du Périgord   Belvès
Arès   Andenge   Labrède   Sauveterre de G.   Eymet   Castillonnés   Villefranche du P.   Gé
Bassin d'Arcachon   Cadillac   Dropt   Castelnau de Montratier
Arcachon   Facture   Podensac   St Macaire   la Réole   Miramont de G.   Cancon   Puyl'Evêque   Luzech   Ca
C. Ferret L.H.   la Teste de Buch   Preignac   Langon   Marmande   Villeneuve s/Lot   Fumel   Penne d'Agenais
Etang de Cazaux   Hostens   Bazas   Tonneins   Ste Livrade   Lanzerte
Belin   LOT ET-GARONNE   Montaigu de Quercy
Parentis en Born   St Symphorien   Grignols   Casteljaloux   Aiguillon   Agen   Valence d'Agen   TARN-ET-GARON
Pontenx les Forges   Captieux   Castelnau   Port Ste Marie   Moissac
Mimizan   Labouheyre   Houeillès   Lavardac   Nérac   Astaffort   Castelsarrasin   Mont
Mézos   Sabres   Roquefort   Mézin   Condom   Lectoure   Montech
Labrit   LANDES   Gabarret   Beaumont de Lomagne   Verdun s/G.   Grisolles
Lit et Mixe   Bourriot Bergonce   Cazaubon   Eauze   Valence s.B.   Grenade s/G.
Morcenx   Mont de Marsan   Douze   Fleurance   Mauvezin   Blagnac   To
Castets   Midouze   Villeneuve de M.   Vic Fezensac   Jegun   ARMAGNAC   GERS   Auch   Gimont   l'Isle Jourdain
Léon   Tartas   Grenade   Négaro   Saramon   Gimone   Lombez   Muret   HAUTE GARON
St Paul   Mugron   St Sever   Adour   Aire s.l'A   Plaisance   Mirande   Miélan   Masseube   l'Isle en Dodon
Soustons   Dax   Hagetman   Riscle   Arros   Rabastens de Bigorre   Castelnau Magnoac   Carbonne
Breton   St Vincent de Tyrosse   Pouillon   Garlin   Maubourguet   Vic en B.   Gers   Cazères   Montesquieu Volvestre
Capbreton   Peyrehorade   Orthez   Arthez   Lescar   Pau   Save   St Gaudens   Salies du S.
Bayonne   Salies de B.   Sauveterre   Tarbes   Tournay   Lannemezan   St Lizier   ARI
Hendaye   Hasparren   Monein   Gan   Pontacq   Htes PYRENEES   le Mas d'Azi
Cambo les B.   St Palais   BASSES-PYRÉNÉES   Nay   St Pé de B.   Lourdes   Bagnères de B.   Montréjeau   St Girons   Massat
La Rhune   Mauléon Licharre   Oloron Ste Marie   Arudy   Bagnères de B.   Salat
St Etienne de Baïgorry   PYRENEES   Pierrefitte   P. du Midi de Bigorre   Arreau   St Béat   Sentein   Seix
Itxassou   St Jean Pied de Port   Tardets Sorholus   Laruns   Nestalas   Col du Tourmalet   Pique   P. de Mauberme   Mt Vallier   Massat
Burguete   Izalzu   P. d'Anie   Cauterets   Luz   Massif de Néouvielle   Bagnères de Luchon   Viella   Pt de Sau   Au
Urdos   P. du Midi d'Ossau   Vignemale   Viella   Pico de Aneto   Esterri de Aneu   P. d'Estats
Aoiz   Canfranc   M. Perdido   Bagnères de Luchon   Montcalm
Lumbier   Jaca   Aragon   Ara   Pico de Aneto   Esterri de Aneu   AND
Sangüesa   Sa de la Peña   Sabiñánigo   Sobrarbe   Vilaller   Montseny   Andorra la Vieja
Tafalla   Sos del Rey Católico   Mte Oroel   Gallego   Anzánigo   Boltaña   Turbon   Seo de Urgel
Petilla de Aragon   Murillo de Gallego   Sierra de Guara   Ainsa   Campo   Pobla de Segur   Rantano de Tremp
Uncastillo   Sadaba   Ayerbe   Ribagorza   Sa
Las Arguedas   Bardenas   Ardisa   ESPAGNE

273

Alpe d'Huez, France

Alpe d'Huez was first used by the Tour in 1952. The late, great Fausto Coppi won the stage – and that year's Tour – and its semi-regular place as one of the race's most decisive and best-loved climbs was sealed.

If mountains can have rivals, then Mont Ventoux is definitely Alpe d'Huez's *bête noire*. It's in terms of the public's affections that the two behemoths war, and in 2013 both climbs featured on the Tour route, although the argument as to which one is 'better' remains undecided.

'The Giant of Provence' certainly has a darker reputation as the site of British rider Tom Simpson's death in 1967; however, the Ventoux shouldn't take all the bad rap – Alpe d'Huez was where, in 1978, Belgian Michel Pollentier failed a dope test – or, rather, was caught trying to pass it – with the use of a concealed pouch of 'clean' urine under his armpit, with a tube running down to his shorts.

Luxembourg's Frank Schleck has both good and bad memories of the Alpe. In 2006, Schleck's attacking style netted him the stage win from Italy's Damiano Cunego. Two years later, Schleck arrived at the base of Alpe d'Huez in the yellow jersey – only to have to witness his CSC team-mate Carlos Sastre attack. While the plan was for Frank and brother Andy to police any riders giving chase, Sastre was simply too strong, and rode away to the stage win, the yellow jersey and the Tour victory, while the Schlecks could only watch.

Arguably the best remembered day on the Alpe was in 1986 when the Tour's top two riders – La Vie Claire team-mates Greg LeMond and Bernard Hinault – called a truce to their rivalry, crossing the line together (below). Hinault had

won the 1985 Tour with LeMond's help; this time it was LeMond's turn to take the overall victory in Paris.

The Tour's two ascents of Alpe d'Huez on stage 18 in 2013 provided a worthy winner in the shape of Frenchman Christophe Riblon, but in 2011 the climb featured as the finale of a short, 109-km stage from Modane, tackling first the Col du Télégraphe, then the Col du Galibier and then the Alpe. It proved to be a veritable fireworks display as Alberto Contador rediscovered his lost form, Cadel Evans had his work cut out containing the Schleck brothers and Thomas Voeckler fought in vain to retain a podium spot, with his faithful Europcar team-mate Pierre Rolland announcing himself as a star of the future by being allowed to ride his own race and take a prestigious stage victory.

> '*In 1986, La Vie Claire team-mates Greg LeMond and Bernard Hinault called a truce to their rivalry, crossing the line together*'

Lyon · Villeurbanne · Crémieu · Belley · Yenne · Aix les B. · L. du Bourget · Faverges · Beaufort s.D. · Albertville · Petit St. Bernard · Bourg · 2157 · St. Maurice · D'AOSTA · Aosta · Domaz · Bie · Ivrea

Bourgoin · la Tour du Pin · Pont de Beauvoisin · les Échelles · Chambéry · St. Pierre d'Alb. · Montmélian · Moutiers · Isère · TIGNES DAM · Gd. de Sassière · 3756 · Gran Paradiso · 4061 · Pont Canavese · Orco · Ceres

Vienne · la Côte St. André · Voiron · Moirans · Allevard · St. Jean de Maurienne · SAVOIE · Massif de la Vanoise · Gde. Casse · 3861 · Lanslebourg · 2084 · Levanna · 3619 · Moncalieri

Rive de Gier · Beaurepaire · Mt. Pilat · 1434 · Rives · Tullins · ISÈRE · 2087 · Gde. Chartreuse · Domène · Gde. des Rousses · Arc · Mt. Thabor · 3177 · St. Michel · Col du Mt. Cenis · Modane · Susa · Dora Riparia · Chivasso · Ton

St. Vallier · St. Marcellin · Grenoble · Vizille · Grave · Aigs. d'Arves · 3514 · Bardonecchia · Moncalieri

Tournon · Romans s. Isère · Vif · le Bourg d'Oisans · 3986 · Meije · 4103 · Col du Lautaret · 2058 · Chisone · PIEM · Dout

Valence · St. Péray · Bourg de Péage · Grand Veymont · 2346 · Drac · la Mure · Corps · les Écrins · Col du Mt. Genèvre · 1854 · Briançon · Alpes · Pinerola · Carn · nastre

Chabeuil · Die · VERCORS · Dévoluy · 2793 · Massif du Pelvoux · l'Argentière · Pic de Rochebrune · 3324 · Torre Pelice · po · Barge

Livron · Crest · HAUT · Col de la Croix Haute · 1180 · St. Bonnet · Dauphiné · Cottiennes · M. Viso · 3841 · Saluzzo · Savig · vas

DRÔME · Loriol · Drôme · 1592 · Col Bayard 1246 · HAUTES-ALPES · Embrun · Guillestre · DAUPHINÉ · Fossan

Montélimar · Dieulefit · Aspres s. Buech · Veynes · Gap · Durance · Parpaillon · Gd. Bérard · 3048 · Maira · Dronero · Cuneo

Valréas · Rémuzat · Serres · Taillard · Seyne · Barcelonnette · Ubaye · Stura · Demonte · Villanov · Mon

Pierrelatte · Nyons · Ouvèze · Laragne · la Motte du Caire · Trois Evêchés · 2927 · Mt. Pelat · 3053 · St. Étienne de T. · C. di Tenda · 1870 · Orn

Buis les Baronnies · Buech · Sisteron · Allos · Gd. Coyer · 2709 · Mt. Mounier · 2818 · Alpes Tinées · St. Martin Vésubie · Tende

Mondragon Dam · Vaison · Aygues · Mt. Ventoux · 1912 · Mgne. de Lure · BASSES-ALPES · Digne · Verdon · Alpes de Provence · Vve. Puget Théniers · ALPES-MARITIMES · Breil

Orange · Sarrains · Carpentras · VAUCLUSE · Bléone · Asse · Annot · 1778 · Mt. Cheiron · Levens · Sospel

Villeneuve les A. · Pernes · Forcalquier · les Mées · Moustiers Ste. Marie · Castellane · Loup · Monte Carlo · Mentor

Avignon · l'Isle s. la Sorgue · Apt · Coulon · Manosque · Durance · Riez · Verdon · Comps · Villefranche · C. Ferrat · Monaco

Tarascon · Cavaillon · M. de Lubéron · Pertuis · Plans de Canjuers · Grasse · Cagnes · Nice · L.H.

St. Rémy · Orgon · Lambesc · Meyrargues · Aups · PROVENCE · Draguignan · Esterel · Antibes · C. d'Antibes · Cannes

Arles · Salon de P. · Aix en P. · Ste. Victoire · Barjols · VAR · Fréjus · G. de la Napoule

Gilles · BOUCHES-DU-RHÔNE · Miramas · Arc · Trets · Argens · les Arcs · St. Raphaël · Côte d'Azur

la Crau · Istres · E. de Berre · Rognac · Gardanne · St. Maximin · Brignoles · Vidauban · Mures · Cogolin · St. Tropez · C. Camarat

G. de Fos · Martigues · Roquevaire · Ste. Baume · 1154 · Carnoules · Solliès Pont · Maures · Cavalaire · L.H.

Port St. Louis · C. Couronne · Marseille · Aubagne · le Beausset · Toulon · Hyères · Bormes

LION · C. Croisette · L.H. · la Ciotat · Bandol · la Seyne · C. Sicié · les Salins · P. Ile de Giens · Porquerolles · L.H. · I. de Port Cros · I. du Levant · Côte · Iles d'Hyères

Col de Portet d'Aspet, France

'Two days later, Casartelli's team-mate, Lance Armstrong, took an emotional stage victory in Tarbes. He had time to celebrate his win, although it was no ordinary celebration. Instead, the American pointed to the sky, and it was Casartelli's life that was celebrated'

The Col de Portet d'Aspet (below) first featured in 1910 – the year that the first Pyrenean climbs appeared at the Tour. The Portet d'Aspet was climbed on stage 9 – the day before the Col du Tourmalet's first appearance – and first over the top was France's Octave Lapize, who also won the stage, and the Tour overall in 1910.

Unfortunately, despite having appeared on the Tour route twenty-nine times (it was last used in 2011), the Portet d'Aspet is best remembered for when it appeared in the 1995 Tour. In 1973, Raymond Poulidor was seriously injured after a crash on the descent of the Portet d'Aspet. It helped to give it a reputation as a mountain with an extremely dangerous descent.

Stage 15 of the '95 Tour took the riders over the Portet d'Aspet, the Col de Menté, the Peyresourde, the Aspin and the Tourmalet before a summit finish at Cauterets.

A lone win by Richard Virenque was overshadowed when news filtered through of a crash on the descent of the first climb. Fabio Casartelli – an Italian riding for the American Motorola outfit –

went down with a number of other rider But while they escaped serious injury, Casartelli hit a concrete barrier at the side of the road.

Just the evening before, the 1992 Olympic road race champion's mother had warned him to wear his helmet. He chose not to, and although it can never be proved whether a helmet might have saved his life, Casartelli died as a result the head injuries he sustained in the impact.

His Motorola team-mates were allowe to take all the prize money the next day which was given to Casartelli's family, and those same team-mates crossed the finish line in Pau at the head of a neutralised stage.

Two days later, Casartelli's team-mate Lance Armstrong, took an emotional stage victory in Tarbes. He had time to celebrate his win, although it was no ordinary celebration. Instead, the American pointed to the sky, and it was Casartelli's life that was celebrated.

A monument now stands at the point which the Italian died, and on each of t ten occasions that the Tour has revisite the climb, the race has paid its respects.

276

de M. Blaye Cavignac S.Astier DORDOGNE Brive Argentat Pleaux
Bourg Coutras Isle Montignac Terrasson Meyssac Aur
Ste Hélène S.André de Cubzac Mussidan le Bugue Sarlat Martel Beaulieu s.D. Maronne
edard en J. Libourne Monpont Bergerac S.t Cyprien Souillac Bretenoux Cère
deaux Ambarès et Lagrave Castillon et Capitourlan le Bugue Domme Gourdon S.t Céré
Pessac Branne Créon Dordogne Ste Foy la G. Lalinde Belvès Domme Gramat Lacapelle Marival Maurs
GIRON Cadillac St. Sauveterre de G. Eymet Beaumont du Périgord Labastide Murat Figeac
Labrède Podensac Macaire Dropt Castillonnès Villefranche du P. LOT Celé Capdenac
Preignac la Réole Miramont de G. Cancon Puy l'Evêque St. Géry Cajarc Deca
Hostens Langon Marmande Tonneins Fumel Luzech Cahors Villefranche de Rouergue Villeneuve d'A. Aubin
elin Bazas Villeneuve s.Lot Penne d'Agenais Castelnau de Montratier Lalbenque Aveyron Rieupeyroux AV
St Symphorien Grignols LOT ET-GARONNE Aiguillon Ste Livrade Montaigu de Quercy Lanzerte Caussade la Salveat
Captieux Casteljaloux Agen Valence d'Agen TARN-ET-GARONNE St Antonin Caylus Viaur
Labouheyre Sabres Houeilles Lavardac Port Ste Marie Astaffort Moissac Nègrepelisse Cordes Carman
Bourriot Bergonce Nérac Lafrancaise Ambia
Labrit LANDES Roquefort Mézin Castelsarrasin Montech Montauban Gaillac Albi
Mont de Marsan Gabarret Condom Lectoure Beaumont de Lomagne Verdun s.G. Villemur s.le T. Isle s.T. TARN
Midouze Villeneuve de M. Cazaubon Eauze Valence s.B. Grisolles Rabastens Realmont
Mugron Grenade Vic Fezensac Fleurance Grenade s.G. St Sulpice Graulhet Dadou Lautrec
St Sever Adour Nogaro Jegun Mauvezin Blagnac Lavaur Agout Cast
Hagetman Aire s.l'A. Riscle Auch Toulouse Girou Labr
Orthez Garlin Plaisance GERS Gimont l'Isle Jourdain Caraman Puylaurens Revel Mazan
Arthez Maubourguet Mirande Saramon Lombez Muret Bazième Villefranche de Lauragais Mgne
Monein Lescar Vic en B. Miélan Masseube Canal HAUTE GARONNE Auterive Castelnandary
Pau Rabastens de Bigorre l'Isle en Dodon Save Garonne Ariège Midi Carcas
PYRÉNÉES Tarbes Castelnau Magnoac Carbonne Montesquieu Saverdun Montréal
Oloron Ste Marie Pontacq Tournay Cazères Volvestre Pamiers Mirepoix
Nay Htes PYRÉNÉES Lannemezan St Gaudens Salies du S. ARIÈGE Limoux S.t Hil
Arudy St Pé de B. Lourdes Gaudens le Mas d'Azil Varilhes Alet
Laruns Pierrefitte Bagnères de B. Montréjean St Lizier St Girons Foix Lavelanet Cor
Nestalas P.du Midi de Bigorre S.t Béat Massat Tarascon Quillan Pic d.
Urdos Canterets Col du Tourmalet Arreau Sentein Seix Quillan
P.du Midi d'Ossau Luz Massif de Néouvielle Bagnères de Luchon P.de Maubermè M.t Vallier Anzat Ax les thermes Madrès
Canfranc Vignemale Viella Pt de Salu P.de Serrère ROU
Aragon Jaca M. Perdido Pico de Aneto Esterri de Aneu P.d'Estas P.Montcalm P de Carlitte PYREN
Peña Mte Oroel Sabiñanigo Vilaller Montseny ANDORRA Col de la Perche Mont Louis
Anzanigo Sobrarbe Turbon Andorra la Vieja Bourg Madame
Sierra de Guara Boltaña Aïnsa Campo Sort Seo de Urgel Cerdaña del Cadi La Pobla de Lillet
Ayerbe Ribagorza Pobla de Segur Rantano de Tremp
ESPAGNE

Luz-Ardiden, France

'Its toughest sections come halfway up the climb, where the gradient touches 9 percent'

The 2003 Tour was the first to see Lance Armstrong really suffer on the way to his seven now-taken-away titles. That edition was his fifth victory at the time, matching Miguel Indurain's five consecutive titles, and equalling the number of Tours won by Jacques Anquetil, Eddy Merckx and Bernard Hinault, but it didn't come easy.

Climbing alongside Spain's Iban Mayo on the lower slopes of Luz-Ardiden, on the day's final climb of stage 15 from Bagnères-de-Bigorre, Armstrong's handlebars caught in a spectator's bag, and he was dumped to the ground, taking Mayo (below right) with him.

The American's main rival that year, Germany's Jan Ullrich, at first appeared to push on, but then clearly took a look back to see what was going on, and waited for Armstrong, who almost came a cropper once more after pulling his foot out of the pedal while pushing hard to make it back up to the front group.

Once Armstrong was safely back with the leaders, Mayo attacked, and Armstrong went with him, then pushed on alone to win the stage by 40 seconds, increasing his overall lead to over a minute from Ullrich.

It was also on Luz-Ardiden at the 1990 Tour that Indurain announced himself to the world. From 1991 to 1995, the Spaniard was a dominant force, but in 1990 the tall climber-cum-time-trial-specialist matched defending champion Greg LeMond pedal-stroke for pedal-stroke. LeMond had turned the screw tight enough at the bottom of the climb to shed yellow-jersey-wearer Claudio Chiappucci from the front group, and then ramped up the speed with only Indurain and Marino Lejarreta still for company. Lejarreta was the next to drop, leaving only Indurain, who looked like a man simply biding his time as he sat calmly on the road-race world champion's wheel.

Hordes of fans – many of them Spanish this being the Pyrenees – roared their young compatriot on to victory. With 400 metres to go, Indurain went to the front and, with a cursory glance behind at the 1989 Tour winner, pushed on for the stage win – and the start of something bigger. LeMond pushed hard all the way to the line, finishing 6 seconds behind Indurain, while taking well over two minutes from Chiappucci, although the Italian still led by 5 seconds overall from LeMond, who would have his opportunity to close the gap a few days later on the time-trial stage at Lac de Vassivière.

Luz-Ardiden may not be that difficult a climb – its toughest sections come halfway up the climb, where the gradient touches 9 percent – and it has only featured on the route eight times, but Armstrong's 2003 fall (a rare occurrence during his riding career), LeMond's vital effort to win the 1990 Tour and Indurain's coming-of-age that day mark out as an important battleground in the Tour's history.

DORDOGNE

Castelnau de M. Blaye Cavignac S.t Astier Terrasson
Lacanau Bourg Coutras Isle Mussidan Montignac
S.te Hélène S.t André Monpont le Bugue Sarlat
S.t Medard en J. de Cubzac Libourne Bergerac S.t Cyprien Domme
Bordeaux Ambarès Castillon Lalinde Gourdo
Pessac et Lagrave et Capitourlan S.te Foy la G.de Beaumont Belvès
Arès GIRONDE Créon Dordogne du Périgord Villefranche
Bassin d'Arcachon Audenge Labrède Sauveterre Eymet Castillonnés du P.
Arcachon de G. Puy l'Evêque Luzech Cah
C. Ferret L.H. la Teste Facture Cadillac Droptt Miramont Cancon Fimel
de Buch Podensac S.t de G. Castelnau S.t Gér
Etang Preignac Macaire la Réole Penne de Montratier
de Cazaux Hostens Langon Marmande d'Agenais Lanzerte
Belin Bazas Tonneins Villeneuve Fumel
Parentis S.t Symphorien Grignols Lot S.te Livrade s.Lot Montaigu Laffaraise
en Born Castetjaloux LOT-ET-GARONNE de Quercy TARN-ET-GARONN
ung de Biscarosse Captieux Aiguillon Moissac Ne
Pontenx les Forges Labouheyre Houeillès Lavardac Agen Valence Monta
Mimizan Sabres Port d'Agen Montech Vil
Mézos Bourriot Nérac S.te Marie Castelsarrasin Grisolles
Labrit Bergonce Mézin Astaffort Beaumont
Lit et Mixe Morcenx LANDES Roquefort de Lomagne Verdun Grenade
Castets Mont de Marsan Gabarret Condom Lectoure s.G. s.G.
Léon Tartas Midouze Cazaubon Eauze Valence Mauvezin Blagnac
Soustons St Paul Villeneuve s.B. Fleurance
Breton de M. Vic Armagnac Gimont l'Isle Jourdain Tou
breton St Vincent Mugron Grenade Fezensac Jegun GERS
de Tyrosse Dax St Sever Nogaro Auch Muret HAUTE-GARONN
Pouillon Adour Aire Plaisance Saramon Lombez
Bayonne Peyrehorade Hagetman s.l'A. Mirande Masseube l'Isle en Dodon
Hasparren Orthez Riscle Carbonne
Cambo Salies de B. Garlin Maubourguet Miélan Castelnau Magnoac Cazères
les B. Sauveterre Arthez Vic en B. Rabastens Montesquieu
St Palais Monein Lescar de Bigorre Volvestre
BASSES-PYRÉNÉES Pau Tarbes Salies du S.
St Etienne Mauléon Oloron Gan Pontacq Tournay St Gaudens St Lizier
de Baigorry Licharre Ste Marie Nay Htes PYRÉNÉES Lannemezan ARIE
St Jean Tardets Arudy St Pé de B. Lourdes Montréjean le Mas d'Azil
Pied de Port Sorholus Bagnères de B. St Béat St Girons
Burguete Laruns Pierrefitte P. du Midi de Bigorre Arreau Massat
Izalzu P. d'Anie Nestalas Col du Tourmalet Sentein Seix
Aoiz Urdos Canterets Luz Massif P. de Mt Vallier
P. du Midi de Néouvielle Bagnères Mauberme
Lumbier Canfranc d'Ossau Vignemale de Luchon Pt de Sau
Aragon Jaca Viella Pico Esterri P. d'Estats
Sangüesa Sos del Rey Sa de la Peña Sabiñánigo M. de Aneto de Aneu ANDO
falla Católico Mte Oroel Perdido Sobrarbe Vilaller Montseny Andorra
Petilla de Aragón Anzánigo Boltaña Turbon la Vieja
gon Uncastillo Murillo Campo Sort Seo
de Gállego Sierra de Guara Ainsa de Urgel
Sadaba Ayerbe Ribagorza Pobla
Bardenas Ardisa de Segur Rantano de Tremp

ESPAGNE

279

Ballon d'Alsace, France

'It was a challenge that the organisers hoped would prove to be a major obstacle. No one was expected to be able to make it to the top without walking'

The Ballon d'Alsace, in the Vosges mountains of northeast France, is widely considered to be the first climb used by the Tour, but that simply isn't the case. True, you could call it the first major climb to be included on the route, in 1905, but the very first stage of the very first Tour, in 1903, featured the Col des Echarmeaux and the Col du Pin-Bouchin – admittedly much smaller climbs than the Ballon d'Alsace – while on stage 2 the same year the riders had to scale the Col de la République, which, at 1161 m (3809 ft), was pretty close to the Ballon d'Alsace's 1178 m (3865 ft).

The 1904 Tour followed the same route as in 1903, so again those three climbs featured on the route. The Ballon d'Alsace was to follow in 1905, on stage 2 between Nancy and Besançon, and it was a challenge that the organisers hoped would prove to be a major obstacle. No one was expected to be able to make it to the top without walking, but René Pottier proved everyone wrong by grinding his way to the top first. It took its toll, though; Pottier later faded and the day's stage winner in Besançon was Hippolyte Aucouturier. Pottier quit the race the next day, but returned in 1906 to win the whole thing.

The Tour has always favoured the climb from St-Maurice-sur-Moselle in the north, from where the climb averag 6.9 percent. Indeed, it was from the san town that the 1967 Tour tackled the Ballon d'Alsace, but it was also to be its first summit finish there. The defendin Tour champion, Lucien Aimar, went on the offensive, and won the stage that time, while another summit finish there in 1969 was won by a certain Eddy Merckx (below) – the young Belgian's first ever Tour stage victory.

leDuc Lerouville Arrouard Semi Sarrebourg Savenne Brumau Bu
Commercy Toul NANCY Lunéville Grey BAS-RHIN Achern
Ligny STRASBOURG Kehl Offenburg Freud
en Barrois Pont St Vincent Dombasle ET-MOSELLE Bruche Molsheim
Ornain Vaucouleurs Bayon Badenviller Donon 1013 Oppenau N
Dizier Vézelise Baccarat Schirmeck Erstein Sü
Gondrecourt 545 Raon Champ du Barr Lahr Wolfach
Joinville Charmes l'Etape Senones Feu 1095 Benfeld Kinzig
Neufchâteau Thaon Rambervillers St Die Ste Marie Ville Sélespat Haslach Schra
Liffol le Grd Mirecourt les V aux Mines Ribeauville Elzach
Andelot 506 Vittel VOSGES Bruyères COLMAR 557 Kandel Villingen Triberg
Bologne Contrexéville Épinal Gérardmer Munster 1241 Breisach Furtwangen
HAUTE-MARNE Mts Faucilles Remiremont Hohneck 1366 Neuf Brisach Neustadt
Chaumont des 504 Bains Cornimont HAUT-RHIN FREIBURG
Nogent Fourchies les B. Plombières les B. Kruth Guebwiller Feldberg St
en B. Bussang Thann Ensisheim 1493 Bonndor
Langres Bourbonne St Loup Ballon Masevaux Cernay Müllheim Blasien Schaffh
les B. s Semouse d'Alsac Girom Mulhouse Wies Zell
Combeaufontaine Luxeuil les B. Lure Giromagny Altkirch Lörrach Waldsh
HAUTE-SAÔNE Héricourt Basel Rheinfelden
Selongey Champlitte Saône Vesoul Montbéliard Delle Liestal Aarau Bad
Béze Arc Fretigney Montbozon Audincourt Ferreu Delémont Olten Bremga
Mirebeau Gray Gy Ognon l'Isle Porrentruy Moutier Aare Zofingen Sursee
Dijon Roulans s le D. St Hippolyte Solothurn Langenthal Re
Pontailler Pesmes Baume Maich Doubs Biel Burgdorf Luzern
s.S. Marnay les Dames Lomont A la Chaux de Fonds Biel er S. Stans
Auxonne Besançon DOUBS Maich Bieler S. Bern SUISSE
St Jean Dampierre Ornans Le Locle Neuchâtel Aare La Sarine
de Losne Lods Aare
me Seurre Dôle Arc Senans Murten Brienzer
Chaussin Salins Pontarlier Fleurier L. de Neuchâtel Thun S. Méiri
Verdun Arbois St Croix Payerne Fribourg Thun Interlaken
s le D. Pierre Poligny Frasne L. des L. de Neuchâtel Thunen S. Spiez Grindelwald
Chalon St Germain St Pon Orbe Yverdon Romont 4278
s Saône du Bois JURA Champagnole Moudon Bulle Alpen 4161 Finster
Lons le Saunier Mt Risoux L.de Zweisimmen Jungfrau
Seille Clairvaux 1384 Joux Saanen Lötschberg
Louhans Cuiseaux St le Brassus Lausanne Sarine Tunnel
Cuisery Laurent Morez Morges Vevey 3250 Leuk Brig Mörel
Pont de Vaux St Amour St Col de Nyon Montreux Be Wildhorn Visp Simplon
Claude la Faucille L. Léman Aigle Sierre 2009
Montrevel Ain 1323 Eviand Rhône Sion Bex
Pont Oyonnax 1723 Gex Thonon les Bains Martigny Evolene Domodossola
de Veyle Crêt de la Neige Chablais Dent du PENNINE Zermatt
Veyle Bourg Nantua Genève Annemasse Midi 260 Orsières L
Bellegarde St Julien Bonneville Rhône Alpi 4481 Matterhorn 4634 Anza
leville en G. Cluses 3097 Col du Gd St Bernard
ombes Pont d'Ain GENISSIAT la Roche s.F. Buet Alpi Matterhorn Monte Rosa Varallo
es.S. Ambérieu DAM Hte SAVOIE Arve Chamonix 2472 VALLE Sesia
Villars St Rambert Annecy Sallanches Mt Blanc Col du Gd St Bernard Alagna
revoux Meximieux L. d'Annecy St Gervais 4810m Chatillon
Miribel Guloz Rumilly 15,781 ft Pré St Didier 281

Lac de Vassivière, France

'The roads surrounding it are perfect for a time-trial stage of the Tour de France'

Lac de Vassivière, in the Limousin region, is one of France's largest man-made reservoirs – and the roads surrounding it are perfect for a time-trial stage of the Tour de France.

At the 1990 Tour, eventual race winner Greg LeMond had chased Claudio Chiappucci across most of France with the Italian left as the last man standing from a first-stage breakaway that had gained over 10 minutes, and the defending champion was still trailing Chiappucci by 5 seconds going into the penultimate stage at Lac de Vassivière.

There were shades of the final stage of the 1989 Tour in Paris the year before when the American had needed to – and managed to – close a gap on Laurent Fignon to win the race. LeMond, resplendent in his road-race world champion's skinsuit – this was still in the days before the introduction of a separate time-trial world championship, – and a pair of 'clip-on tri bars', set to work. This time, the 5-second deficit to Chiappucci seemed much more within reach, and so it proved.

Also counting in LeMond's favour had been the fact that he knew the route well,

having ridden a stage of the 1985 Tour there – also run as a time trial – which h won, funnily enough, by 5 seconds from Bernard Hinault. It was a kick in the tee for Hinault, who was LeMond's team leader, but the American's assistance during the rest of the race ensured that Hinault tied up a fifth Tour title, which remains the last by a French rider. The stage win was ample compensation for LeMond in any case: it made him the first American winner of a Tour stage.

In 1995 – the third and still the last time that the Tour has visited the lake – Miguel Indurain (above) stamped his authority all over it by winning the stag there, which was again held as a time trial. Already in yellow, the Spaniard sewed up his fifth Tour title by increasin his lead to 4 minutes 35 seconds over Switzerland's Alex Zülle in second place overall. Ominously, the rider who finished in second place on the stage, ju 48 seconds off the pace, was Bjarne Riis inching ever closer to Indurain, it seeme Riis finished third in Paris behind Indurain and Zülle in 1995; a year later, the Dane was to oust Indurain altogeth

Coulonges s. l'Autise
St Maixent
Lusignan
Montmorillon
St Benoit du Sault
Eguzon
Aigurande
Boussac
Huriel
Vivonne
Gençay
Lussac les Chatx
Sèvre Niortaise
Niort
Couhé
Lezay
Usson du P.
Vienne
Clain
l'Isle Jourdain
Gartempe
Dun le Palleteau
Creuse
Bonnat
le Souterraine
le Dorat
Frontenay Rohan Rohan
Melle
s. Bretonne
Civray
Magnac Laval
M A R C H E
Guéret
Gouzon
Mauzé
Bellac
Bénévent l'Ab.
Chénérailles
Chef Boutonne
Boutonne
Aulnay de Saintonge
Pressac
Charente
Availles Limouzine
Bessines s. G.
C R E U S E
Ruffec
St Sulpice Laurière
Confolens
Nantiat
Taurion
Aubusson
Bellegarde
St Jean d'Angély
Mansle
Roumazières
St Junien
HTE-VIENNE
Bourganeuf
Felletin
Matha
Aigre
Chasseneuil
Rochechouart
Ambazac
Pontaumur
A N G O U M O I S
St Léonard de Noblat
Aix s. V.
Limoges
Vienne
Rouillac
Vars
Tardoire
Oradour s. Vayres
Eymoutiers
la Courtine
Saintes
C H A R E N T E
la Rochefoucauld
Cognac
Jarnac
Pierre Buffière
de Eygurande
Angoulême
Châlus
St Germain les Belles
Pons
Châteauneuf s. Charte
Nontron
Villebois Lavalette
St Pardoux la Rivière
Isle
St Yrieix
Vézère
Millevaches
Treignac
Ussel
Meymac
Jonzac
Barbezieux
Mareuil
Uzerche
Egletons
Mirambeau
Verteillac
Thiviers
Auvezère
Vigeois
C O R R È Z E
Neuvic
Montmoreau
Lizonne
Montendre
Chalais
Aubeterre
Dronne
Brantôme
Juillac
Seilhac
Tulle
Dordogne
Montlieu
Périgueux
Ribérac
Hautefort
Donzenac
Mauriac
St Savin
Montguyon
St Aulaye
Blaye
Cavignac
St Astier
Thenon
Brive
Argentat
Pleaux
Bourg
D O R D O G N E
Corrèze
Maronne
Coutras
Isle
Terrasson
Montignac
Meyssac
St Cernin
St André de Cubzac
Mussidan
Libourne
Monpont
Martel
Beaulieu s. D.
Aurillac
Ambarès et Lagrave
Castillon et Capitourlan
le Bugue
Vézère
St Cyprien
Sarlat
Souillac
Bretenoux
Cère
Bergerac
Branne
Dordogne
Ste Foy la Gde
Lalinde
Domme
St Céré
Créon
Beaumont du Périgord
Belvès
Gramat
Lacapelle Marival
Maurs
Sauveterre de G.
Eymet
Gourdon
Garonne
Cadillac
Podensac
St Macaire
Dropt
la Réole
Miramont de G.
Castillonnès
Villefranche du P.
Labastide Murat
Figeac
Capdenac
Decazeville
Preignac
L O T
Célé
Langon
Cancon
Puy l'Evêque
St Géry
Cajarc
Aubin
Hostens
Marmande
Bazas
Ciron
Villeneuve s. Lot
Fumel
Luzech
Cahors
Lot
Villeneuve d'A.
Villefranche de Rouergue
Rodez
St Symphorien
Tonneins
Penne d'Agenais
Grignols
Ste Livrade
Castelnau de Montratier
Lalbenque
Aveyron
Captieux
L O T - E T - G A R O N N E
Montaigu de Quercy
A V E Y R
Casteljaloux
Aiguillon
Rieupeyroux
Lauzerte
Caylus
la Salvetat
Houeillès
Lavardac
Port Ste Marie
Agen
Caussade
Bourriot Bergonce
Lafrançaise
Nérac
Valence d'Agen
T A R N - E T - G A R O N N E
St Antonin
Viaur
Baïse
Astaffort
Mézin
Moissac
Roquefort
Castelsarrasin
Nègrepelisse
Cordes
Carmaux
Gabarret
Condom
Lectoure
Montauban
Ambialet
Cazaubon
Montech
Tarn
Gaillac
Albi
Villeneuve de M.
Eauze
Valence s. B.
Beaumont de Lomagne
Verdun s. G.
Villemur s. le T.
Grenade
Grisolles
l'Isle s. T.
Rabastens
T A R N
St Sernin
Vic Fezensac
Fleurance
Réalmont
Adour
St Sever
Nogaro
A r m a g n a c
Jegun
Grenade s. G.
St Sulpice
Graulhet
Dadou
Montredon Labessonié
Aire s. l'A.
G E R S
Mauvezin
Lavaur
Agout
Riscle
Plaisance
Auch
Blagnac
Lautrec
Toulouse
Garlin
Arrats
Gimont
l'Isle Jourdain
Castres
Mirande
Saramon
Caraman
Puylaurens
Douze
Midouze
Gironde
L A N D E S
Armagnac

Col d'Izoard,
France

'*In the Casse Déserte is one of the more haunting monuments... silent and windswept, with a very real sense of the battles man and machine, combined, have had against the forces of nature*'

The most iconic images of the Col d'Izoard are those of lone riders struggling up through the moonscape of the Casse Déserte section of the climb, on its southern side, from Guillestre. It's here, around two kilometres from the summit, that you'll also catch a glimpse of the memorial to Italy's Fausto Coppi and Frenchman Louison Bobet – names both synonymous with the climb – whose profiles are mounted on plaques, mounted in turn to one of the many jagged rocks. Along with the memorial to Fabio Casartelli on the Col de Portet d'Aspet and the one in honour of Tom Simpson on Mont Ventoux, the Coppi/Bobet one in the Casse Déserte is one of the more haunting monuments to riders past that can be found in the Alps and Pyrenees. Part of it, of course, is due to the legend of the riders concerned, but an equal part is the location – silent and windswept, with a very real sense of the battles man and machine, combined, have had against the forces of nature.

In 1949, on stage 16 from Cannes to Briançon, the Izoard was the site of a duel between Coppi and compatriot Gino Bartali, who rode together up through the Casse Déserte and on down the other side to Briançon, where Bartali took the stage win and Coppi, later, the overall Tour title.

A year later, Coppi was a non-starter at the Tour with a broken pelvis sustained at the Giro, while Bartali pulled himself and the entire Italian team out of the race midway through after complaining of feeling threatened by French fans.

That opened the door to the start of Bobet's relationship with the Izoard and, with no Coppi or Bartali to get in the way, the Frenchman used the Izoard as a springboard to win stage 18 between

Gap and Briançon. Switzerland's Ferdi Kübler and Belgium's Constant 'Stan' Ockers were the only riders capable of finishing within three minutes of Bobet, and Kübler went on to win that 1950 Tour with some ease.

The stage between Gap and Briançon over the Izoard was key in 1953, during which Bobet rode alone up the climb to finish over five minutes ahead of Holland's Jan Nolten. Bobet won his first Tour that year, and the Izoard played just as important a role the next year when Bobet won the second of his three Tours. Bobet won again in Briançon on stage 18 thanks to his knowledge of 'his' mountain, although that man Kübler finished only 1 minute 49 seconds behind on that occasion.

Crémieu · Belley · Faverges · Beaufort s.D. · Aosta · Romagnan

la Tour du Pin · Yenne · Aix les B. · Albertville · Petit S.Bernard · D'AOSTEA · Biella · Cervo

Pont de Beauvoisin · Chambéry · St Pierre d'Alb · Bourg St Maurice · 2157 · G.de Sassière · Gran · Pont Canavese · Santhia

e St André · les Échelles · Montmélian · Moutiers · Isère · TIGNES DAM · 3756 · 4061 Paradiso · Ivrea

Rives · Voiron · Allevard · St Jean · SAVOIE · G.de Casse · 3619 · Levanna · Ceres · Vercelli

Moirans · St Jean de Maurienne · 3861 · Lanslebourg · Orco · T

Tullins · ISÈRE · 2087 · Dômène · G.des Rousses · St Michel · 2084 · Col du M.Cenis · Chivasso · Casale

Grenoble · Vizille · Aig. d'Arves 3514 · Mt Thabor 3177 · Modane · Susa DoraRiparia · TORINO · Monferra · Va

Vif · laGrave · 3470 · Col du Lautaret 2058 · Bardonecchia · Moncalieri · PIEMONTE

le Bourg d'Oisans · 3986 Meije · Chisone · Pinerola · Carmagnola · Asti

Grand Veymont 2346 · la Mure · 4103 les Écrins · Col du M.Genèvre · Briançon · Alpes · Torre Pelice po · Bra · Tanaro · Alba

Corps · Massif du Pelvoux · Pic Roch.une · 324 · Cottiennes · Barge

Die · 2793 · l'Argentière · Guillestre · 3841 · M.Viso · Saluzzo · Savigliano · Fossano

1180 · Col de la Croix Haute · St Bonnet · HAUTES-ALPES · Durance · Ubaye · M.Viso · Dronero · Mondovi

ÔME 1592 · Col Bayard 1246 · Embrun · Parpaillon · 3048 · Maira · Villanova Mon. · Demonte

Die · Veynes · Gap · Gd Bérard · Stura · Cuneo · Ormea

Aspres s.Buech · Tallard · Seyne · Barcelonnette · Maira

Serres · laMotte du Caire · Trois Evêchés 2927 · Mt Pelat 3053 · St Etienne de T. · C.di Tenda 1870 · Tende

Rémuzat · Allos · Alpes Maritimes

Nyons Ouvèze · Laragne · Sisteron · Gd Coyer 2709 · Mt Mounier 2818 · St Martin Vésubie · Alassio

Buis les Baronnies · BASSES-ALPES · Verdon · Var · Puget Théniers · ALPES- · Breil · Imperia · Pto Maur

Vaison · Mt Ventoux 1912 · Ch.au Arnoux · Digne · Annot · MARITIMES · Sospel · L.H.

Carpentras · Mgne de Lure · Bléone · les Mées · Asse · Castellane · Mt Cheiron 1778 · Levens · San Remo

VAUCLUSE · Pernes · Forcalquier · Moustiers Ste Marie · Loup · Monte Carlo · Menton

l'Isle s. la Sorgue · Apt · Manosque · Riez · Annot · Villefranche · Monaco · 1000 m.

Cavaillon · Coulon · Durance · Verdon · Comps · Grasse · Cagnes · Nice · C.Ferrat · L.H.

M. de Lubéron · Pertuis · Plans de Canjuers · Draguignan · Antibes · C.d'Antibes

Lambesc · Meyrargues · Aups · PROVENCE · Grasse · Cannes · G.de la Napoule

ES-DU-RHÔNE · Aix en P. · Ste Victoire · Barjols · VAR · Esterel · Fréjus · Côte

Miramas · Arc · Frets · Argens · les Arcs · Draguignan

E.de Berre · Rognac · Gardanne · St Maximin · Brignoles · Vidauban · St Raphael · d'AZUR

Martigues · Romevaire · Ste Baume 1154 · Carnoules · Cogolin · St Tropez · 2000 m.

Couronne · Marseille · Aubagne · Solliès Pont · Maures · C.Camarat · L.H.

C.Croisette L.H. · la Ciotat · le Beausset · Hyères · Cavalaire

Bandol · Toulon · Bormes

C.Sicié · la Seyne · les Salins · I. du Levant · Côte

P.Ile de Giens · I. de Port Cros · Iles d'Hyères

I. Porquerolles L.H.

285

Col d'Aubisque,
France

'Van Est's front wheel slipped on the wet first corner while descending off the mountain, and he skidded off the barrier-less road. It was truly miraculous that he didn't plunge to his death'

In 1985, the Col d'Aubisque featured as the final climb in what was a relatively short stage of 52 km from Luz-St-Sauveur to the summit of the Aubisque, which also took in the Col du Soulor.

Stephen Roche arrived in Luz-St-Sauveur that morning meaning business and wearing a skinsuit, rather than a standard, separate jersey and shorts, proving that modern-day usage by David Zabriskie and Team Sky is nothing new. Zabriskie talked of sniggers when he turned up for the start of Paris-Tours in 2008 wearing a skinsuit in order to give himself every aerodynamic advantage, and eyebrows have been raised at Sky often plumping for one for road racing in the past couple of years, so you can only imagine the kind of reception Roche got in the mid-1980s.

It worked, though – Roche won that stage to the top of the Aubisque. Two years later, Roche would be winning the Tour overall.

The 1709-m (5607-ft) Aubisque first featured in the Tour on 1910. On that occasion Octave Lapize famously rode over the top accusing the race organisers of being murderers, such was the severity of the climbs in the Pyrenees that had been introduced that year.

In 1951, Dutchman Wim Van Est (right) struggled going down the Aubisque more than going up. Clad in the yellow jersey as Tour leader, Van Est's front wheel slipped on the wet first corner while descending off the mountain, and he skidded off the barrier-less road. It was truly miraculous that he didn't plunge to his death, saved instead by a precipice 'just' 70 m down the ravine. No one had a rope long enough to reach him, so instead his manager strung together all forty of the team's tyres, which were used to haul him back up to safety.

DORDOGNE

Blaye · Cavignac · St Astier · Ténon · Montignac · Ter
Bourg · Coutras · Isle · Mussidan · le Bugue · St Cyprien
Castelnau de M. · Ste Hélène · St André de Cubzac · Libourne · Monpont · Bergerac · Lalinde · Dom
Lacanau · St Medard en J. · Ambarès et Lagrave · Castillon et Capitourlan · Beaumont du Périgord · Belvès
Bordeaux · GIRON US · Branne · Ste Foy la Gde · Castillonnès · Villefranche du P.
Pessac · Créon · Sauveterre de G. · Eymet · Miramont de G. · Cancon · Puy l'Evêque · Luzec
Arès · Garonne · Cadillac · St Macaire · Drott · Marmande · Villeneuve s. Lot · Penne d'Agenais · Castel de Montr
Bassin d'Arcachon · Andenge · Labrède · Podensac · la Réole · Tonneins Lot · Ste Livrade · Montaigu de Quercy · Lanzerte
Arcachon · Facture · Preignac · Langon · LOT-ET-GARONNE · Aiguillon · Agen · TARN-ET-
C. Ferret L.H. · la Teste de Buch · Hostens · Bazas · Casteljaloux · Port Ste Marie · Valence d'Agen
Etang de Cazaux · Belin · St Symphorien · Grignols · Houeillès · Lavardac · Nérac · Astaffort · Moissac
Parentis en Born · Captieux · Castelsarrasin
Etang de Biscarosse · Pontenx les Forges · Labouheyre · Bourriot Bergonce · Roquefort · Mézin · Condom · Lectoure · Montech
Mimizan · Sabres · Gabarret · Eauze · Valence s.B. · Beaumont de Lomagne · Verdun s.G.
Mézos · LANDES · Mont de Marsan · Cazaubon · Vic Fezensac · Fleurance · Grenade s.G.
Lit et Mixe · Morcenx · Tartas · Midouze · Villeneuve de M. · Armagnac · GERS · Mauvezin
Castets · Léon · St Paul · Mugron · Grenade · Nogaro · Auch · Blagnac
Soustons · St Vincent de Tyrosse · Dax · St Sever · Aire s.l'A. · Plaisance · Gimont · l'Isle Jourdain
Cap Breton · Capbreton · Pouillon · Hagetman · Riscle · Mirande · Saramon · Lombez · Muret
Boucau · Peyrehorade · Garlin · Maubourguet · Miélan · Masseube · l'Isle en Dodon · HAUTE G.
Biarritz · Adour · Orthez · Luy · Vic en B. · Rabastens de Bigorre · Save · Carbonne · Garonne
St Jean de Luz · **Bayonne** · Salies de B. · Arthez · Lescar · Castelnau Magnoac · Cazères · Montr Volve
Hendaye · Hasparren · Sauveterre · Monein · Pau · Pontacq · Tournay · St Gaudens · Salies du S.
Irun · 900 · Cambo les B. · St Palais · BÉARN · Gan · Tarbes · Lannemezan · St Lizier · le Ma
la Rhune · BASSES-PYRÉNÉES · Mauléon Licharre · Oloron Ste Marie · Nay · Htes PYRENEES · St Girons
St Etienne de Baïgorry · St Jean Pied de Port · Arudy · St Pé de B. · Lourdes · Bagnères de B. · Montrejean · St Béat · St Girons
Elizondo · Tardets Sorholus · Laruns · Betrefitte Nestalas · P. du Midi de Bigorre 2877 · Arrean · Sentein · Seix
PYRENEES · 2504 P.d'Anie · Cauterets · 2114 · Col du Tourmalet · 2880 Mt Vallier · 2839
Burguete · Izalzu · Urdos · 2887 P. du Midi d'Ossau · Luz · 3092 · Bagnères de Luchon · P. de Mauberme · Pt de San
Aoiz · 3298 · Vignemale · Massif de Néouvielle · Pic du Sai 2052
NARRA · Lumbier · Canfranc · M. Perdido · Pico de Aneto · Esterri d'Aneu · P. d'Estés
Sangüesa · Jaca · Aragon · 3404 · Viella · Montseny 2883 · And la Vie
Tafalla · Sa de la Peña · Sabiñánigo · Sobrarbe · Vilaller · Sort · Se
Olite · Sos del Rey Católico · 1767 · Mte Oroel · Turbon 2492 · Pobla
Petilla de Aragón · 1523 · Anzánigo · Gallego · Boltaña · Ainsa · Campo · Rantano
Uncastillo · Murillo de Gallego · Sierra de Guara · Vilaller · Ribagorza · Pobla de Segur
Arguedas · Sadaba · Ayerbe · 2077 · Pallaresa
Ardisa

ESPAGNE

Sestriere, Italy

The ski resort of Sestriere sits just over the border from France in Italy, and has been the scene of some truly epic Tour de France stages.

In 1992, Claudio Chiappucci – who'd risen to prominence on the back of having worn the yellow jersey at the 1990 Tour, holding off eventual race winner Greg LeMond until the penultimate stage – attacked early on stage 13 from St-Gervais-les-Bains, on the Col des Saisies. By the Col de l'Iseran, the breakaway group was down to just the Italian and France's Richard Virenque, whom Chiappucci (below) promptly dropped, pushing on alone, dressed in the polka-dot 'king of the mountains' jersey.

It was a seemingly suicidal move, but as the race headed across the border, and the roadside fans turned from French to Italian, you began to sense that Chiappucci was onto something special. Even the Italians – who will always favour their beloved Giro – knew what the Tour's polka-dot jersey signified. Chiappucci really was king of the mountains that day, and the crowds on the final climb up to Sestriere were simply enormous, vociferous and seemingly unwilling to let Chiappucci and the phalanx of polic motorbikes through until the very last moment. A spectacular stage culminate in the stage win for Chiappucci, but Miguel Indurain stood firmly enough to take a second overall Tour title.

In 1996, the finish of stage 9 in Sestri saw Denmark's Bjarne Riis take the yellow jersey for the first time in the rac and then defend it all the way to Paris. The snow-hit stage saw the route reduc to just 46 km (28.5 miles), missing out the originally scheduled climbs of the Col de l'Iseran and the Col du Galibier. Riis won alone at Sestriere, but we now know that it was medically assisted: he admitted in 2007 to having used EPO during his riding career, which feels a lot like a kick in the teeth for Sestriere, almost devaluing a climb renowned for epic acts of attacking riding – all the more so when you consider that Lance Armstrong won alone there in 1999, effectively sewing up his first Tour title

'It was a seemingly suicidal move, but as the race headed across the border, and the roadside fans turned from French to Italian, you began to sense that Chiappucci was onto something special'

Aosta
D'AOSTA
Petit St Bernard
Beaufort s.D.
Busto Arsizio
Romagnano
Faverges
Albertville
Aix les B.
Yenne
Chambéry
St Pierre d'Alb
Bourg St Maurice
2157
Gde Sassière 3756
Isère TIGNES DAM
Gran Paradiso 4061
Donnaz
Dora Baltea
Biella
Cervo
Ivrea
Novara
Moutiers
les Echelles
Montmélian
SAVOIE
Gde Casse 3861
3619 Levanna
Pont Canavese
Santhia
Ceres
Orco
Vercelli
Mortara
Allevard
Gde Chartreuse
Massif de la Vanoise
Lanslebourg
2084
Moirans
St Jean de Maurienne
St Michel
Col du Mt Cenis
Chivasso
Lome
2087
Arc
Modane
Mt Thabor
Susa
Dora Riparia
Torino
Casale Monferrato
Po
Domène
Gdes Rousses
Aigs d'Arves 3514
3470
3177
Valenza
Vizille
la Grave
Col du Lautaret 2058
Bardonecchia
Moncalieri
Alessandria
Vif
le Bourg d'Oisans
3986 Meije
Col du Mt Genèvre 1854
Chisone
PIEMONTE
4103 les Ecrins
Briançon
Pinerola
Carmagnola
Asti
la Mure
Massif du Pelvoux
Alpes Cottiennes
Tanaro
Drac
Corps
Pic de Rochebrune 3324
Torre Pelice
Po
2793
l'Argentière
Bra
Alba
Ovada
Dévoluy
Dauphiné
Barge
Acqui
St Bonnet
3841 M. Viso
Guillestre
Saluzzo
Savigliano
HAUTES-ALPES
Embrun
Durance
Parpaillon
Ubaye
Fossano
Bormida
Appennino
Col Bayard 1246
Gap
Dronero
Voltri
Veynes
3048 Gd Bérard
Maira
Aspres s.Buech
Tallard
Cuneo
Mondovi
Varazze
Serres
Seyne
Barcelonnette
Stura
Villanova Mon
Savona
Buech
la Motte du Caire
Trois Evêchés 2927
Mt Pelat 3053
Demonte
Laragne
Allos
St Etienne de T.
Tanaro
Ormea
Finale Ligure
Baronnies
Sisteron
C. di Tenda 1870
BASSES-ALPES
Gd Coyer 2709
Mt Mounier 2818
Alpes Maritimes
Tinée
Tende
Albenga
Chau Arnoux
Mgne de Lure
Digne
Verdon
St Martin Vésubie
Alassio
Bléone
Puget Théniers
Var
ALPES-MARITIMES
Breil
L.H.
Imperia
(Pto Maurizio Oneglia)
les Mées
Asse
Provence
Annot
Sospel
Forcalquier
Moustiers Ste Marie
1778 Mt Cheiron
Levens
San Remo
Manosque
Castellane
Monte Carlo
Menton
Luberon
Riez
Loup
Monaco
1000 m.
Durance
Verdon
Villefranche
C. Ferrat
Pertuis
Comps
Nice
L.H.
Plans de Canjuers
Grasse
Cagnes
Aups
Antibes
Meyrargues
PROVENCE
Alpes
Cannes
C. d'Antibes
Aix
Ste Victoire
Barjols
Draguignan
Esterel
L.H.
G. de la Napoule
Argens
VAR
Trets
les Arcs
Fréjus
St Maximin
Gardanne
Vidauban
St Raphael
Brignoles
2000 m.
Ste Baume 1154
Côte d'Azur
Marseille
Maures
St Tropez
Carnoules
Aubagne
Cogolin
C. Camarat
le Beausset
Sollies Pont
L.H.
Cavalaire
Toulon
Hyères
Bormes
La Ciotat
Bandol
les Salins
I. du Levant
C. Sicié
la Seyne
P. Ile de Giens
L.H.
I. de Port Cros
I. Porquerolles
Iles d'Hyères
LI

Col du Galibier,
France

'On the menu was the giant that is the Col du Galibier. At 2556 m (8386 ft), it was by far the highest pass the race had used'

Having included the Pyrenees for the first time in 1910, the Tour paid its first visit to the Alps the following year – and on the menu was the giant that is the Col du Galibier. At 2556 m (8386 ft), it was by far the highest pass the race had used, dwarfing the Pyrenees' 2115-m (6939-ft)-high Col du Tourmalet.

The Galibier would feature on the Tour route, as the highest point, in every edition until 1938, when it was superseded by the introduction of the Col de l'Iseran (2770 m/9088 ft), although the Galibier still appeared on the same stage that year, and both climbs were there again in 1939.

After the Second World War, the Galibier featured in the next two editions, in 1947 and 1948, but has since been used sporadically – although still often. Since 1947 the climb has featured a further thirty-three times, making sixty-two appearances in all.

Before 1976, when the tunnel near the summit was closed for repair, the riders had crossed the top of the Galibier at 2556 m (8386 ft). Without the tunnel, however, a new road took the riders right up to 2645 m (8678 ft).

The Galibier should have featured in the 1996 Tour, but the climb's altitude, and therefore its propensity for snow, meant that it was omitted from stage 9

between Val d'Isère and Sestriere due to it being unpassable along with the Col de l'Iseran. That shortened stage allowed Denmark's Bjarne Riis to attack and punish his rivals to the tune of 30 seconds, while also gaining him the yellow jersey, which he then held all the way to Paris. Might the Galibier have slowed him down?

It certainly did for the runner-up that year, Riis's young Telekom team-mate Jan Ullrich, in 1998. Having usurped Riis to win the 1997 Tour, Ullrich was up against Italy's Marco Pantani the following year, and 'The Pirate' used his superior climbing ability to outwit the defending champion, who suffered on the Galibier in the freezing rain, allowin Pantani to go on and win the 1998 title.

In 2011, marking 100 years since the first appearance of the Alps at the Tour, the race climbed the Galibier from both sides on consecutive stages. The tunnel was reopened in 2002, and the 2011 route took the riders over the high road on stage 18, while the tunnel was employed for stage 19. Luxembourg's Andy Schleck (above) was the first to the summit on both occasions – winning stage 18 when it was the final climb, while on stage 19 it appeared en route to the finish at Alpe d'Huez, won by Frenchman Pierre Rolland.

Bordeaux, France

'It was first used as a stage finish and start in the first Tour de France in 1903, and has been used eighty times between then and 2010'

After Paris, the French west coast city of Bordeaux is the Tour's most-used destination – for stage starts or finishes – most often acting as the finish for a massed sprint. It was first used as a stage finish and start in the first Tour de France in 1903, and was used eighty times between then and 2010.

English speakers have had great success in Bordeaux over the years: American Davis Phinney won the second of his two Tour stage wins there in 1987, from Dutch sprint star Jean-Paul Van Poppel and Great Britain's Malcolm Elliott, while Brits Barry Hoban and Mark Cavendish have also won there.

Hoban (above) won in Bordeaux on stage 18 of the 1969 Tour, and then won again the following day between Bordeaux and Brive-la-Gaillarde, becoming the first British rider to win two consecutive stages, and remaining the only British rider to do so before Mark Cavendish came along.

Cavendish won his own Bordeaux stage in 2010, which is the last time the Tour has finished in the city.

The Bordeaux stages used to finish at the outdoor Lescure velodrome, which

later became the home of the Girondins de Bordeaux football club, and is now called the Stade Chaban-Delmas after former city mayor Jacques Chaban-Delmas.

The city's indoor Vélodrome du Lac was cleverly used by British rider Chris Boardman to break the Hour Record, o the same day as stage 18 of the 1993 To de France between Orthez and Bordeau (won by Uzbekistan's 'Tashkent Terror' Djamolidine Abdoujaparov from the USA's Frankie Andreu). The publicity helped secure Boardman a pro contract later in the year with the French Gan team.

The following April, the velodrome was used by Scotland's Graeme Obree t break Boardman's record, then used ag in September, October and November 1994 by Miguel Indurain, Tony Roming and Rominger again, respectively, each rider breaking the previous record.

Today, the velodrome hosts a round of the UCI Track World Cup, while the city of Bordeaux will continue as a popular stage town for the Tour.

GOLFE

DE

ASCOGNE

200 m.

25 m.

la Tremblade CHARENTE Marennes Matha
Pte de la Coubre Saintes Saujon Rouillac CHARENTE la Roc
L.H. Royan MARITIME Pons Cognac Jarnac Angoulême
Pte de Grave Gémozac Châteauneuf s. Charte Villebois
le Verdon Girone Jonzac Barbezieux Lavalette M
St Vivien de M. Mirambeau Montmoreau Verteilla
Médoc Montendre Montlieu Chalais Aubeterre Dro
Lesparre Pauillac St Savin Montguyon Aulaye St Ribéra
Houtin Montlieu St André Muss
Etang de Carcans St Laurent et Benon St Savin Coutras Isle Monpont
Castelnau de M. Blaye Bourg Cavignac St André de Cubzac Libourne Castillon et Capitourlan Be
Lacanau Ste Hélène Ambarès et Lagrave Branne Dordogne Ste Foy la Gde
St Medard en J. Bordeaux Créon Us Sauveterre de G. Eymet
Arès GIRON Garonne Cadillac Macaire la Réole Miramo de G.
Bassin d'Arcachon Andenge Labrède St Macaire Dropt
Arcachon Facture Podensac Preignac Langon Marmande
C. Ferret L.H. la Teste de Buch Leyres Bazas Tonneins Lot
Etang de Cazaux Belin Hostens Ciron Grignols LOT ET GAR
Parentis en Born St Symphorien Captieux Casteljaloux Aiguille
Etang de Biscarosse Sabres Bourriot Bergonce Houeillès Lavardac Port
Pontenx les Forges Labouheyre Nérac Mézin
Mimizan Labrit Roquefort LANDES
Mézos Morcenx Mont de Marsan Gabarret Condo
Lib et Mixe Castets Tartas Midouze Cazaubon Eauze Valen s.B.
Léon St Paul Mugron Villeneuve de M. Grenade Vic Fezensac Jeg
Soustons Dax St Sever Nogaro Armag Ger Auch
Breton St Vincent de Tyrosse Hagetman Aire s.l'A Riscle Plaisance
Gouf de Cap Capbreton Pouillon Peyrehorade Garlin Mirande S
Boucau Salies de B. Orthez Luy Maubourguet
Biarritz Bayonne Arthez Vic en B. Miélan
San Sebastián St Jean de Luz Hasparren Sauveterre Monein Lescar Rabastens de Bigorre Castel
C. Higuer L.H. Cambo les B. St Palais Saison Gave de Pau Pau Tarbes
GUIPÚZCOA Hendaye St Étienne de Baïgorry Mauléon Licharre Oloron Gan Pontacq Tournay Htes PYRÉNÉES
Tolosa Irun la Rhune Elizondo St Jean Pied de Port Ste Marie BASSES-PYRÉNÉES Nay St Pé de B. Lourdes Lanneme
Vergara Beasain Lecumberri Burguete Tardets Sorholus Arudy Bagnères de B.
Alsásua Irurzun Izalzu Irati P. d'Anie Laruns Pierrefitte Nestalas P. du Midi de Bigorre Arrea
Andia 2504 2877 2114 293

Île de Noirmoutier/ Passage du Gois, France

'It created chaos
as a huge pile-up
affected a number
of race favourites'

The Île de Noirmoutier is an island that sits just off the Vendée coast of western France. It's joined to the mainland by both a road bridge and the Passage du Gois – a 4.15-km (2.58-mile)-long road submerged by the tide twice a day.

There's an annual running race across the Passage du Gois, at which the starting gun is fired when the tide first covers the road, with the slower runners getting very wet feet indeed. The Tour has used it only twice – with very different results.

The 1999 Tour started at the nearby Puy du Fou theme park. Stage 2, two days later, was between Challans and St-Nazaire, and featured the Passage du Gois (below) along the way. It created chaos as a huge pile-up affected a number of race favourites, including Switzerland's Alex Zülle, Italy's Ivan Gotti and France's Christophe Rinero, who was considered one of the favourites by virtue of his fourth place overall and the king of the mountains title he won at the doping-scandal-hit 1998 Tour.

All three limped home more than six minutes behind the lead group, which had included Richard Virenque, Fernando Escartin and eventual overall winner Lance Armstrong, although Zülle battled gamely for the rest of the race to finish second in Paris to Armstrong by just 7 minutes 37 seconds.

The 'homonymic pair' of Marc Wauters and Jonathan Vaughters, as American cycling writer Samuel Abt described them at the time in *The New York Times*, were both forced to abandon the race entirely due to their injuries, with American Vaughters taken to hospital having sustained a fractured chin.

The Noirmoutier bridge was used for the stage-1 time trial of the 2005 Tour – the organisers seemingly happy to av[o]the slippery stones of the Passage du G[ois] that year. Young American rider David Zabriskie recorded the the Tour's faste[st] ever individual time-trial stage – 54.676 kph (33.974 mph) – over the 19-km (11.8-mile) course between Fromentine, on the mainland, and Noirmoutier. However, following the 2012 USADA investigation into Armstrong and Zabriskie's former tea[m,] US Postal, Zabriskie's admission to having doped during part of his career resulted in a six-month ban and the annulment of his results between May 2003 and July 2006.

The Passage du Gois reappeared in 2011, although this time the Tour got under way with a 'neutralised start' – i.e[.] a procession – onto the 'passage' from Noirmoutier, and the race was only officially waved on its way once the riders had safely ridden to the end of the road where it joined the mainland.

The bridge will undoubtedly be used again in the future, but it remains to be seen whether the Tour will ever race across the Passage du Gois in anger aga[in.]

Brittany, France

'Both three-time Tour winner Louison Bobet and five-time champion Bernard Hinault come from the windswept region, and grew up spending hours battling the often harsh Breton winters on their bikes, moulding themselves into the tenacious riders they became'

Like Normandy, Brittany is a regularly visited region by the Tour and, although it might lack the guaranteed excitement of the climbs of the Pyrenees or the Alps, these flatter regions have nevertheless between them been the scene of a number of significant escapades.

Rennes had become the first Breton town to host a stage of the Tour in 1905, and the race has returned to Brittany almost every year since.

In 2008, Brest hosted the Tour's *Grand Départ* with an opening stage run as a massed-start road race – the first time that the Tour had started without a time trial since 1966 (the opening stages in 1971 and 1988 were held as team time trials). Spain's Alejandro Valverde – who was racing under the cloud of having been named in the 2006 investigation into infamous doctor Eufemiano Fuentes and his high-profile sporting clients, and would in 2009 receive a two-year ban for blood doping – jumped clear of his rivals on the uphill finish in Plumelec to take the race's first yellow jersey.

Just three years later, in 2011, when it was the neighbouring Vendée's turn to host the *Grand Départ*, it was followed by no fewer than four stages in Brittany,

showcasing the region through sprint wins by Tyler Farrar and Mark Cavendi in Redon and at Cap Fréhel, respectivel while eventual overall winner Cadel Evans showed what was yet to come by outsprinting Alberto Contador at the finish at Mûr-de-Bretagne.

Is it a coincidence that two of the greatest Tour riders of all time hail from Brittany? Probably not. Both three-tim Tour winner Louison Bobet and five-time champion Bernard Hinault come from the windswept region, and grew u spending hours battling the often harsh Breton winters on their bikes, mouldin themselves into the tenacious riders they became.

In 1985, the Tour started in Plumelec where, appropriately enough, Hinault (below) won the prologue time trial. Despite pressure from Ireland's Stephe Roche and his own team-mate, Greg LeMond, along the way 'The Badger' recorded his fifth and final Tour victory in Paris that year. Although it may be hard to believe, that 1985 win remains t last by a French rider, and so the home nation could do a lot worse than to loo to Brittany to again produce its next gr cycling champion.

ÎLES ANGLO-NORMANDES
(rattachées à la Grande-Bretagne)

Hurd Dp Alderney
L.H.
St Pierre L.H. pte de l
Église
Octaville Barfle
Cherbourg

Guernsey
Valognes
L.H. Sto
PeterPort Sark
Bricquebec
Cotentin
Carteret
Douve
Gr.
Isi

Ecréhou
la Haye du Puits Carentan
Jersey
Lessay
Li
St Helier Périers
St
Coutances

les Sept Iles
Perros Guirec
Sillon de Talbert
Regnéville MANCHE
I. Bréhat
Minquiers
I. Chausey
Gavray
I. de Batz
L.H. Roscoff Lannion Treguier Paimpol
Golfe de St Malo
Granville Villedieu
Pontrieux Baie de Fréhel St Malo
See
Avranches
Ignogan St Pol de Léon Begard Plouha Erquy St Servan s. Mer Cancale
Mt S. Michel
Lesneven Morlaix St Brieuc Dinard
Landivisiau Plouaret Guingamp Pléneuf Plancoët Dol
Ezeau
est Landerneau Mtss d'Arrée Belle Isle en Terre St Brieuc Lamballe Plancoët Pontorson St H
du H
Daoulas Mtss d'Arrée Trieux St Brieuc Jugon Dinan Trans Antrain
Crozon Huelgoat Callac CÔTES-DU-NORD Combourg Fougèr
FINISTÈRE R. Quintin Broons Rance Hédé St Aubin du Cormier
Châteaulin Carhaix Corlay Plouguenast Merdrignac ILLE-ET-VILAINE
Pleyben Rostrenen Mûr St Méen Montfort Châteaubourg Vilaine
Douarnenez Châteauneuf du Faou Mts Noires Loudéac le Grand s. Meu
Odet Guéméné Scaër Le Faouët Mauron Mordelles Rennes Vitré
Andierne Quimper Rosporden Plouay Blavet Josselin Ploërmel Guichen Argentré du Pl
Pont l'Abbé Fouesnant Quimperlé Baud Locminé Guer Maure de B. Janzé la Guerche de B.
Concarneau Hennebont MORBIHAN Brest Semnon
I. Glénans Lorient Landes de Lanvaux Malestroit Bain de B. Pousancé
Pt Louis Pluvigner Vannes Arz Ust Vilaine Derval Châteaubriant
I. de Groix Auray Questembert Redon Guéméné Penfao Candé
Le Muzillac Nozay Erdre
Quiberon B. de Morbihan la Roche Blain Nort St G
Sarzeau Bernard Pontchâteau
Belle le I. Houat Guérande Pazanne Savenay Ancenis C
Ile Palais I. Hoëdic LOIRE-INFÉRIEURE Varades St
L.H. pte du Croisic la Baule Nantes Beaupréa
Croisic St Paimbœuf Vertou Vallet
Nazaire L. de Loire
Pte de St Gildas Pornic Ste Grandlieu Clisson A
Bourgneuf en Retz St Philbert de Grand
Noirmoutier Machecoul Montaigu Me
I. de Noirmoutier Boulogne Legé les Herbiers
Beauvoir s. Mer Challans Vie les Essarts
St Jean de Monts P
L.H. VENDÉE
I. d'Yeu

100 m

297

Champs-Élysées,
France

Belgian Walter Godefroot was the stage winner on the Champs-Élysées when Paris's famous boulevard was first used as the finish of the Tour in 1975, having previously finished in the Parc de Princes velodrome since the race's inception in 1903 until 1967. For the next seven years, it finished at another Paris velodrome, the 'Cipale', in the Bois de Vincennes.

Traditionally, the Tour's final stage has nearly always been one of fun and high jinks, with the overall result having already been decided on the previous day. The 1979 edition provided an exception, though, when second-placed Joop Zoetemelk attacked race leader Bernard Hinault, despite being more than three minutes in arrears on the general classification. Hinault had no choice but to react, and proceeded to win the stage and teach the Dutchman a lesson.

Even on more sedate final stages, once the race actually hits the Place de la Concorde just ahead of the Champs-Élysées, all hell tends to break loose as the riders jockey for position and put on a show.

It becomes a show for the sprinters, and the speed ramps up and up as all the riders realise that the finish line is in sight after three tough weeks.

Uzbekistan's DjamolidineAbdoujaparov never really had the line in sight when he put his head down and failed to see the feet of a Coca-Cola crash barrier at the side of the road during the final stage of the 1991 Tour. The beefy sprinter hit the ground hard, but was helped – bleeding and confused – across the finish line by doctors and officials in order to sew up that year's green jersey competition, before going for some stitches of his own.

The Champs-Élysées stage is called 'the sprinters' world championships' due to the attention focused on it each year, and official 2011 world champion Mark Cavendish won on the famous boulevard an astonishing four times in a row from 2009 to 2012, and was thwarted from taking a fifth in 2013, finishing third to stage winner Marcel Kittel and Andre Greipel

It hasn't all been sprints, however: in recent times, both Eddy Seigneur (199 and Alexandre Vinokourov (2005) have eluded the sprinters' teams to take sol stage victories. In 1989, the Tour create the most suspenseful finish to the race them all when the final stage was run a an individual time trial. The USA's Gre LeMond trailed French favourite Laure Fignon (below) by 50 seconds, which seemed an impossible gap to close over the 24-km course from Versailles. But close it the American did, tacking on ar extra 8 seconds to win the Tour by wha remains the smallest ever margin.

In 2013, the Tour had a twilight finish on the avenue — a spectacular finish that also saw the race circle the Arc de Triomphe for the first time, which it's set to do again in 2014.

> *'It becomes a show for the sprinters, and the speed ramps up and up as all the riders realise that the finish line is in sight after three tough weeks'*

Index

Note: page numbers in **bold** refer to picture captions. Page numbers in *italics* refer to maps.

Acknowledgments

Photographs
Cover: Miguel Indurain in yellow during stage 11, Serre Chevalier to Isola 2000, of the 1993 Tour de France © Offside Sports Photography
All other photographs featured in Mapping le Tour are © Offside Sports Photography, with the exception of pages 7 and 220 © GettyImages and pages 17 and 250 which are © Shutterstock.com

Maps
The publisher would like to thank David Edwards-May of Euromapping and Sandrine Lombard of the Bibliothèque d'étude et d'information Grenoble for sourcing, supplying and arranging reproduction rights of historic maps.

1903–1914: © *Onésime Reclus map, 1913, Bibliothèque municipale de Grenoble, FGC.10238*
1919–1939: © *Atlas général, Vidal-Lablache, 1931, Bibliothèque municipale de Grenoble, 98546*
1947–1959: © *The Times Atlas of the World, Mid-Century Edition, 1955*
1960–1979: © *George Philip & Son, 11th Edition, 1975*
1980–1999 and 2000–2013: © CollinsBartholomew, 2013
The Tour's most memorable places: © *The Times Atlas of the World, Mid-Century Edition, 1955*